ILLEGAL TRANSACTIONS IN INTERNATIONAL TRADE

Theory and Measurement

STUDIES IN INTERNATIONAL ECONOMICS

Editors

JAGDISH N. BHAGWATI
JOHN S. CHIPMAN

Volume 1

NORTH-HOLLAND PUBLISHING COMPANY – AMSTERDAM · OXFORD
AMERICAN ELSEVIER PUBLISHING COMPANY, INC. – NEW YORK

ILLEGAL TRANSACTIONS IN INTERNATIONAL TRADE

Theory and Measurement

Edited by

JAGDISH N. BHAGWATI

Professor of Economics
Massachusetts Institute of Technology

1974

NORTH-HOLLAND PUBLISHING COMPANY – AMSTERDAM · OXFORD
AMERICAN ELSEVIER PUBLISHING COMPANY, INC. – NEW YORK

Library of Congress Catalog Card Number 73–88164
ISBN North-Holland for this series 0 7204 8500 2
ISBN North-Holland for this volume 0 7204 8501 0
ISBN American Elsevier for this volume 0 444 10581 6

Publishers

NORTH-HOLLAND PUBLISHING COMPANY – AMSTERDAM
NORTH-HOLLAND PUBLISHING COMPANY, LTD. – OXFORD

Sole distributors for the U.S.A. and Canada

AMERICAN ELSEVIER PUBLISHING COMPANY, INC.
52 VANDERBILT AVENUE
NEW YORK, N.Y. 10017

PRINTED IN THE NETHERLANDS

INTRODUCTION TO THE SERIES

This series is intended to embrace all aspects of international economic analysis: theoretical, empirical and econometric. It will equally encompass contributions to pure and monetary theory.

The series will include the publication of collected essays, conference proceedings of exceptional professional quality and interest, and edited volumes addressed to specific phenomena of importance in the analysis of international economics. It will particularly encourage, however, the publication of hitherto unpublished studies which represent fresh and valuable contributions to the analysis of international economic problems.

The *Journal of International Economics* now provides an excellent outlet for original scientific work in international economics in article length form. For pamphlet length contributions, the different series published by the *International Finance Section* at Princeton have long been of exceptional value, even though they have not generally extended beyond international monetary issues. It is the hope of the editors that the launching of this series, *Studies in International Economics*, will now fill the lacuna in the systematic publication of monograph and volume length research output of international economists, and succeed in doing so consistently with the high quality that the promotion of scientific study of international economic issues requires.

THE EDITORS

TO

Sukhamoy
and
TN

CONTENTS

Introduction to the Series v

Acknowledgements xi

JAGDISH N. BHAGWATI
Introduction 1

Part I – The pure theory of international trade

Chapter 1
JAGDISH N. BHAGWATI and BENT HANSEN
A theoretical analysis of smuggling 9
(reprinted from the Quarterly Journal of Economics, May 1973)

Chapter 2
JAGDISH N. BHAGWATI and T. N. SRINIVASAN
An alternative proof of the Bhagwati–Hansen results on smuggling and welfare 23

Chapter 3
JAGDISH N. BHAGWATI and T. N. SRINIVASAN
Smuggling and trade policy 27
(reprinted from the Journal of Public Economics, Aug. 1973)

Chapter 4
HARRY G. JOHNSON
Notes on the economic theory of smuggling 39
(reprinted from the Malayan Economic Review, May 1972)

Part II – Balance of payments and developmental effects

Chapter 5
GORDON C. WINSTON
Overinvoicing, underutilization, and distorted industrial growth 49
(reprinted from the Pakistan Development Review, Summer 1969)

Chapter 6
JAGDISH N. BHAGWATI
Fiscal policies, the faking of foreign trade declarations, and the balance of payments 66
(reprinted from the Bulletin of the Oxford University Institute of Statistics, Feb. 1967)

Part III – Partner-country data comparisons and faked invoicing

Chapter 7
OSKAR MORGENSTERN
On the accuracy of economic observations: Foreign trade statistics 87
(reprinted from Chapter IX, The Accuracy of Economic Observations, Princeton University Press, 1950)

Chapter 8
SEIJI NAYA and THEODORE MORGAN
The accuracy of international trade data: The case of Southeast Asian countries 123
(reprinted from the Journal of the American Statistical Association, June 1969)

Chapter 9
JAGDISH N. BHAGWATI
On the underinvoicing of imports 138
(reprinted from the Bulletin of the Oxford University Institute of Statistics, Nov. 1964)

Chapter 10
JAGDISH N. BHAGWATI, ANNE KRUEGER and CHAIYAWAT WIBULSWASDI
Capital flight from LDCs: A statistical analysis 148

Part IV – Detecting smuggling

Chapter 11
C. G. F. SIMKIN
Indonesia's unrecorded trade 157
(reprinted from the Bulletin of Indonesian Economic Studies, March 1970)

Chapter 12
H. V. RICHTER
Problems of assessing unrecorded trade 172
(reprinted from the Bulletin of Indonesian Economic Studies, March 1970)

Chapter 13
RICHARD N. COOPER
Tariffs and smuggling in Indonesia 183

Part V – Miscellany

Chapter 14
G. C. HUFBAUER and J. P. O'NEILL
Unit values of U.S. machinery exports 195
(reprinted from the Journal of International Economics, Aug. 1972)

Index 207

ACKNOWLEDGEMENTS

Thanks are due to the following for permission to reprint the papers included in this volume: the *Quarterly Journal of Economics*, the *Journal of Public Economics*, the *Journal of International Economics*, the *Bulletin of the Oxford University Institute of Statistics*, the *Pakistan Development Review*, the *Malayan Economic Review*, the *Journal of the American Statistical Association*, the *Bulletin of Indonesian Economic Studies* and Princeton University Press. The volume also includes previously unpublished research papers by T. N. Srinivasan, Richard Cooper, Anne Krueger and the editor. The editor's research was supported by the National Science Foundation.

INTRODUCTION

Jagdish N. BHAGWATI

International trade economists, when they seek to translate the results of pure theory into policy advice, typically run into the phenomena of smuggling (which implies the use of illegal channels of importation and exportation) and faked invoicing (which implies the use of legal channels of trade but evasion). These illicit phenomena are important in scope in the less developed countries, in particular, where frequently the methods of enforcement are lax, the frontiers many and large, and the rewards from illegal activity high relative to the returns from legal activity.

These illicit phenomena vitiate not merely the accuracy and use of foreign trade statistics. They must also affect the policy prescriptions from the theory of trade and welfare that economists would bring to the policymaker. There is urgent need therefore to integrate the analysis of illegal trade phenomena into the pure theory of international trade; and it is necessary also to develop techniques for detecting the presence, and assessing the magnitude, of such phenomena in specific contexts.

This volume brings together a number of contributions in different journals across the world (including one written by Richard Cooper especially for this volume) which are aimed at precisely these tasks. And, while they are essentially in the nature of pioneering efforts, and will undoubtedly lead to further analytical work, they already provide the economist with a set of tools with which he may detect and analyse the presence and consequences of illicit trade activity.

1. Pure theory

Part I contains three papers which develop systematically a simple technique for integrating illicit trade activity into the general equilibrium theory of international trade. The paper by Bent Hansen and myself (ch. 1) does this simply by introducing a smuggling transformation curve, with legal trade occurring subject to the tariff and illegal trade without the tariff. This technique is used then to analyse the welfare impact of trade with and without smuggling. A brief note by T.N. Srinivasan and myself (ch. 2) then provides a formal, alternative proof of the central Bhagwati–Hansen results. A paper by T.N. Srinivasan and myself (ch. 3) then extends the analysis (mainly) to the questions of optimal and maximal-revenue tariffs, ranking them in the presence of smuggling and in its absence. The note by Harry Johnson (ch. 4) also uses the technique introduced by Hansen and myself to explore some of these questions, using a geometrical technique which is a most useful and valuable supplement to the mathematical analysis of the Bhagwati–Srinivasan paper (ch. 2) with which it partially overlaps.

These analyses, aimed essentially at the smuggling of 'goods', need to be supplemented by analyses of the smuggling of 'bads' (e.g. heroin) and assets (e.g. gold). They also make a number of simplifying (though *not* necessarily unrealistic) assumptions which could be relaxed with profit: e.g. the enforcement expenditure could be introduced and readily made a policy variable set at an optimal level; the assumption that (homogeneous) legally and illegally imported products are cleared at the same price in domestic markets could be amended to allow for differential prices; and so on. Among the more interesting extensions will be the formal extension to many-good models. Two important implications may be spelled out here:

(1) Take, for example, Lerner's well-known 'symmetry theorem'. According to this theorem, it makes no (real) difference whether a tariff is levied on the exportable or the importable good. This theorem *would* carry over, in the case of smuggling, *if* there were a unique smuggling transformation curve. This is, however, not a plausible assumption. The cost of smuggling will vary with its feasibility which must depend, in turn, on the physical characteristics of the commodity. It follows therefore that an export tax at the same rate as an import tax could, and generally would, lead to *differential* results thanks to the differential impact of each on the smuggling transformation curve.

(2) The other example relates to the fact that differential smuggling feasibilities among different tradeable goods will have a bearing also on the question of optimal policy structures. T.N. Srinivasan and I have analysed four non-economic objectives – production, consumption, import level and factor employment in a sector – and shown that each is optimally achieved by policies which affect the relevant market – production, consumption, trade and factor-use tax-cum-subsidies, respectively (Bhagwati and Srinivasan, 1969). Vandendorpe (1974), in a brilliant recent paper, has extended this analysis to a multiple-good model to show that the same policies carry over and the optimal policy structures would require uniform tax rates. Thus, if the government desires to reduce *overall* imports by a fixed value, the prescription for a *small* country is to use uniform tariff rates on each importable. However, smuggling will generally be characterised by non-

constant costs, so that (as Vandendorpe shows for the case of monopoly power in trade) the optimal policy structure will cease in general to be uniform[1].

It is also clear that the Bhagwati–Hansen technique for incorporating smuggling into the theory of international trade conceives of the real cost of smuggling as incurred in the form of the (two) produced goods which enter the utility function: this is an assumption which is identical with that used by Paul Samuelson in his celebrated analysis of transport costs in the transfer problem. That, therefore, no primary, domestic factors are deployed in undertaking smuggling is not necessarily however an unrealistic assumption: a totally realistic form of smuggling costs is the perishing of smuggled goods, including their forced "loss" owing to dumping to avoid detection (as in the notorious example of slaves being literally dumped into the sea during the illegal slave trade from the West African coast). If, nonetheless, one wished to postulate that domestic, primary factors were used in undertaking illegal trade, one would have the option of using at least two different types of models for this purpose, as contrasted with the Bhagwati–Hansen model.

Either one could assume that legal and illegal trade utilised domestic primary factors *indirectly* via the input of a "third" intermediate commodity/service called "transportation" which, in turn, uses primary domestic factors. One could make this model as complicated as one wishes, including the modification of the utility function to allow for the direct consumption of this "third" commodity/service. A simplified version of such a model, where the "third" commodity enters in fixed-proportion into illegal trade but not at all into the utility function or into legal trade, has just been constructed by Munir Sheikh in a paper forthcoming in the *Journal of International Economics* (and brought to the Editor's attention only as this volume was at the final proof stage).

Alternatively, one could allow the domestic primary factors to enter the foreign trade (legal and illegal) transformation functions *directly*, instead of constructing the "third" commodity which then enters trade. In many trade situations, this may well be a more appropriate way of portraying reality. An analysis of smuggling in this type of model is currently under way by Bhagwati and Hansen.

Clearly, therefore, the analytical papers reprinted here represent the beginning of theoretical work that should pay handsome dividends in improving our understanding of the impact of illegal trade phenomena on the policy dimensions of trade theory.

[1] A formal analysis of this problem could further distinguish between the level of total and the level of legal imports.

2. Balance of payments and developmental effects

At the same time, two other papers are brought together here, by Winston (ch. 5) and myself (ch. 6), which extend the analysis of the effects of illegal trade to areas of policy which go beyond the normal preoccupations of the pure theory. Thus, Winston analyses the effects of overinvoicing of imports in Pakistan on the choice of technique and on the level of capacity utilisation in the industrial sector importing capital goods, whereas my paper, arising from Indian analysis, is primarily addressed to the question of how illegal trade may affect the legal trade and the balance of payments as compiled by statistical offices: a matter of obvious significance in interpreting official statistics and changes therein.

3. Detection of faked invoicing

As the ramifications of illegal trade are clearly various and significant, the question of detecting their presence, and hopefully their magnitude, is of vital concern. This volume therefore brings together a number of papers which have been addressed precisely to this problem.

Naturally, the methods of detecting (rather than estimating the magnitude of) illegal trade have been more conspicuous in the literature. The principal technique of detecting illegal trade – other than the apprehension of smugglers, the checking of invoices against exogenously obtained 'true' prices and the interview technique – owes its origin in essence to Morgenstern's well-known work on the accuracy of foreign trade statistics. Because of its historic interest in this context, it is reprinted here at length (ch. 7). The technique of partner-country-data comparisons is developed there with great mastery and elegance, and with a keen eye for all the *statistical* reasons why these data may not match.

A modern version of Morgenstern's work is the paper by Naya and Morgan (ch. 8), which extends the technique of partner-country-data comparisons to Asian countries in recent trade, again focusing on the statistical aspects of these discrepancies.

But the use of such partner-country-data comparisons, addressed specifically to the detection of faked invoicing, is explicitly to be found in the policy-orientated work of other economists. Thus, in my paper on the underinvoicing of Turkish imports (ch. 9), I explicitly link up the discrepancies between the import data of Turkey and the export data of her partner countries to the *economic* rationale that import duties higher than the black-market premium on foreign exchange provide a systematic reason to underinvoice the imports carrying those high duties. This is a difficult, and almost elusive, technique – as should be evident from the Morgenstern and Naya–Morgan analyses – but it did 'work' reasonably plausibly for Turkey during 1961 and 1962, and it may work elsewhere, if the 'noise' from the *statistical* factors discussed by Morgenstern is not excessive.

Yet another application of such a technique is the small paper by Krueger, Wibulswasdi and myself (ch. 10) on detecting capital flight from less developed countries.

4. Detection of smuggling

While the partner-country-data technique may be able to reveal faked invoicing, the smuggling trade will clearly not be caught by this technique as it bypasses legal trade channels altogether.

Possible techniques for detecting smuggling, however, are also to be found in the papers on Indonesia by Simkin (ch. 11), Richter (ch. 12) and Cooper (ch. 13) reprinted in this volume. While Simkin and Richter discuss the difficulties of assessing unrecorded trade, they also make sophisticated use of techniques to evaluate it: note, in particular, Simkin's attempt at estimating, from production and inventory data, the 'true' export of rubber to Malaya as distinct from the recorded export of rubber.

Of particular interest is Cooper's analysis of smuggling by setting the market prices of imported goods against the tariff-inclusive prices. Where the latter price exceeds the former, there is clearly presumption that the goods are being smuggled and tariffs evaded. A similar analysis was undertaken earlier by King (1970) for Mexico, using unit values of goods in domestic production and of 'similar' imported goods – showing that smuggling was widely present. Interestingly, in both King's and Cooper's analyses, the proportionate differential between the tariff-inclusive price and the actual market price tends to rise with the tariff rate – a phenomenon on which Cooper comments at some length in his interesting paper. Note also that this technique is available only when tariffs are used to restrict imports (or exports); with quantitative restrictions, there would be no 'tariff-inclusive' price available for such an exercise.

Finally, reprinted here is a paper by Hufbauer and O'Neill (ch. 14) which is of some interest in the empirical analysis of illegal trade phenomena although it is directed at explaining cross-sectional differences in the unit values of U.S. exports of machinery to different destinations. Hufbauer and O'Neill examine a number of alternative hypotheses, including the possibility of faked invoicing to examine these differences; in so doing they point to yet another possible implication of the presence of illegal trade in general, and of faked invoicing in particular, in the analysis of international trade. While their analysis of faked invoicing is based on the premise that incentives to fake invoices by importing countries will result in faked invoices in the exporting country (U.S.A.) as well – a premise that seems to me to be less than plausible because to fake the invoices at both ends would be to make the U.S. exporter liable for faking to his own government, for which there could be serious penalties; further this also is a premise that contradicts the partner-country-data comparison approach which, of course, presumes that the faking occurs only at one end and not both, as is indeed often the case – the analysis nonetheless points to some interesting implications of the presence of illegal trade on one's customary way of handling trade data in economic analysis.

This collection of papers on the economic analysis of illegal trade, therefore, should point the way to a far greater awareness of the significance of illegal trade, of both faked invoicing and smuggling, in the analysis of trade data, and also in the economic analysis of issues in trade and welfare. As such, this collection should be of importance and interest to both policy advisers and to the theorists of international trade.

References

Bhagwati, J. and T. N. Srinivasan, 1969, Optimal intervention to achieve non-economic objectives, Review of Economic Studies XXXVI, January.

King, T., 1970, Mexico: Industrialization and Trade Policies since 1940 (Oxford University Press, London).

Vandendorpe, A., 1974, On the theory of optimal policy structures in an open economy, Journal of International Economics, February.

PART I

THE PURE THEORY OF INTERNATIONAL TRADE

Chapter 1

A THEORETICAL ANALYSIS OF SMUGGLING

Jagdish N. BHAGWATI and Bent HANSEN

1. Introduction

In some underdeveloped countries smuggling takes on large proportions and is a major economic problem. In Afghanistan as much as one-quarter to one-fifth of total foreign trade is believed to be smuggling trade (Hansen, 1971; Smith et al., 1969). Other countries in the East, certainly Indonesia, and a number of African countries also have this problem. There is a need, therefore, to look at smuggling not only as a moral and legal problem but also as a purely economic phenomenon.

It is commonly argued that smuggling must improve economic welfare since it constitutes (partial or total) evasion of the tariffs (or quantitative restrictions), which, for a small country, would signify a suboptimal policy. We propose to demonstrate in sect. 2 of this paper the falsity of this view, while also investigating the restrictive conditions under which smuggling may improve welfare.

Since, however, the tariff may be, and often is, levied to achieve specific objectives, such as protecting import-competing production or collecting revenue, we should also want to compare the welfare levels reached under tariffs with and without smuggling, *subject to such exogenously specified objectives.* In sect. 3 we do this for the case of protecting production and show that the achievement of a given degree of protection to domestic importable production, in the presence of smuggling, produces lower welfare than if smuggling were absent. In sect. 4 we extend our analysis to the phenomenon of faked invoices[1].

[1] Alan Manne has called our attention to an early attempt to analyze smuggling by the famous Italian eighteenth-century (1738–1794) criminologist and economist Cesare Bonesana, Marchese di Beccaria (Beccaria, 1764–1765). Beccaria's problem seems to be to find a method for rational determination of tariff rates and for that purpose he sets up a condition for smuggling to break even. Beccaria does not explain his symbols very precisely, but there can be no doubt that the following interpretation is correct.

Assume that a merchant's investment in merchandise is u and that the tariff duty to be paid thereon is t. The rate of tariff is thus $\tau = t/u$. With smuggling the value of the merchandise successfully brought through the controls without payment of tariffs is x. Thus $(u - x)$ has been con-

2. Smuggling and welfare

In the following analysis, we apply the Hicks–Samuelson value theoretical framework, which is customarily used in the traditional theory of international trade. We further assume that primary factors, in perfect competition, produce (two) traded goods and that the country is small, i.e. the terms of trade are fixed. We shall assume a given, well-behaved community indifference map. This assumption could be given up without altering any conclusions: it is retained for convenience of exposition.

Since smuggling merely represents, from a welfare point of view, yet another way in which exportables are transformed into importables, we must represent it as a smuggling transformation (or offer) curve. However, it is clear that this transformation curve must be less favorable than the terms of trade[2].

We next have the option of assuming that smuggling is either competitive or monopolistic and that the smuggling offer curve is characterized by either a constant rate of transformation or an increasing rate of transformation. We consider all these options in the following analysis[3]. For the sake of simplicity we shall assume that the individual smuggler has a constant marginal rate of transformation. When we assume increasing marginal rates of transformation for the smuggling industry as a whole, we retain the assumption of individual constant

fiscated. Since the successfully smuggled commodities may be sold at domestic market price, the condition for smuggling to break even is clearly $x(1 + \tau) = u$, or, as Beccaria presents it, $x + tx/u = u$. He then develops this expression into something that perhaps can be described as isoprofit curves, but does not get anywhere with his analysis, and finally expresses the hope that it may prove useful as a starting point for further analysis.

It is, indeed, easy to develop Beccaria's analysis. Let p denote the smuggler's total profit. We then have $p = x(1 + \tau) - u$. Let $p/u = r$ be the rate of profit and $x/u = z$ be the probability for success in smuggling. We have then immediately $1 + r = z(1 + \tau)$. Assume now that the 'normal' rate of profit is r^*. For smuggling to be unprofitable the tariff rate has to be set so that $\tau < \{(1 + r^*)/z\} - 1$. If, on the other hand, the sovereign can work on the probability of successful smuggling through increased supervision – the more supervision, the lower is z – our relation shows the trade-off between increased supervision and increased tariff rates (revenues). To judge from his text it was precisely this trade-off that Beccaria was looking for – natural for a criminologist.

From a national point of view commodities are not lost because they are confiscated, of course. Nonetheless, Beccaria's analysis introduces a private cost factor, the risk of being caught, that certainly is important for determining the volume of smuggling and that our analysis does not deal with. (Pierluigi Molajoni translated Beccaria's article and has helped us with the interpretation.)

[2] As James Kearl has remarked to us, however, there may be relatively minor instances of smuggling at *more* favorable terms of trade – as when LDC-resident Americans with *subsidized* PX sources of foreign goods may be willing to resell these goods in their host LDCs at prices that fall below legal channel prices.

[3] We disregard the petty smuggling of tourists that is done at zero marginal costs (economically). Our concern is large-scale smuggling on a commercial basis.

rates of transformation. The industry's increasing rate of transformation is thus exclusively due to intra-industrial, interfirm diseconomies of scale. This assumption permits us in a simple way to deal with both perfect competition and monopoly without loss of generality.

With perfect competition in smuggling, both the foreign price (the terms of trade) and the domestic price are given to the individual smuggler. With monopoly in smuggling, however, several possibilities are open. We shall use a minimum assumption to the effect that, whereas the monopolistic smuggler knows and takes into account the form of the (smuggling) industry's transformation curve, he does not consider the effect on domestic prices of a change in the volume of smuggling[4]. We have in fact also studied the case in which the monopolistic smuggler does consider domestic price effects. But our conclusions remain valid in this case as well. Hence, for reasons of space, we do not present this analysis here. Moreover, we cannot possibly take up here all possible cases of imperfect competition.

We also assume that, in the monopolistic smuggling case, the smuggler is a 'nonresident' whose profits therefore do *not* constitute welfare for the country that experiences smuggling[5]. The question of the residence of the smuggler clearly does not arise, however, in the case of competitive smuggling; for, under our assumptions, the smuggling profits under competition would be zero[6].

2.1. Perfect competition in smuggling at constant costs

In fig. 1, AB is the production possibility curve and the slope of $P_f C_f$ (= the slope of $P_t C_t$) is the fixed, international terms of trade. The domestic price, inclusive of the tariff but in the absence of smuggling, is tangent to AB at P_t. If free trade

[4] At constant costs our monopolistic smuggler clearly behaves in exactly the same way as a competitive smuggling industry would do. At increasing costs he behaves as a competitive smuggling industry does at increasing costs for the individual smuggler without intra-industry diseconomies.

[5] We could assume that the smuggler is a resident of the country or, which is very realistic in some primitive countries where smuggling is a large industry, that the smugglers really belong to **no** country. In Afghanistan nomadic tribes move across the borders to and from Pakistan and Iran, and some of them make a living from smuggling (Smith et al., 1969, p. 328). They are 'countries without fixed territory'. Either country, or both, may include the nomads in their population and national income estimates, but such statistical conventions do not integrate the nomads with either country!

[6] We should clarify, however, that the results for the monopolistic smuggling case, showing that smuggling may be harmful, do *not* critically depend on the assumption that the smuggler is a nonresident. While it may be thought that the country must be worse off from the exercise of monopoly power from abroad, it must be remembered at the same time that the monopolistic smuggler maximizes along an 'inferior' transformation curve and *not* along the 'legal' offer curve.

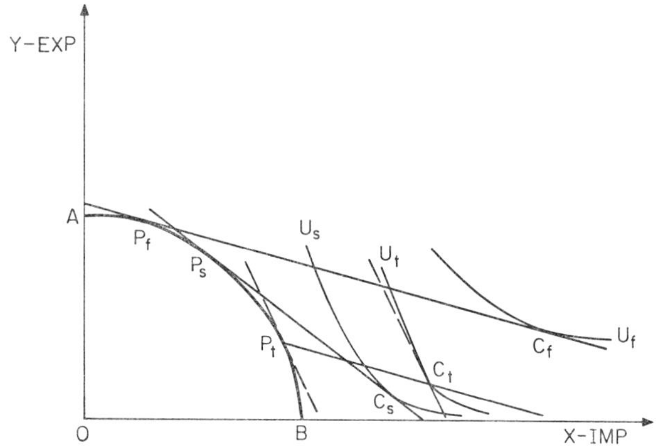

Fig. 1. Perfect competition in smuggling at constant costs. With free trade, production possibility curve AB, and given international price line P_fC_f, the welfare (maximum) is at U_f. With tariff, the production, consumption and welfare are at P_t, C_t and U_t, respectively, provided that no smuggling takes place. With smuggling, at constant price line (transformation line) P_sC_s, less steep than the tangent to AB at P_t, *legal trade ceases* and welfare ends up at $U_s < U_t$. Hence, smuggling *reduces* welfare.

prevailed, welfare would be at U_f, whereas with the tariff, but without smuggling, it would be at U_t.

With smuggling, however, the smuggling transformation curve is P_sC_s (steeper than P_fC_f, but less steep than the tangent at P_t); the domestic price faced by producers and consumers is P_sC_s and the welfare is U_s.

Since $U_s < U_t$, we have here a case where smuggling has reduced welfare below what it would be in the absence of smuggling. Smuggling becomes a welfare-reducing phenomenon, contrary to common belief.

On the other hand, fig. 2 depicts a case where $U_s > U_t$: smuggling has improved welfare. We can therefore conclude: *for nonprohibitive tariffs, and constant costs smaller than the tariff-included price and perfect competition in smuggling, smuggling cannot be uniquely welfare-ranked* vis-à-vis *non-smuggling.*

The rationale underlying this conclusion is readily seen by analogy with the analysis of the welfare effects of a trade-diverting customs union. Smuggling is analogous to admitting a 'partner country' as an importer at higher cost than the 'outside country'; smuggling therefore imposes a terms of trade loss, but the production and consumption gain may outweigh this loss, as they do in fig. 2, but not in fig. 1. Thus, we cannot tell in general whether smuggling is welfare-improving or not – compared to legal trade with the tariff[7].

[7] We might add, however, that, if we were to draw the tangent to the production possibility curve AB and the no-smuggling tariff situation utility curve U_t in figs. 1 and 2, and define the

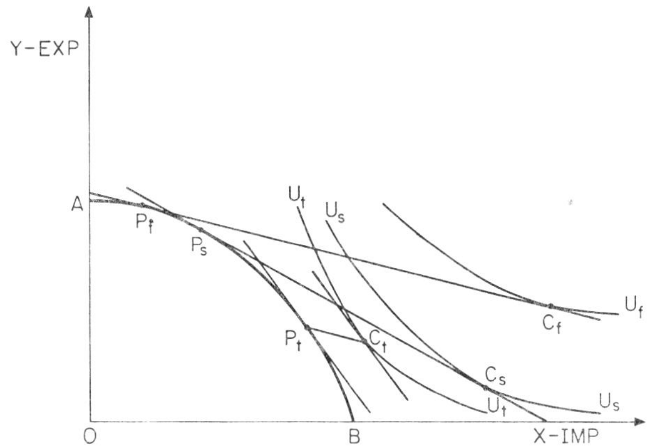

Fig. 2. Perfect competition in smuggling at constant costs (contd.). This figure is identical with fig. 1, except that now smuggling *improves* welfare: $U_s > U_t$. With the smuggler's transformation line less steep than the tangent at P_t legal trade is again eliminated.

In both figs. 1 and 2 legal trade is eliminated, given the assumption that the smugglers' transformation line is less steep than the tangent to the country's production frontier at P_t; when the competitive smugglers' costs are constant and lower than the tariff-included price, legal trade cannot survive[8]. Were the smugglers' transformation line steeper than the tangent at P_t, smuggling would, on the other hand, cease completely, and legal trade prevail. But there is here a borderline case in which smuggling and legal trade may coexist. When the smugglers' transformation line coincides with the tangent at P_t, smugglers' constant costs are equal to the tariff-included price and smuggling may or may not prevail. Unfortunately our assumptions leave, strictly speaking, the division of trade between smuggling and legal trade indeterminate. Nevertheless, we can state unequivocally that in this case smuggling must be a welfare-reducing activity. Fig. 3 shows that no matter how much or how little smugglers trade, trade exclusively on a legal basis would be better. If the smugglers have all trade, as at point C_s at welfare level U_s, C_t at the

point of tangency with AB as P_z, we can distinguish two zones (in analogy with the trade-diverting customs union theory): zone I, defined as the range of smuggling offers that would yield smuggling situation equilibrium production between P_f (excluded) and P_z (excluded), where the smuggling must necessarily improve welfare over the nonsmuggling situation; and zone II, defined similarly over the range from P_z (excluded) to P_t (included), where the smuggling must necessarily worsen welfare.

[8] John Pettengill has remarked to us, however, that governmental agencies may be compelled to buy through legal channels, in which case legal imports at higher cost *could* coexist with illegal imports by the nongovernmental sector at lower cost. We exclude this possibility in the analysis in the text.

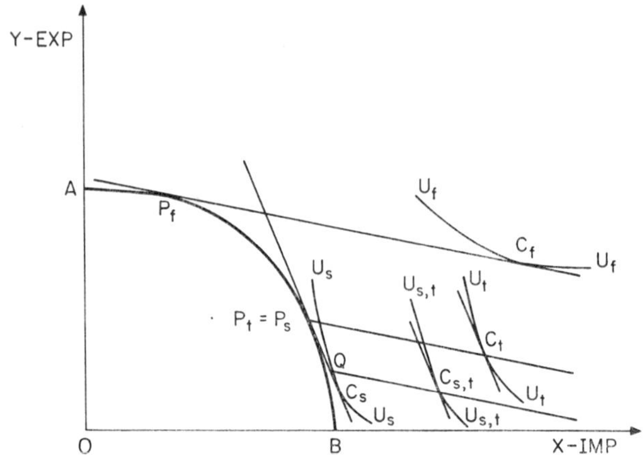

Fig. 3. Perfect competition in smuggling at constant costs (contd.). In this figure, the smugglers' transformation line, $P_s C_s$, coincides with the tangent to AB at P_t ($=P_s$). If the smugglers have all trade, the welfare level will be U_s with the consumption point C_s. C_s is clearly inferior to C_t; therefore $U_s < U_t$. With smuggling at Q, legal trade will lead to the consumption point $C_{s,t}$ at welfare level $U_{s,t}$. We have always $U_s < U_{s,t} < U_t$. The first inequality is obvious; it means that some legal trade is better than no legal trade. The second inequality follows from the circumstance that, if $U_t < U_{s,t}$, which is easily seen to be possible, there would exist at least one more equilibrium point on the trade line, $P_t C_t$, at a higher welfare level than $U_{s,t}$ (Bhagwati, 1968).

welfare level U_t must clearly be better: $U_t > U_s$. And with smuggling at Q and legal trade at $C_{s,t}$, we have $U_t > U_{s,t}$. We have thus the following result. *For nonprohibitive tariffs, and constant costs equal to the tariff-included price and perfect competition in smuggling, legal trade and smuggling may coexist. In this case, no smuggling is better than any amount of smuggling; and the less smuggling the better.*

2.2. Perfect competition in smuggling at increasing costs

We now consider the case where there are increasing costs in smuggling, while it continues to be competitive. It is clear that, in this case, we can have smuggling coexisting with legal trade, whereas in the preceding case, with constant costs in both smuggling and legal trade, smuggling, if profitable at all, eliminated legal trade apart from a special borderline case. This possibility of legal trade coexisting with smuggling is not merely a theoretical curiosum: in real life it is probably the most common case, and, as we show below, it turns out to be critical to the welfare effects of smuggling (indeed, as we have already seen in the borderline case above).

Let us initially discuss the cases where smuggling eliminates trade, despite increasing costs. Fig. 4 illustrates this possibility. The smuggling transformation

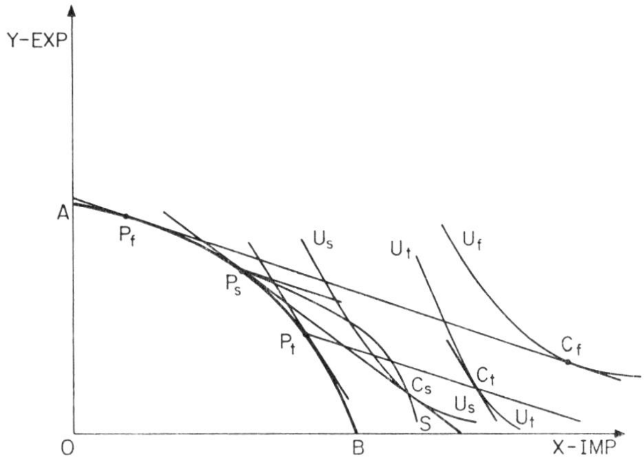

Fig. 4. Perfect competition in smuggling at increasing costs. This figure is identical with fig. 1, but we now have increasing costs in smuggling. The transformation curve for smuggling is P_sC_sS, and the equilibrium for the smuggling situation is characterized by production at P_s, where the *average* (recall the assumption of individual constant rate of transformation) transformation rate in smuggling (the straight line, P_sC_s) is tangential to AB and by consumption at C_s, where the same rate is tangential also to U_s. Again, legal imports are eliminated, and $U_s < U_t$.

curve, P_sC_s, now exhibits diminishing returns, and the equilibrium under smuggling shows the domestic price ratio, at which production and consumption take place, to be the line P_sC_s. Since P_sC_s is steeper than the legal trade price line, P_fC_f, legal

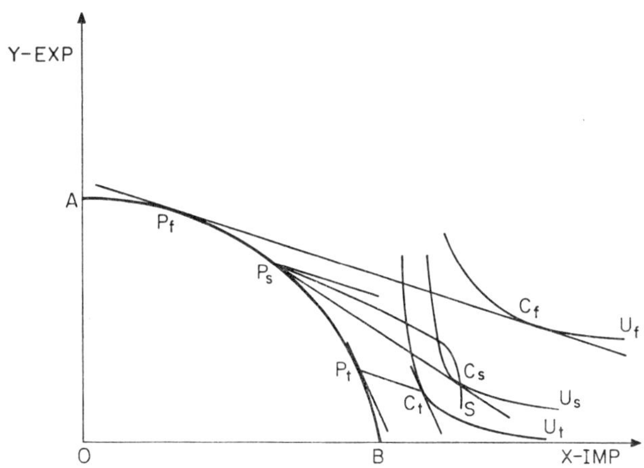

Fig. 5. Perfect competition in smuggling at increasing costs (contd.). This figure is identical with fig. 4, except that we now show smuggling to result in greater welfare than legal trade: $U_s > U_t$. Again, in the smuggling situation, legal imports are eliminated.

trade has been eliminated. Smuggling is shown to lower welfare *vis-à-vis* the nonsmuggling situation: $U_s < U_t$.

On the other hand, fig. 5 shows just the opposite: $U_t < U_s$, and smuggling has improved welfare. Thus, we have the following result. *For nonprohibitive tariffs, and increasing costs and perfect competition in smuggling, smuggling cannot be uniquely welfare-ranked* vis-à-vis *nonsmuggling when legal trade is eliminated by smuggling.*

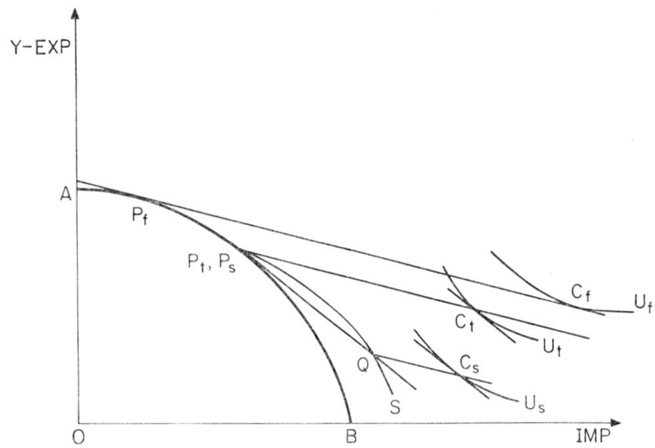

Fig. 6. Perfect competition in smuggling at increasing costs (contd.). This figure shows a situation where smuggling and legal trade *coexist* in equilibrium. The production points, P_t and P_s, therefore coincide; smuggling takes the availability point to Q and legal trade takes it then, at international prices, to C_s and welfare $U_s < U_t$ (the welfare that would be achieved under legal trade alone); see caption for fig. 3 concerning the possibility of $U_s > U_t$, in case of multiple equilibria.

Consider, however, the case where legal trade is *not* eliminated in the smuggling situation. Fig. 6, which is a variant of figs. 4 and 5, illustrates this case. In the smuggling situation, the domestic price will now be the tariff-inclusive price: so both production (at P_s) and consumption (at C_s) must be at tariff-inclusive prices. The point of trade on the *smuggling* transformation curve, P_sQS, must be (at Q) where the *average* terms of trade (we have individual constant returns) are again the same as the *domestic* price ratio. However, *legal* trade must occur at the *international* price ratio, the slope of QC_s. It is clear, then, that smuggling worsens welfare, and we thus have the result: *for nonprohibitive tariffs, and increasing costs and perfect competition in smuggling, when legal trade is not eliminated, smuggling necessarily reduces welfare* vis-à-vis *the nonsmuggling situation.*

The rationale for this result is again readily seen. The smuggling situation, *vis-à-vis* the nonsmuggling situation, now imposes *identical* production and consumption distortions on the economy, while *also* imposing a terms of trade loss; smuggling must therefore necessarily be a welfare-reducing phenomenon in this instance.

2.3. Monopoly in smuggling at constant costs

When smuggling is monopolistic, the *marginal* rate of transformation in smuggling will be equated with the domestic price ratio. However, for constant costs in smuggling, the marginal and average rates of transformation are identical, and hence the results are identical with the case where smuggling is competitive. Hence we can conclude: *for nonprohibitive tariffs, and constant costs and monopoly in smuggling, smuggling cannot be uniquely welfare-ranked* vis-à-vis *nonsmuggling.*

2.4. Monopoly in smuggling at increasing costs

However, when there are increasing costs in smuggling, we have to distinguish between marginal and average terms of trade in smuggling. As with the competitive case, we find that the ranking of smuggling *vis-à-vis* nonsmuggling is critically dependent on whether smuggling eliminates legal trade.

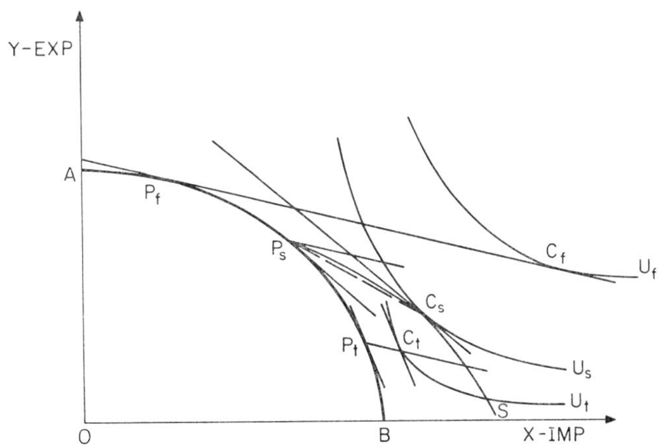

Fig. 7. Monopoly in smuggling at increasing costs. This figure is similar to fig. 5: legal trade is eliminated and $U_s > U_t$. However, instead of depicting smuggling on the perfectly competitive assumption, we now equate the *marginal* rate of transformation in smuggling (at C_s) with the marginal rate of transformation in domestic production and domestic prices (at P_s). Smuggling improves welfare over the legal trade situation.

In fig. 7, we illustrate a case where smuggling does eliminate legal trade. The difference from fig. 5, where the case of competitive smuggling under increasing costs was discussed, is that the smuggling equilibrium is characterized by equality of domestic prices and the *marginal* rate of transformation in smuggling – the tangents to the production possibility curve AB at P_s, to the transformation curve P_sS at C_s, and to the social indifference curve U_s at C_s are parallel. We here depict a case where $U_s > U_t$: smuggling is welfare-improving. We could, however, equally readily have redrawn the diagram to show $U_s < U_t$, i.e. that smuggling had reduced welfare.

Thus we have the following proposition. *For nonprohibitive tariffs, and increasing costs and monopoly in smuggling, smuggling cannot be welfare-ranked* vis-à-vis *nonsmuggling when legal trade is eliminated by smuggling.*

We note, therefore, that the conclusions are identical regardless of whether smuggling is competitive or monopolistic.

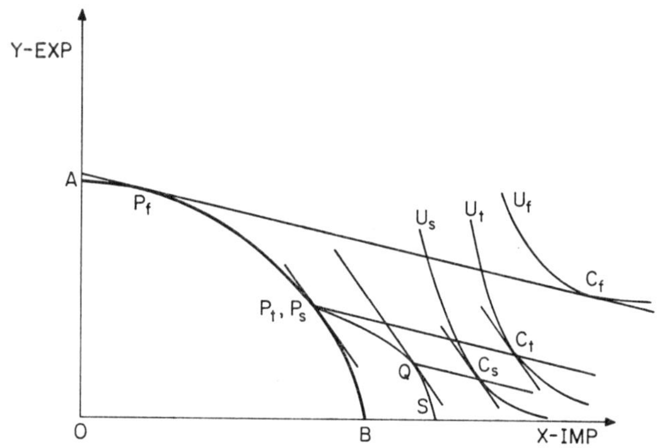

Fig. 8. Monopoly in smuggling at increasing costs (contd.). This figure shows the *simultaneous* presence of smuggling and legal trade in equilibrium. It is easy to see that, *in this case of continued legal trade in the presence of smuggling*, smuggling is necessarily inferior to nonsmuggling: $U_t > U_s$. Concerning the possibility that $U_t < U_s$ in case of multiple equilibria, see caption to fig. 3.

Consider now, however, the case where smuggling fails to eliminate legal trade. Fig. 8 illustrates this case. As with the competitive smuggling case, we find that $U_s < U_t$ and that smuggling necessarily reduces welfare. Again, it is easy to see why: with legal trade continuing, the distortion in domestic production and consumption must be *identical* between the smuggling and nonsmuggling situations, whereas the presence of smuggling imposes an (additional) terms of trade loss. Thus we can conclude: *for nonprohibitive tariffs, and increasing costs and monopoly in smuggling, smuggling is necessarily inferior to nonsmuggling when smuggling does not eliminate legal trade.*

2.5. *Prohibitive tariffs*

Note, however, that we have explicitly qualified all our propositions by stating them as valid for *nonprohibitive tariffs* alone. The reason for this is clear enough. When we consider a prohibitive tariff, the nonsmuggling situation is autarkic. Smuggling then makes trade feasible; the appropriate analogy now is with a *trade-creating* customs union, as distinct from a trade-diverting customs union, and clearly gains must necessarily accrue from smuggling. We can thus conclude: *for prohibitive tariffs, smuggling is necessarily superior to nonsmuggling, whether smuggling is competitive or monopolistic, and whether subject to constant or increasing costs.*

2.6. *Perfect competition vs. monopoly in smuggling*

A comparison between figs. 6 and 8 leads directly to the following conclusion. *When legal trade and smuggling coexist at nonprohibitive tariffs and increasing costs in smuggling, monopoly in smuggling is better than perfect competition.*

In other words, the more smugglers we put in jail, the better! This sounds quite reasonable and proper: economics and morality coincide in their prescriptions! (When legal trade is eliminated, however, monopoly and competition cannot be ranked thus. And at constant costs the two are identical (on our assumptions).) Our result is analogous to the familiar proposition in optimum tariff theory that the exercise of monopoly power by a country improves its welfare. In this instance the smuggler's exercise of his monopoly power is tantamount (on our assumptions) to the country's adopting an optimum tariff policy along the smuggling transformation curve; hence it clearly yields a superior welfare level than if smuggling were competitive.

3. Exogenously specified objectives: target increase in importable production

The preceding analysis is essentially of interest where the economist thinks either that the tariff policy is misconceived or that it is an historical accident. In either case, the economist is likely to argue – and indeed such arguments are frequently asserted in practice – that smuggling *must* be welfare-improving, a notion that we have just demonstrated to be unsustainable as a general proposition.

But suppose now that the tariff has been imposed to achieve some definite end. Assume that the government wishes to achieve a prespecified degree of protection for the import-competing industry. We then have the following proposition. *To attain a feasible target increase in domestic production of the importable good, a tariff with no smuggling is superior to a tariff with smuggling.*

This proposition is illustrated in fig. 9. With the production point fixed by the target specification at $P_s(P_t)$, it follows that $U_s < U_t$. Again, the rationale of this result can be readily grasped by noting that the *fixing* of the production point makes the production distortion *identical* between the smuggling and the non-smuggling situations, whereas the terms of trade under smuggling are inferior to those under legal trade. Consumption is again at identically distorted prices (at C_t and C_s under the nonsmuggling and the smuggling situations, respectively). Hence smuggling must necessarily worsen welfare.

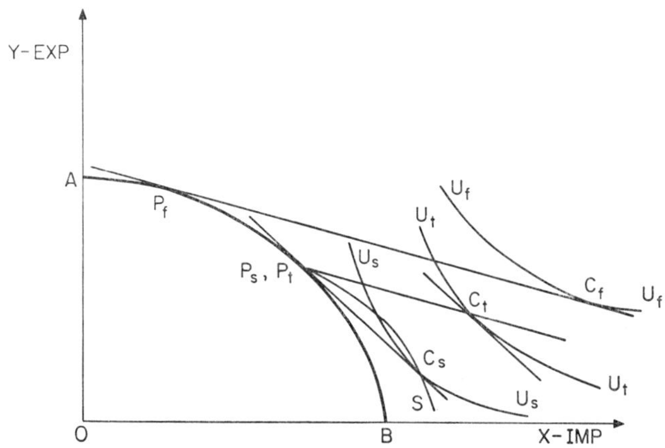

Fig. 9. Smuggling at predetermined production point. Note that the production of X, the importable commodity, cannot fall below $P_s = P_t$. A suitable tariff, in the absence of smuggling, will take welfare to U_t. A *higher* tariff, in the presence of smuggling (at transformation curve P_sC_sS), would (necessarily) produce lower welfare at U_s. The same result could be illustrated for the case where smuggling does *not* eliminate legal trade, as also for monopolistic smuggling.

This result is of interest not merely because it reinforces our critique of the customarily complacent view of smuggling, but also because it would seem to us to provide yet another argument in support of the view that, for a *production* noneconomic objective, a production tax-cum-subsidy policy is superior to a tariff policy (Corden, 1957; Bhagwati and Srinivasan, 1969). In the presence of smuggling, the tariff rate needed to encourage domestic import-competing production is clearly *greater* than if smuggling is not present, and this conclusion is clearly of considerable significance to countries such as Afghanistan and Indonesia, where smuggling assumes significant dimensions.

4. Overinvoicing and underinvoicing of transactions

Our analysis of smuggling can also be readily extended to quasi-smuggling phenomena, such as the overinvoicing and underinvoicing of transactions on *legal* trade. For earlier analyses of such phenomena, seeking different answers, see Bhagwati (1969); Bhagwati and Desai (1970); and Winston (1970). We demonstrate how this can be done for the case where the presence of a tariff duty leads to underinvoicing of imports.

We should distinguish between two possibilities: (1) where the underinvoicing of imports amounts merely to a *de facto* reduction in the tariff, so that the smuggling situation is equivalent to a lowering of the tariff; and (2) where the resulting gain to the importer has to be shared, in some degree, with the exporter who collaborates in the faking of the invoices, in which case the effective c.i.f. price of importation to the importing country rises, entailing a terms of trade loss.

Clearly, the latter case is equivalent to our analysis of smuggling, and therefore no modification in our conclusions is necessary. However, in the former case, our conclusions get critically affected. For, with underinvoicing amounting only to a lower tariff, it follows that it must necessarily be superior to a non-underinvoicing situation, and for the case where a target-specified degree of domestic production of the importable must be achieved, it clearly makes no difference now whether there is faking of invoices or not; with faking, the tariff will just have to be set higher, and the faking-inclusive real situation will then be identical with that which would have been obtained without faking but with a lower tariff[9].

5. Conclusions

We have thus managed to incorporate successfully the phenomena of smuggling and faked invoicing into the welfare analysis of tariffs. Our analysis is clearly generalizable, and in a sequel to this paper we propose to extend our analysis into two major areas: (1) the welfare analysis of domestic taxation; and (2) other propositions in the theory of trade and welfare[10].

[9] As with smuggling, however, the degree of protection sought may be unattainable in the presence of faking of invoices.

[10] In particular, our analysis must be extended to a multiple-good model, while the present analysis has explored only the two-good model throughout. Further, we have dealt in the present

Acknowledgements

Helpful comments were received on an earlier draft of this paper from Abba Lerner, Earl Rolph, Murray Kemp, and Ernest Nadel. Bhagwati's research has been supported by the National Science Foundation.

References

Beccaria, C., 1764–1765, Tentativo Analitico Sui Contrabbandi, Estratto dal foglio periodico intitolato: il Caffé, vol. I (Brescia), reprinted in: Scrittori Classici Italiani di Economia Politica, 1804, parte moderna, tomo XII (Milano), 235–241.

Bhagwati, J., 1968, The gains from trade once again, Oxford Economic Papers XX, 137–148.

Bhagwati, J., 1969, Fiscal Policies, the Faking of Foreign Trade Declarations and the Balance of Payments, Trade, Tariffs, and Growth (M.I.T. Press, Cambridge, Mass.), 266–294.

Bhagwati, J. and T. N. Srinivasan, 1969, Optimal intervention to achieve non-economic objectives, Review of Economic Studies XXXVI, 27–38.

Bhagwati, J. and P. Desai, 1970, India: Planning for Industrialization (Oxford University Press, London).

Corden, W. M., 1957, Tariffs, subsidies, and the terms of trade, Economica XXIV, 235–242.

Hansen, B., 1971, Economic Development in Afghanistan: An Appraisal (submitted to Secretariat of United Nations ECAFE, Bangkok).

Smith, H. H. et al., 1969, Area Handbook for Afghanistan (U.S. Government Printing Office, Washington, D.C.).

Winston, G., 1970, Overinvoicing, underutilization and distorted industrial growth, Pakistan Development Review X, 405–421.

paper only with the smuggling of goods rather than bads (such as heroin) or of assets (such as gold), whose analysis must be conducted in the framework of differently constructed models. Finally, we may note explicitly that we (correctly, in our view) conceive of smuggling as necessarily taking place in the presence of governmental attempts at enforcing the tariff. (Norman Mintz has pointed out to us that if we were to postulate instead that the government does not do so, the smuggling equilibrium would be identical with the free-trade equilibrium: the real cost of smuggling trade would be no different from that of legal trade in this case because the smugglers would be merely walking past the customs officers, choosing not to pay the tariff and not being penalized for doing so! This situation would be both nonsensical and unrealistic; we have therefore assumed that smuggling necessarily takes place in the context of enforcement.) As with traditional analysis, however, where the cost of operating the tariff is not explicitly taken into account by, say, a shrunk-in production possibility curve, we have simply ignored this aspect of the tariff-enforcement costs. We should also add that our analytical technique for treating smuggling costs is identical to the well-known Samuelson technique for treating transportation costs as using one or both of the two goods, rather than domestic primary factors, within the standard two-good model; and that this technique also has empirical justification when trade goods are literally lost or perish in illegal transit. If, however, we were to consider legal and illegal trade as both using *primary* domestic factors, then we would have to work with a more complex production-and-trade model.

Chapter 2

AN ALTERNATIVE PROOF OF THE BHAGWATI–HANSEN RESULTS ON SMUGGLING AND WELFARE

Jagdish N. BHAGWATI and T. N. SRINIVASAN

1. Introduction

In this note we formally analyse the impact of smuggling on welfare, for a small country, and derive the basic results in the Bhagwati–Hansen paper.

Consider a country with no monopoly power in trade, producing two goods at level X_1, $G(X_1)$ when G is the transformation function ($G > 0$, $G' < 0$, $G'' < 0$ for $0 \leqslant X_1 \leqslant \bar{X}_1$). Assume perfect competition in domestic markets. Let foreign trade take place through two channels: legal and smuggler's. Let the first commodity be imported, and the second commodity (exportables) be the numéraire. Let there be no production taxes or subsidies, nor consumption taxes or subsidies (other than tariffs).

Let p_d be the domestic price ratio and p_ℓ, p_s the foreign price ratios for legal trade and smuggler's trade. Let C_i be the consumption of commodity i. Let x_ℓ, x_s be the imports of commodity 1 through the legal and smuggler's channels respectively. Let $U(C_1, C_2)$ be the social utility function. Now,

$$C_1 = X_1 + x_\ell + x_s, \tag{1}$$

$$C_2 = G(X_1) - p_\ell x_\ell - p_s x_s, \tag{2}$$

$$U_1 = p_d U_2, \tag{3}$$

and

$$-G'(X_1) = p_d. \tag{4}$$

The first two equations are commodity balance equations. Eqs. (3) and (4) follow from utility and profit maximization under competition, given p_d and the budget and transformation constraints. There are in all eight unknowns: C_1, C_2, X_1, x_ℓ, x_s, p_ℓ, p_d, p_s. To determine an equilibrium, in general we need four more equations, describing the determination of p_ℓ, p_s and the relationship of the domestic price ratio p_d to p_ℓ and p_s. To this we turn.

2. Case I: Legal trade eliminated by smuggling

Consider a country with no monopoly power in trade, i.e. $p_{\ell} = \bar{p}_{\ell}$. Assume that it imposes a tariff at the *ad valorem* rate t and that the tariff succeeds in eliminating legal trade, i.e. $x_{\ell} = 0$. Assume further that there is perfect competition in smuggling, so that $p_s = p_d$. If smugglers face constant costs, then $p_s = \bar{p}_s$; otherwise $p_s = h(x_s)/x_s$ where $h(x_s)$ represents the exports of commodity 2 needed to be smuggled out for getting smuggled imports of commodity 1 at level x_s. We shall assume that $h(0) = 0$, $h' > 0$, $h'' > 0$, implying that p_s is an increasing function of x_s and $p_s < h'$. Thus, the equations

$$p_{\ell} = \bar{p}_{\ell},\ x_{\ell} = 0,\ p_s = p_d,\ p_s = \bar{p}_s,$$

or

$$p_{\ell} = \bar{p}_{\ell},\ x_{\ell} = 0,\ p_s = p_d,\ p_s = h(x_s)/x_s,$$

taken with eqs. (1)–(4), determine the equilibrium.

We now wish to compare the welfare level U^s achieved under smuggling with the welfare level U^t under the given tariff t with no smuggling. Clearly if the domestic price ratio p_d $(= p_s)$ coincides with $\bar{p}_{\ell}(1 + t)$, the tariff-inclusive price of legal imports, then welfare without smuggling will be higher than that with smuggling. For, in this case, production levels are the same in the two situations, but smuggling involves inferior terms of trade compared to the tariff situation. Thus, $U^s < U^t$ when $p_d = p_s = \bar{p}_{\ell}(1 + t)$.

Let us now compute the derivation of U^s as $p_d = p_s$ falls *below* $\bar{p}_{\ell}(1 + t)$:

$$\begin{aligned}
\frac{dU^s}{dp_d} &= U_1^s \frac{dC_1}{dp_d} + U_2^s \frac{dC_2}{dp_d}, \\
&= U_2^s\left(p_d \frac{dC_1}{dp_d} + \frac{dC_2}{dp_d}\right), \text{ using (3)}, \\
&= U_2^s\left\{\frac{d}{dp_d}(p_d C_1 + C_2) - C_1\right\}, \\
&= U_2^s\left[\frac{d}{dp_d}\{p_d X_1 + G(X_1)\} - C_1\right], \text{ using } p_d = p_s,\ x_{\ell} = 0, \\
&= U_2^s(X_1 - C_1), \text{ using (4)}, \\
&= -U_2^s x_s, \text{ using (1) and } x_{\ell} = 0, \\
&< 0.
\end{aligned}$$

This implies that as p_d falls from $\bar{p}_\ell(1 + t)$, U^s increases. If p_d falls to $\bar{p}_\ell$, we reach free-trade equilibrium and hence $U^s > U^t$. Hence there exists a unique p_d^* such that $U^s = U^t$ and $U^s \gtreqless U^t$ according as $p_d \lesseqgtr p_d^*$.

Thus, when legal trade is eliminated by competitive smuggling given the tariff, smuggling will improve welfare provided the smuggling equilibrium p_d is below the critical value p_d^* and will worsen it for p_d above p_d^*.[1]

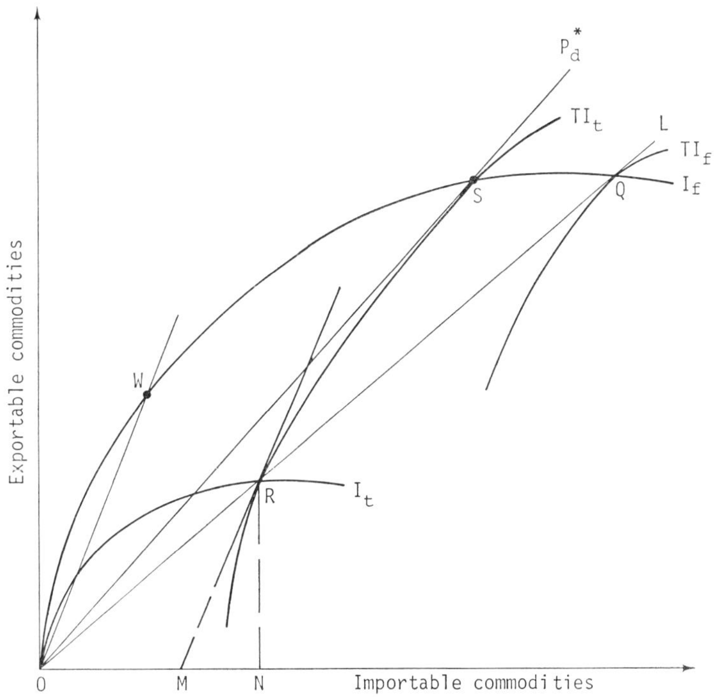

Fig. 1.

This proposition can be readily illustrated with the aid of the trade-indifference curve technique. In fig. 1, OI_f is the country's free-trade offer curve, OL the legal-trade offer curve facing it, and with the tariff at rate OM/MN, the tariff-ridden offer curve is OI_t. The country's trade-indifference curve touching the domestic tariff-inclusive price-ratio MR at R is TI_t. It follows that P_d^* is the smuggler's offer which, under smuggling, would bring the economy to the *same* welfare level

[1] It is clear that when the tariff is prohibitive so that the equilibrium in the absence of smuggling is one of autarky, p_d* coincides with the autarky equilibrium price and hence smuggling, by setting p_d below p_d*, necessarily improves welfare.

TI_t at S. We can thus distinguish the following regions: (1) *zone I:* where the smugglers' offer curve lies between OQ and OS: in this zone, smuggling clearly must improve welfare; (2) *zone II:* where the smugglers' offer curve lies between OS and OW (= MR): here, smuggling will worsen welfare; and (3) *zone III:* where the smugglers' offer curve lies to the left of OW: in this case smuggling will cease and welfare will be unchanged, at level TI_t (at R)[2].

3. Case II: Legal trade co-existing with smuggling

Assume now that, in the smuggling situation, legal trade is *not* eliminated. This case will arise only when $p_s = p_d = \bar{p}_\ell(1 + t)$. When this is so, however, we have already seen that smuggling must result in inferior terms of trade and the consequent loss therefrom is maximal if smuggling replaces legal trade fully and is zero if smuggling does not occur – these two being the extreme possibilities in this situation. It follows that, in the smuggling situation, if the two forms of trade actually co-exist, the welfare level must be lower than in the non-smuggling situation.

[2] At OW, smuggling may be zero, in which case welfare will be unchanged; if positive smuggling occurs, as it can (because $OW = MR$), welfare will have reduced below the level in the absence of smuggling.

Chapter 3

SMUGGLING AND TRADE POLICY

Jagdish N. BHAGWATI and T. N. SRINIVASAN

1. Introduction

Bhagwati and Hansen (1973) have shown that the phenomenon of smuggling in an open economy can be incorporated readily into standard trade-theoretic analysis by treating smuggling as essentially involving a less favourable transformation curve insofar as smuggling involves a real cost[1].

In this paper, we utilise the same analytical device and extend the Bhagwati–Hansen analysis to a number of other issues traditionally considered in the theory of international trade policy. We use the same analytical simplifications:

(i) Smuggled goods and legal imports are cleared at the same final price: consumers do not discriminate in their purchases between the two sources of supply.

(ii) Changes in social welfare are analysed by reference to a standard Crusoe-type social utility function defined on the *current* availability of goods and services.

(iii) Goods constituting consumption and directly entering the utility function are smuggled, and *not* bads (e.g. heroin) or assets (e.g. gold): the model used for our analysis is the traditional trade-theoretic model where non-traded primary factors produce traded final goods entering the utility function.

(iv) Expenditure on enforcement of the tariff is held implicitly constant in comparing the tariff-with-smuggling and tariff-without-smuggling situations and is not explicitly considered, in keeping with the tradition of trade theory, in comparing either with the free-trade situation: one important effect is to rule out analysis of the possible trade-offs between increased enforcement expenditure and reduced smuggling.

(v) Finally, the bulk of our formal analysis is based on the two-traded-goods model.

Section 2 considers a country with monopoly power in (legal) trade (the small-

[1] This real cost arises insofar as the avoidance of normal trade channels leads to increased costs, e.g. more expensive transport and higher f.o.b. price for imports.

country analytical results then being derivable as a special case) and derives the first-order conditions for an optimal solution when smuggling is possible and examines the set of policies that would yield this optimum. Noting that this set of policies is not operationally feasible in general, we proceed to examine therefore in sect. 3 the following issues in the 'second-best' domain where a tariff is the only policy instrument available. The following questions are considered:

(i) How does the optimal tariff without smuggling – which is clearly the first-best policy instrument – rank with the optimal tariff with smuggling – which is clearly, in light of sect. 3, *not* a first-best policy instrument?

(ii) How does the maximal-revenue tariff in the presence of smuggling[2] compare with the optimal tariff in the presence of smuggling?

(iii) How does the maximal-revenue tariff in the presence of smuggling compare with the maximal-revenue tariff in its absence?

(iv) Is the maximal revenue that can be collected with smuggling lower than the maximal revenue in the absence of smuggling?

(v) For any *given* revenue, is the tariff rate with smuggling greater than the tariff rate without smuggling?

In sect. 4, we summarise our results in tabular form.

2. First-best solution

Consider a country producing two goods at levels X_1, $G(X_1)$ when G is the transformation function ($G > 0$, $G' < 0$, $G'' < 0$ for $0 \leqslant X_1 \leqslant \bar{X}_1$). Let foreign trade take place through two channels: legal and smuggler's. Let the first commodity be imported, and the second commodity (exportables) be the numéraire.

Let p_d be the domestic price ratio and p_ℓ, p_s the foreign price ratios for legal trade and smuggler's trade. Let C_i be the consumption of commodity i. Let x_ℓ, x_s be the imports of commodity 1 through the legal and smuggler's channels respectively. Let $U(C_1, C_2)$ be the concave social utility function.

Let $p_\ell = g(x_\ell)/x_\ell$ where $g(x_\ell)$ represents the exports of commodity 2 needed for getting imports of x_ℓ units of commodity 1 through legal trade. We shall assume that $g(0) = 0$, $g' > 0$, $g'' \geqslant 0$ (where primes denote derivatives of appropriate order) implying that p_ℓ is a non-decreasing function of x_ℓ and $p_\ell < g'$. Clearly the case where $g'' \equiv 0$ will correspond to a situation where there is no monopoly power in trade. Analogously, let us assume $p_s = h(x_s)/x_s$ where $h(0) = 0$, $h' > 0$, $h'' \geqslant 0$. Again, the case where $h'' \equiv 0$ will correspond to the case where there are constant costs in smuggling:

[2] It has been shown that, without smuggling, the maximal revenue tariff is greater than the optimal tariff (Johnson, 1950).

$$C_1 \leqslant X_1 + x_\ell + x_s, \tag{1}$$

$$C_2 \leqslant G(X_1) - g(x_\ell) - h(x_s), \tag{2}$$

$$C_1, C_2, X_1, x_\ell, x_s \geqslant 0.$$

Maximising the Lagrangean $\Phi = U - \lambda_1[C_1 - X_1 - x_\ell - x_s] - \lambda_2[C_2 - G + g + h]$, we get (for our interior solution)

$$U_1 = \lambda_1, \tag{3}$$

$$U_2 = \lambda_2, \tag{4}$$

$$\lambda_1 + \lambda_2 G' = 0, \tag{5}$$

$$\lambda_1 - \lambda_2 g' = 0, \tag{6}$$

$$\lambda_1 - \lambda_2 h' = 0, \tag{7}$$

or

$$U_1/U_2 = -G' = g' = h'. \tag{8}$$

In other words, the marginal rate of substitution in consumption is equated to the marginal rate of transformation in production, in legal trade and in smuggling.

If we do not wish to rule out corner solutions we can rewrite eqs. (3)–(7) as follows:

$$U_1 - \lambda_1 \leqslant 0 \quad \text{with equality if } C_1 > 0,$$

$$U_2 - \lambda_2 \leqslant 0 \quad \text{with equality if } C_2 > 0,$$

$$\lambda_1 + \lambda_2 G' \leqslant 0 \quad \text{with equality if } X_1 > 0,$$

$$\lambda_1 - \lambda_2 g' \leqslant 0 \quad \text{with equality if } x_\ell > 0,$$

$$\lambda_1 - \lambda_2 h' \leqslant 0 \quad \text{with equality if } x_s > 0.$$

One particular corner solution is of some interest. Suppose there is no monopoly power in legal trade, i.e. $g = p^f x$ where p^f is the fixed world terms of trade. Ruling out specialisation in consumption and production, the optimal solution will be characterised by free trade and no smuggling if

$$U_1 = \lambda_1,\ U_2 = \lambda_2,\ \lambda_1 + \lambda_2 G' = 0,\ \lambda_1 = \lambda_2 g' = \lambda_2 p^f,$$

and

$$h'(0) \geqslant \lambda_1/\lambda_2 = p^f.$$

In other words, free trade will be the optimal policy in the absence of monopoly power in trade if, as we have assumed, the marginal terms of trade of the smuggler at zero level of smuggling is not superior to the legal world terms of trade, i.e. there is no incentive for smuggling when free trade prices prevail in domestic markets.

Returning, however, to an interior solution and the case of monopoly power in trade, and assuming competitive smuggling, production and consumption, we can sustain the optimal solution obtained above by:

(i) consumption tax at an *ad valorem* rate c so that $\{h(x_s)/x_s\}$ $(1 + c) = h'$;

(ii) tariffs (subsidies) on legal imports at an *ad valorem* rate t so that $\{g(x_\ell)/x_\ell\}$ $(1 + t) = h(x_s)/x_s$;

(iii) production subsidies at the rate s so that $\{h(x_s)/(x_s)\}$ $(1 + s) = -G'$.

In this framework, if we introduce a non-economic objective of raising the production of importables X_1 to some preassigned level X_1^* in the form of a constraint $-X_1 \leqslant -X_1^*$, we add the expression $-\lambda_3(-X_1 + X_1^*)$ to the Lagrangean and maximise. The first-order conditions (3), (4), (6) and (7) continue to hold. Eq. (5) gets modified to

$$\lambda_1 + \lambda_2 G' + \lambda_3 = 0. \tag{9}$$

Of course, the solutions for C_1, C_2, X_1, X_2, x_ℓ, x_s, λ_1, λ_2 will be different with the non-economic objective present. The form of policy interventions, however, are the same[3]: consumption tax, tariff (subsidy) on legal imports and a production subsidy. In the presence of the non-economic objective, the production subsidy at rate s that equates $\{h(x_s)/x_s\}$ $(1 + s)$ to $-G'$ will be higher than the consumption tax c that equates $\{h(x)_s/x_s\}$ $(1 + c)$ to h' since

$$-G' = \frac{\lambda_1}{\lambda_2} + \frac{\lambda_3}{\lambda_2} = h' + \frac{\lambda_3}{\lambda_2} > h',$$

whereas in the absence of the non-economic objective the two rates will be equal.

3. Optimal tariff and revenue questions

While the analysis of the optimal policy mix in the presence of smuggling and monopoly power in (legal) trade that we have just set out is technically correct, it does assume the oddity that the smuggled goods be subject to consumption

[3] Other non-economic objectives analysed by Bhagwati and Srinivasan (1969) can be introduced in the presence of smuggling with exactly the same type of policy consequences as for the case of production analysed in the text.

taxes in the same way as legally-traded goods. If we rule this out, and assume instead that smuggled goods fetch to the smuggler the tariff-inclusive price plus or minus the tax or subsidy on consumption of the legal imports and production, then the achievement of the optimal solution is impossible. We then have a second-best problem which we propose to tackle in a subsequent paper.

Instead we proceed to examine the question of the optimum level at which the tariff can be set, in the presence of smuggling, when the tariff is the only policy instrument available[4]. We also extend the analysis, using only the tariff as a policy variable, to questions posed by revenue as an objective.

Let us then set out the conditions of equilibrium, given a tariff rate t, in the absence of smuggling A and in the presence of smuggling P:

A		P	
$C_{1A} = X_{1A} + x_{\ell A}$	(10A)	$C_{1P} = X_{1P} + x_{\ell P} + x_{sP},$	(10P)
$C_{2A} = G(X_{1A}) - g(x_{\ell A})$	(11A)	$C_{2P} = G(X_{1P}) - g(x_{\ell P}) - h(x_{sP}),$	(11P)
$U_{1A}/U_{2A} = p_{dA}(t)$	(12A)	$U_{1P}/U_{2P} = p_{dP}(t),$	(12P)
$-G'(X_{1A}) = p_{dA}(t)$	(13A)	$-G'(X_{1P}) = p_{dP}(t),$	(13P)
$\dfrac{g(x_{\ell A})(1+t)}{x_{\ell A}} = p_{dA}(t)$	(14A)	$\dfrac{g(x_{\ell P})(1+t)}{x_{\ell P}} = p_{dP}(t),$	(14P)
		$h(x_{sP})/x_{sP} = p_{dP}(t).$	(15P)

As a preliminary to deriving the tariff rates that maximise revenue or welfare, let us derive the rates of change of the equilibrium values of some of the variables (denoted by a dot over the variable) with respect to changes in tariff. It can be shown that

$$\dot{X}_{1A} = \frac{G'}{G''}\frac{(1-\theta_A)}{(1+t)} > 0 \qquad \dot{X}_{1P} = \frac{G'}{G''}\frac{(1-\theta_P)}{(1+t)} > 0,$$

$$\dot{x}_{\ell A} = \frac{-\theta_A}{(1+t)\{(g'/g) - (1/x_{\ell A})\}} < 0 \qquad \dot{x}_{\ell P} = \frac{-\theta_P}{(1+t)\{(g'/g) - (1/x_{\ell P})\}} < 0,$$

$$\dot{p}_{dA} = \frac{p_{dA}(1-\theta_A)}{(1+t)} > 0 \qquad \dot{p}_{dP} = \frac{p_{dP}(1-\theta_P)}{(1+t)} > 0,$$

[4] This is a problem of policy relevance as a number of LDCs are not equipped to utilise other instruments (such as production and consumption taxes) with quite the same efficacy.

$$\dot{x}_{sP} = \frac{(1 - \theta_P)}{(1 + t)\{(h'/h) - (1/x_{sP})\}} > 0,$$

where

$$\theta_A = \frac{P_A/G'' + U_2}{P_A/G'' + U_2 - Q_A/p_{dA}} \qquad \theta_P = \frac{P_P/G'' + U_2 - R_P/p_{dP}}{P_P/G'' + U_2 - (Q_P + R_P)/p_{dP}},$$

$$P_A = (U_{11} - p_{dA}U_{21}) - p_{dA}(U_{12} - p_{dA}U_{22}) < 0 \qquad P_P = (U_{11} - p_{dP}U_{21}) - p_{dP}(U_{12} - p_{dP}U_{22}) < 0,$$

$$Q_A = \frac{(U_{11} - p_{dA}U_{21}) - g'(U_{12} - p_{dA}U_{22})}{(g'/g) - (1/x_{\ell A})} < 0 \qquad Q_P = \frac{(U_{11} - p_{dP}U_{21}) - g'(U_{12} - p_{dP}U_{22})}{(g'/g) - (1/x_{\ell P})} < 0,$$

$$R_P = \frac{(U_{11} - p_{dP}U_{21}) - h'(U_{12} - p_{dP}U_{22})}{(h'/h) - (1/x_{sP})} < 0.$$

Since $U_2 > 0$, $G'' > 0$ it is clear that $0 < \theta_A, \theta_P < 1$. Neither good is assumed inferior in consumption to ensure P_A, P_P, Q_A, Q_P, R_P are negative.

Maximal-revenue tariffs: Let us first consider the maximisation of revenue: T_A, T_P. Now,

$$T_A = g(x_{\ell A})t \qquad T_P = g(x_{\ell P})t,$$

$$\dot{T}_A = g + tg'\dot{x}_{\ell A} \qquad \dot{T}_P = g + tg'\dot{x}_{\ell P}.$$

Let us assume that T_A and T_P attain a unique maximum at the solution of $\dot{T}_A = 0$ and $\dot{T}_P = 0$ respectively. Let us denote the solutions by t^*_{AT} and t^*_{PT}. By definition[5], $\dot{T}_A \gtreqless 0$ according as $t \lesseqgtr t^*_{AT}$ and $\dot{T}_P \gtreqless 0$ according as $t \lesseqgtr t^*_{PT}$. By substituting for $\dot{x}_{\ell A}$, $\dot{x}_{\ell P}$ in the expressions for $\dot{T}_A$ and $\dot{T}_P$ respectively we can then show that

$$\frac{1+t}{t} \gtreqless \frac{\theta_A(g'/g)}{(g'/g) - (1/x_{\ell A})} \quad \text{according as } t \lesseqgtr t^*_{AT},$$

and

$$\frac{1+t}{t} \gtreqless \frac{\theta_P(g'/g)}{(g'/g) - (1/x_{\ell P})} \quad \text{according as } t \lesseqgtr t^*_{PT}.$$

[5] This is true, in general, only for values of t in a neighbourhood of $t_{AT}{}^*$ and $t_{PT}{}^*$, respectively.

Optimal tariffs: Denoting the welfare levels achieved in the absence and in the presence of smuggling by U_A and U_P, we can next show that

$$\dot{U}_A = U_2(p_{dA} - g')\dot{x}_{\ell A}; \quad \dot{U}_P = U_2\{(p_{dP} - g')\dot{x}_{\ell P} + (p_{dP} - h')\dot{x}_{sP}\}.$$

Let us assume that U_A and U_P attain their unique maximum at the solution t^*_{AU} and t^*_{PU} respectively of $\dot{U}_A = 0$ and $\dot{U}_P = 0$. Then, by definition, $\dot{U}_A \gtrless 0$ according as $t \lessgtr t^*_{AU}$ and $\dot{U}_P \gtrless 0$ according as $t \lessgtr t^*_{PU}$. By substituting for $\dot{x}_{\ell A}$, $\dot{x}_{\ell P}$, $\dot{x}_{sP}$ in the expression for $\dot{U}_A$ and $\dot{U}_P$ respectively, we can thus show that

$$\frac{1+t}{t} \gtrless \frac{(g'/g)}{(g'/g) - (1/x_{\ell A})} \text{ according as } t \lessgtr t^*_{AU},$$

$$\frac{1+t}{t} \gtrless \frac{(\theta_P)(g'/g) - (1-\theta_P)\{(g'/g) - (1/x_{\ell P})\}(h/g)}{\{(g'/g) - (1/x_{\ell P})\}\{(\theta_P) - (1-\theta_P)(h/g)\}}$$

$$\text{according as } t \lessgtr t^*_{PU}.$$

These inequalities hold in a neighbourhood of t^*_{AT} and t^*_{PT} respectively. We can now proceed to answer the questions which we posed in the introduction.

3.1. Comparison of maximal-revenue and optimal tariffs in the absence of smuggling

This implies ranking t^*_{AT} and t^*_{AU}; and, as is already known from Johnson's classic analysis (Johnson, 1950–1951), $t^*_{AT} > t^*_{AU}$. This follows because $(1+t)/t$ is a decreasing function of t; t^*_{AT} and t^*_{AU} are the solutions of

$$\frac{1+t}{t} = \frac{\theta_A(g'/g)}{(g'/g) - (1/x_{\ell A})} \quad \text{and} \quad \frac{1+t}{t} = \frac{g'/g}{(g'/g) - (1/x_{\ell A})},$$

and θ_A lies between 0 and 1, and

$$\frac{g'/g}{(g'/g) - (1/x_{\ell A})}$$

crosses $(1+t)/t$ from below at $t = t^*_{AU}$.

3.2. Comparison of optimal tariffs in the presence and in the absence of smuggling

We can see that, for constant-elasticity offers such that $\eta_g = xg'(x)/g(x)$ is constant for all $x \geqslant 0$, $t^*_{PU} < t^*_{AU}$, i.e. the optimal tariff in the presence of smuggling is less than in the absence of smuggling. This follows from the facts that $t^*_{AU} = (\eta_g - 1)$ and

$$t^*_{PU} = (\eta_g - 1)\left\{1 - \left(\frac{1}{\theta_P} - 1\right)\frac{h}{g}\right\} < \eta_g - 1.$$

However, η_g is in general a function of the particular x at which it is evaluated: hence, *in general*, we cannot rank t^*_{AU} and t^*_{PU}.

3.3. Comparison of the maximal-revenue and optimal tariffs in the presence of smuggling

We can show that, with smuggling, $t^*_{PT} > t^*_{PU}$, i.e. the maximal-revenue tariff is higher than the optimal tariff, just as in the (traditional) case without smuggling. Note that t^*_{PT} and t^*_{PU} are respectively solutions of

$$\frac{1+t}{t} = \frac{(g'/g)\theta_P}{(g'/g) - (1/x_{\ell P})} \quad \text{and}$$

$$\frac{1+t}{t} = \frac{(\theta_P)(g'/g) - (1-\theta_P)h/g\{(g'/g) - (1/x_{\ell P})\}}{\{(g'/g) - (1/x_{\ell P})\}\{(\theta_P) - (1-\theta_P)h/g\}}.$$

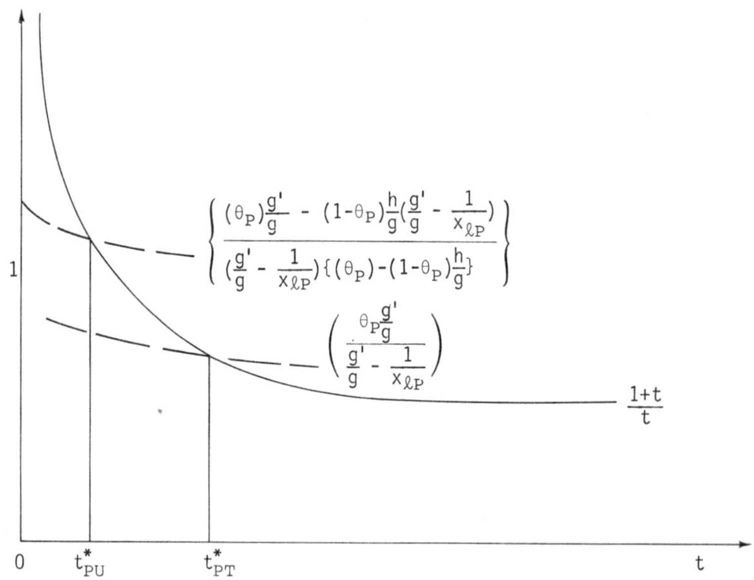

Fig. 1.

Further, $(1 + t)/t$ is a decreasing function t. It can be shown that, when $t = t^*_{PU}$,

$$\frac{1 + t^*_{PU}}{t^*_{PU}} > \frac{\theta_P(g'/g)}{\{(g'/g) - (1/x_{\ell P})\}}.$$

Since

$$\frac{\theta_P(g'/g)}{\{(g'/g) - (1/x_{\ell P})\}}$$

crosses $(1 + t)/t$ from below at $t = t^*_{PT}$, we can conclude that $t^*_{PT} > t^*_{PU}$. Fig. 1 illustrates the situation.

3.4. Comparison of maximal-revenue tariffs in the presence and in the absence of smuggling

As we noted earlier,

$$\frac{1 + t^*_{AT}}{t^*_{AT}} = \frac{\theta_A(g'/g)}{\{(g'/g) - (1/x_{\ell A})\}} = \frac{\theta_A\, \eta_g}{\eta_g - 1} \quad \text{and}$$

$$\frac{1 + t^*_{PT}}{t^*_{PT}} = \frac{\theta_P(g'/g)}{(g'/g) - (1/x_{\ell P})} = \frac{\theta_P\, \eta_g}{\eta_g - 1}.$$

Now θ_A and θ_P involve second derivatives of the welfare and transformation functions and in general we cannot assert anything about the ratio of θ_A to θ_P. Thus even if we were to assume that η_g is a constant, we cannot rank t^*_{AT} and t^*_{PT} and this conclusion holds *a fortiori* if η_g was not a constant.

3.5. Comparison of revenue collected, given the tariff rate, in the presence and in the absence of smuggling

We may now investigate whether the revenue collected, given the tariff rate, will reduce in the presence of smuggling. This is readily shown as follows.

First, we can show that $x_{\ell A}$ reduces as the tariff increases. Let $\bar{t}$ be the tariff that reduces $x_{\ell A}$ to zero. Clearly $\bar{t}$ is determined by $(1 + \bar{t})g'(0) = -G'(X^*_1)$ where X^*_1 is the output of X_1 under autarky[6]. Let us confine ourselves to tariffs in the range $(0, \bar{t})$. Given our assumptions about G, U and g already made and

[6] Implicitly we are assuming $g'(0) < -G'(X_1{}^*)$. This simply means that there is an incentive to import commodity 1 at the autarky point, if there is no tariff.

assuming further that neither good is inferior, corresponding to any tariff t there exists a unique equilibrium in the absence of smuggling.

Consider now a tariff t under which an equilibrium exists in the absence as well as in the presence of smuggling. It is clear that $p_{dP}(t) < p_{dA}(t)$. For if $p_{dP}(t) \geqslant p_{dA}$, then:

(i) (13A) and (13P) will imply $X_{1A} \leqslant X_{1P}$ since $G'' < 0$;

(ii) (14A) and (14P) will imply $x_{\ell A} \leqslant x_{\ell P}$ since $\{g(x)\}/x$ is an increasing function of x;

(iii) by assumption, $x_{sP} > 0$; and

(iv) (10A), (10P), (11A) and (11P) will imply $C_{1A} < C_{1P}$ and $C_{2A} > C_{2P}$. However, given the concavity of U and non-inferiority of either good, $C_{1A} < C_{1P}$, $C_{2A} > C_{2P}$ will imply $U_{1A}/U_{2A} = p_{dA} > U_{1P}/U_{2P} = p_{dP}$, contradicting the assumption that $p_{dP} \geqslant p_{dA}$.

Thus, for the same tariff, $p_{dP} < p_{dA}$ and consequently $x_{\ell P} < x_{\ell A}$. Since at $t = \bar{t}$, $x_{\ell A} = 0$ it follows that the maximal tariff $\bar{\bar{t}}$ for co-existence of smuggling and legal trade will be less than $\bar{t}$. Let us now confine our attention to tariffs in the interval $(0, \bar{\bar{t}})$. Clearly at $t = \bar{\bar{t}}$, $x_{\ell P} = 0$ and $x_{\ell A} > 0$.

From the above it immediately follows that given a tariff, the revenue that can be collected in the presence of smuggling is less than the revenue in the absence of smuggling. For the same tariff, the equilibrium domestic price ratio and legal imports are higher in the absence of smuggling: hence the tariff revenue will be higher. This also means that the maximum tariff revenue that can be collected is greater in the absence of smuggling. However, as we have already argued, we cannot in general rank the tariff rates that generate maximum revenue in the two cases.

3.6. Comparison of tariff rates generating given revenue, in the presence and in the absence of smuggling

We may now investigate yet another problem: in generating a given, feasible revenue, can we argue that smuggling will require necessarily a higher or a lower tariff than if smuggling were not possible?

To analyse this question, consider any tariff revenue $\bar{T}$ that can be collected in the presence and absence of smuggling. If we assume that the revenue $\{T_A(t), T_P(t)\}$ collected by a tariff to increase, reach a maximum and then decrease as t increases[7], there will be pairs of tariffs $(\hat{t}_A, \hat{\hat{t}}_A)$ and $(\hat{t}_P, \hat{\hat{t}}_P)$ that yield $\bar{T}$. Since $T_A(t) > T_P(t)$

[7] This *is* an additional restriction to those we have specified earlier: in general, there is no reason to assume that the revenue collected is not identical at more than two values.

for all relevant t, it is clear that $\hat{t}_A \leqq t_{AT} \leqq \hat{\hat{t}}_A$, $\hat{t}_P \leqq t_{PT} \leqq \hat{\hat{t}}_P$ and $\hat{t}_A < \hat{t}_P \leqq \hat{\hat{t}}_P < \hat{\hat{t}}_A$. Thus, of the two tariffs that collect a given revenue in the absence of smuggling, the *lower* one is *less* than the lower tariff that collects the same revenue in the presence of smuggling, and the *higher* one is *larger* than the higher one.

4. Summary

The results reached in sect. 3 may now be summarised in table 1, as follows[8]:

Table 1.
Summary of results obtained in sect. 3.

Variables \ State of the economy	Absence of smuggling	Presence of smuggling	Ranking
1. Optimal tariff rate	t^*_{AU}	t^*_{PU}	no ranking[a]
2. Revenue maximising tariff rate	t^*_{AT}	t^*_{PT}	no ranking
3. Revenue collected given a tariff	T_A	T_P	$T_A > T_P$
4. A given revenue R is collected by:[b]	$[\hat{t}_A, \hat{\hat{t}}_A]$	$[\hat{t}_P, \hat{\hat{t}}_P]$	$\hat{t}_A < \hat{t}_P$ $\hat{\hat{t}}_A > \hat{\hat{t}}_P$
Ranking	$t^*_{AU} < t^*_{AT}$	$t^*_{PU} < t^*_{PT}$	

[a] for constant elasticity offers it is shown that $t^*_{PU} < t^*_{AU}$.

[b] the revenue collected by a tariff is assumed to increase, reach a maximum and then decrease as the tariff rate increases. $(\hat{t}_i, \hat{\hat{t}}_i)$ refer to the lower and higher rate that collects the given revenue; see illustrative diagram.

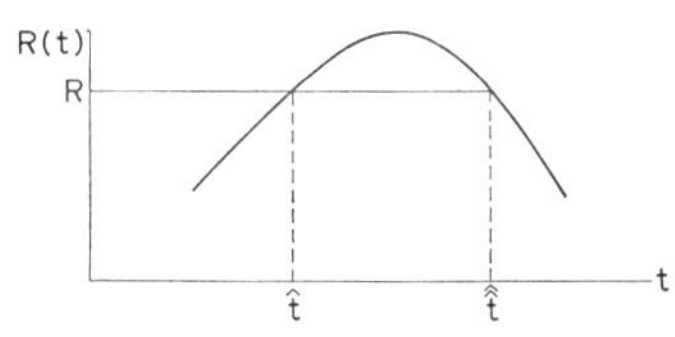

Acknowledgements

The research for this paper was supported by the National Science Foundation. The paper was written while T. N. Srinivasan was Visiting Professor of Economics at M.I.T. Thanks are due to Yasuo Uekawa and the referees for their very helpful comments.

[8] We are thankful to an anonymous referee for having suggested this tabular presentation.

References

Bhagwati, J. and T. N. Srinivasan, 1969, Optimal intervention to achieve non-economic objectives, Review of Economic Studies XXXVI.

Bhagwati, J. and B. Hansen, 1973, A theoretical analysis of smuggling, Quarterly Journal of Economics 87.

Johnson, H. G., 1950–1951, Optimum welfare and maximum revenue tariffs, Review of Economic Studies XIX.

Chapter 4

NOTES ON THE ECONOMIC THEORY OF SMUGGLING*

Harry G. JOHNSON

1. Summary of previous results

Smuggling is an ancient phenomenon, and remains widespread in the modern world. In some countries, even today, it accounts for a high proportion of imports and, by implication, of exports as well. The effects of smuggling on the economic welfare of the country affected are therefore both an interesting and a potentially important question. To assess these welfare effects, it is necessary to have some standard for welfare evaluation. Two general standards are available: one is that of the government which imposes the tariffs that lead to smuggling, the other is that of the traditional private welfare economics of international trade.

On the basis of the former standard, that is, from the government's view, there are various reasons why smuggling may be held to have adverse welfare effects. One is the moral judgment that the successful breaking of laws is bad for society's moral fibre. Another, more mundane, is that smuggling of imports is bad because it reduces the government's (import) tax revenue below what it otherwise would be, and so reduces the amount, or increases the economic cost, of the provision of public goods through government[1]. A third and more specific argument is that, if the 'public good' in question is a given level of domestic production of import-substitutes to be achieved by a tariff, smuggling increases the social cost of providing this public good because smuggling of imports as contrasted with legal importation entails higher real costs of importation without reducing the (tariff-determined) final price to consumers. There is a fourth possibility, which is excluded from this section by the assumption that the country's terms of trade are given by the world market, namely that the tariff imposed by the government

* The first section of these notes is simply a condensation of the paper by Bhagwati and Hansen (1973a), republished in this volume as ch. 1, and entitled 'A theoretical analysis of smuggling'. The second section is more original.

[1] This argument is subject to a possible qualification, that smuggling by increasing exports may increase the tax revenue collected on exports.

is the theoretical optimum tariff, so that smuggling worsens the country's welfare by undermining the optimum tariff policy.

Adopting the private welfare view, on the other hand, and regarding tariffs as merely an arbitrary governmental intervention in the efficient allocation of resources, it may be argued that smuggling increases welfare by reducing or eliminating the arbitrary distortions. This view could be based on the purely ideological belief that anything that reduces the power of the state must be beneficial, regardless of its economics; but that argument belongs in the previous paragraph, and will be ignored henceforward in order to concentrate attention on the traditional criteria of private welfare maximization.

The view that smuggling, by undermining arbitrary governmental barriers to international trade, increases private welfare would obviously be correct if smuggling were a costless operation, because then it would amount merely to a *de facto* elimination of arbitrary barriers to trade. If smuggling involves extra costs by comparison with legal trade, as is obviously the case, the conclusion just stated is not necessarily correct. The problem that then arises can be thought of fruitfully by analogy with the formation of a customs union, the smuggling sector being the partner country in the union. Insofar as smuggling brings in imports that replace domestic production of import-substitutes at a lower social cost, there is beneficial trade creation; but insofar as smuggling also brings in imports that replace imports that otherwise would have entered the country through lower-cost legal channels, there is welfare-reducing trade diversion.

The two extreme possibilities are those already mentioned, namely, where smuggling involves no excess cost of importation over legal trade and its results are purely trade-creating and beneficial, and where smuggling is subject to rising costs for smugglers as a group[2], such that smuggling activity merely replaces legal importation without lowering the cost of imports to consumers. In the latter case it is evident that the social loss from smuggling will be less, the less smuggling there is, i.e. the more steeply rising are the average costs of smuggling. However, insofar as the average costs of smuggling are determined by the enforcement activities of customs officers, there is an obvious trade-off between the costs of such enforcement activities and the social benefits achieved in terms of reduction of the aggregate excess cost of smuggled imports. It is also evident that the social loss from smuggling would be reduced if smuggling were monopolized, since a monopolist would equate the marginal and not the average cost of smuggled goods with their domestic (tariff-inclusive) price.

In between these two extremes is the case in which smuggling raises the social

[2] In line with traditional theory, the rising cost must be interpreted as external to the smuggling firm but internal to the smuggling industry.

cost of imports to the economy while reducing the price to domestic consumers and producers – in the process necessarily replacing legal trade. In this case there are production cost and consumption cost gains to the economy from the *de facto* lowering of the tariff; but these have to be balanced against the fact that erstwhile tariff proceeds (at the *de facto* lower rate due to smuggling) are replaced by the excess costs of the smuggled imports. Whether private welfare increases or decreases depends, as in the more familiar case of a customs union, on whether the production and consumption gains from trade-creation due to lower domestic prices more or less than offset the loss from diversion of trade from lower-cost legal to higher-cost smuggled sources.

The borderline between the two possibilities, for the case in which the excess costs of smuggling are constant, is illustrated in fig. 1. *WW* (not shown for

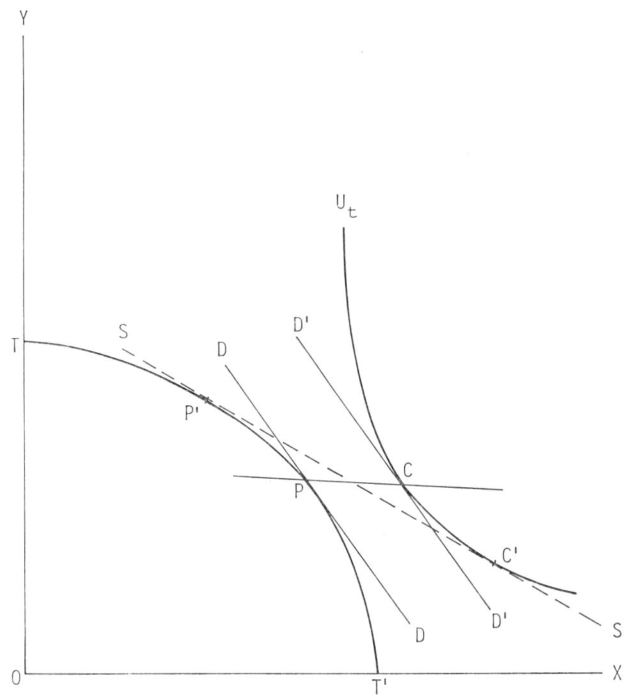

Fig. 1.

simplicity) is the world price ratio, *SS* is the cost ratio in the presence of smuggling, *DD* and *D'D'* are the domestic price ratios set by the tariff, *P* and *C* are the production and consumption points achieved under the tariff in the absence of smuggling, *P'* and *C'* the production and consumption points prevailing with smuggling, and U_t is the welfare level achieved in both cases. It is clear that if the import–export cost ratio with smuggling were steeper than the slope of SS the country would lose by the replacement of legal trade by smuggling, and vice versa.

Note that with constant world prices and constant excess cost of smuggling, it would not matter whether smuggling were competitive, or monopolistically organized. If, on the contrary, the average excess cost of smuggling were an increasing function of the volume of smuggled trade, the combinations of goods the economy could obtain through smuggling, starting from the production position P', would be represented by a curve concave to the origin passing through P' and C'. This curve would contain a segment passing to the north-east of U_t, indicating the possibility of a welfare gain from the replacement of competition by monopoly in smuggling. Of course, if smuggling were monopolized, the production point would not remain at P' (where the marginal cost of production of import substitutes would be less than the marginal cost of obtaining imports through smuggling) but would shift south-easterly along the transformation curve TT'.

2. Revenue and optimal tariffs

The foregoing notes merely summarize results already arrived at by Bhagwati and Hansen (1973a). More can be said, however, about the effects of allowing for the presence of smuggling as an economic activity responsive to the incentive offered for it, in those cases where the tariff is imposed in pursuit of a particular governmental purpose.

First, however, it would be noted that, if the disincentives to and extra costs of smuggling are attributable to customs-enforcement activity, there is a maximization problem for government in the allocation of governmental expenditure to enforcement. The obvious maximization principle is that the marginal unit of expenditure on enforcement should bring in an equivalent amount in extra tariff revenue on trade directed by enforcement from illicit to legal tariff-paying channels. Formally, this criterion can easily be shown to be $E = t\pi S\eta_{\mathrm{SE}}$ where E is expenditure on enforcement, t the tariff rate, π the foreign price of imports, S the quantity of smuggled goods, and η_{SE} the elasticity of the quantum of smuggled imports, written with a reversed sign.

Where the purpose of the imposition of the tariff is a non-economic objective, such as establishing a given level of production of import-substitutes or some desired 'self-sufficiency' level of imports, it is obvious that smuggling makes the achievement of the objective more expensive than it would otherwise be, owing to the excess costs of smuggling over legitimate trade. It is also obvious that there will be an optimum level of expenditure on customs-enforcement, as determined by the formula presented above.

Where the government's objective is to maximize its collection of tariff revenue, it is evident that the possibility of smuggling reduces the maximum-revenue tariff rate by increasing the elasticity of demand for legitimate (tariff-paying) imports. Assuming a fixed level of enforcement expenditure, and a supply of smuggled imports governed by the difference between the foreign price (assumed fixed to avoid optimum tariff complications) and the domestic price (the foreign price augmented by the tariff), the government's tariff revenue is $t\pi(C - P - S)$, where t is the tariff rate, π the fixed foreign price of imports, and C, P and S, are domestic consumption, production and smuggling, each a function of the domestic price $p = (1 + t)\pi$ of imports. The government maximizes revenue by setting

$$\frac{t}{1+t} = \frac{1}{\dfrac{C}{C-P-S}\eta_c + \dfrac{P}{C-P-S}\varepsilon_p + \dfrac{S}{C-P-S}\varepsilon_s},$$

where η_c is the price-elasticity (with positive sign) of domestic consumption of importables, ε_p the price-elasticity of domestic production of importables, and ε_s the price-elasticity of smuggled imports. The revenue-maximizing tariff rate will be lower in the presence than in the absence of smuggling, both because smuggling reduces the quantity of imports to which the tariff applies (the term $C - P - S$), indirectly increasing the elasticity of import demand, and because the supply of smuggling is elastic with respect to the tariff rate (the term ε_s).

Let us now abandon the convenient assumption of fixed terms of trade and consider the implications of the presence of smuggling for the familiar optimum tariff argument. The foregoing argument on maximum-revenue tariffs, together with the standard proposition that in the absence of smuggling the optimum tariff rate must be below the maximum-revenue tariff rate, suggests that the optimum tariff rate will be lower in the presence than in the absence of smuggling. This cannot, however, be proven to be true in general, though it must be true under certain restrictions on the elasticity of the foreign offer curve[3], and there is a presumption that it will be true.

In fig. 2, *OPI* and *OPII* are the offer curves of countries *I* and *II* under free trade, *P* being the free trade equilibrium and *OPT* (not shown for simplicity) the free trade price ratio. Country *I* imposes an optimum tariff (in the absence of

[3] Bhagwati and Srinivasan (1973b) have shown, in their paper which is republished in this volume as ch. 3, that it will be true for a constant elasticity of the quantity of exports demanded in legal trade in exchange for given quantities of imports. I am grateful to Bhagwati for pointing out the need to correct my earlier published analysis in the light of their results, though I cannot as yet establish their criterion geometrically.

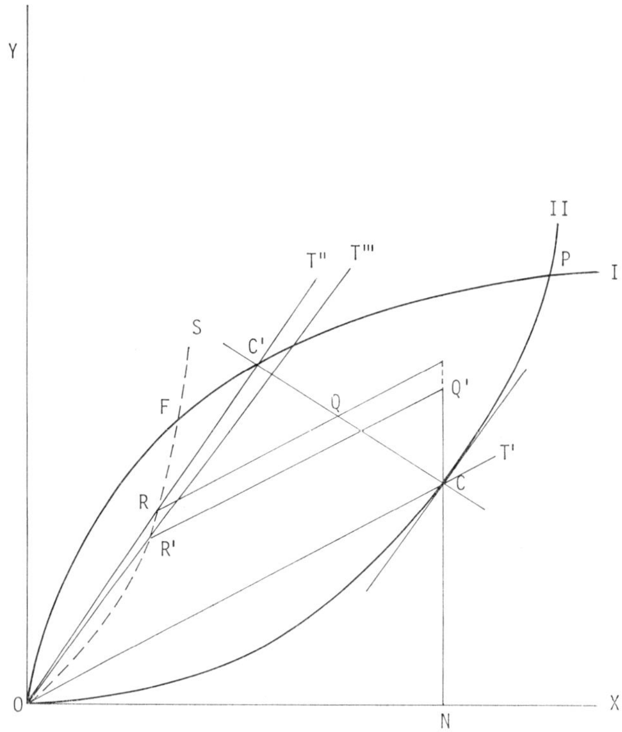

Fig. 2.

smuggling) determined by the tangency of one of its community indifference curves to the foreign offer curve at C; OT' is the world market terms of trade and OT'', parallel to the tangent at C, the domestic price ratio. Now assume the possibility of smuggling at the rising average cost curve ORS[4]. At the domestic price OT'', OR of imports would be smuggled and the community's opportunity line through trade would become ORQ extended. But at the domestic price ratio OT'', the community would choose to consume at point Q, on the income-expansion line $C'C$. There would be a deficiency of import demand and export supply by comparison with the foreign offer of ON imports for CN exports at the terms of trade OT'. To restore equilibrium at the terms of trade OT' the tariff would have to be reduced, lowering the domestic price of imports to the slope of $OT''OT'''$, reducing smuggling to OR', and shifting the country's trade opportunity line to $OR'Q'$, where Q' is determined by the two requirements that the community

[4] The rising cost may be attributed to a rising risk of detection as smuggling increases; expenditure on detection must be assumed to be constant, in order to exclude it from the analysis.

indifference curve passing through Q' has the same tangent slope as OT''' and that Q' lies vertically above C on NC produced[5].

Q' is the trade equilibrium point under smuggling with the initially optimal terms of trade, but it will only be by accident the optimum trade point with smuggling. By repetition of the derivation of the location of Q' for different terms of trade OT', one can trace out a locus of possible trade equilibrium points running from P through Q' to point F – where all imports are smuggled and legitimate trade ceases, so that further tariff increases become irrelevant[6].

Because both the quantity and the average cost of smuggled imports increase as trade is restricted, the opportunity line with smuggling must both lie above and have a less steep slope than the foreign offer curve (the opportunity line without smuggling) at any volume of imports. If the $PQ'F$ line lies wholly above the free trade price line OPT, the country cannot gain from imposing a tariff in the presence of smuggling and the optimum tariff rate is zero. If, as is shown by the location of Q' in fig. 2, the $PQ'F$ locus dips below the free trade price line OPT, the country can still gain from the imposition of a tariff.

The tariff required to maximize welfare will be that associated with a position on $PQ'F$ at which a community indifference curve is tangent to that locus. Given the less steep slope condition on $PQ'F$ relative to OCP, the tangency position must lie to the right of $C'C$ on $PQ'F$. However, it may involve either a larger or a smaller quantity of imports than the former optimum tariff quantity ON; and this raises the question of the relation of the optimum tariff rate with smuggling to that in the absence of smuggling.

To investigate the problem, assume first that Q' is in fact the optimum welfare point in the presence of smuggling. As already demonstrated, the optimum tariff rate with smuggling must be lower than this rate; and since a lower tariff rate than the non-smuggling optimum tariff rate is required to move Q' to a level of imports right of point N, the with-smuggling optimum tariff rate in this case (where optimization requires a larger volume of imports in the presence than in the absence of smuggling) must also be lower than the optimum tariff rate in the absence of smuggling. But if the optimum welfare point under smuggling involves less imports than ON, the two forces of raising the tariff rate to restrict imports below the optimum tariff level in the absence of smuggling, and lowering the tariff rate to make the restricted level of imports an equilibrium point in the presence of

[5] It is to be noted that the slope of OT''', and the locations of R' and Q' have to be simultaneously determined.

[6] For complete accuracy, the ORS curve for the cost of smuggling should be assumed to be added vertically onto the terms of trade line OT', and hence to tilt towards the right as foreign trade is increasingly restricted, so that the terminal F for the opportunity line $PQ'F$ would lie towards the right on OPI from the point shown in fig. 2.

smuggling, pull in opposite directions, and the optimum tariff rate with smuggling could be higher with than without smuggling.

The nature of the argument, however, suggests that a higher optimum tariff rate in the presence than in the absence of smuggling will constitute an exceptional case[7].

There is a partial parallel here with the theory of optimal tariff retaliation. In the case under analysis, the country imposes an optimum tariff, the smugglers retaliate by smuggling, and the country first adjusts its tariff rate to maintain the initially optimum-tariff level of imports. It may then retaliate against the smugglers either by restricting trade still further (raising the tariff as compared with that producing equilibrium at Q') in order to obtain better terms of trade, or by reducing the degree of trade restriction (lowering the tariff as compared with that producing equilibrium at Q') in order to benefit from a larger volume of trade. In the latter case, the with-smuggling optimum tariff rate must be lower than the non-smuggling optimum tariff rate; in the former case, it might be higher.

It is clear from the earlier analysis that if smuggling can be curtailed by additional customs-enforcement expenditure, the country should carry such expenditure up to the point where the marginal expenditure is just equal to the cost saving achieved by diverting goods back from smuggled to legal channels, or, what is the same thing, the extra tariff revenue produced. What the effect of variability of enforcement-expenditure on the optimal with-smuggling tariff rate may be is a problem that will not be pursued here, though it may be conjectured that in general the effect will be to raise the optimal with-smuggling tariff rate.

References

Bhagwati, J. and B. Hansen, 1973a, A theoretical analysis of smuggling, Quarterly Journal of Economics, May, reprinted in this volume.

Bhagwati, J. and T. N. Srinivasan, 1973b, Smuggling and trade policy, Journal of Public Economics, August, reprinted in this volume.

[7] This is also suggested by the detailed mathematical analysis of Bhagwati and Srinivasan (1973b) in ch. 3.

PART II

BALANCE OF PAYMENTS AND DEVELOPMENTAL EFFECTS

Chapter 5

OVERINVOICING, UNDERUTILIZATION, AND DISTORTED INDUSTRIAL GROWTH

Gordon C. WINSTON

1. Introduction

With an artificial exchange rate, a government establishes a set of prices that makes certain transactions highly profitable at the same time that it establishes laws making those transactions illegal. We usually call it 'corruption' when people follow the government's *price* incentives instead of its contradictory *legal* incentives. In Pakistan, the dollar sells for 4.75 rupees in the official market, but for two to three times that much in the free market. Handsome profits are made by those who can trade in both.

This paper describes overinvoicing of capital-equipment imports in Pakistan industry. Moral dimensions of the problem are not at issue. The central question is how overinvoicing affects the allocation of investment and, therefore, the structure of industry – how (and by how much) overinvoicing changes the costs of capital to the men who make investment decisions[1]. The logic of the problem can be developed with simple equations but an understanding of overinvoicing and its consequences does not depend on algebra. The reader who finds equations more a hindrance than a help can omit them and still get a clear sense of the shape and magnitude of the problem.

For those unfamiliar with the system, overinvoicing works like this: an industrialist whose new factory has been sanctioned, i.e. approved officially, will arrange with a foreign supplier to sell him equipment at a fictitious invoice price, higher than the price he actually pays. Presentation of the partly fictitious invoice to the foreign-exchange authorities entitles the industrialist to buy the full invoice

[1] After completing this paper, I discovered Bhagwati's analysis of the statistical and financial problems created by faking foreign trade declarations (Bhagwati, 1967). It is nicely complementary, both in generalizing the devices and incentives for faking invoices – over- and under-invoicing of imports and exports – and in analysing their impact on real and apparent balance-of-payments accounts. On the subject of this paper, however, Bhagwati does not touch.

amount of foreign exchange at the official rate of 4.75 rupees to make payment. The portion of the invoiced amount that represents overpayment is then deposited by the supplier to the industrialist's account in a foreign bank and, because of the disequilibrium exchange rate, it can be sold for rupees at the higher black-market rate. Therein lies the foreign-exchange profit to the industrialist. The deception of overinvoicing, of course, is necessary because the government has made it illegal for anyone openly to trade foreign exchange between the official and the black markets.

Sect. 2 devises a way to measure the incentive effects of overinvoicing through the financial – foreign-exchange market – profits that reduce the real costs of capital equipment to the industrialist. The size of these financial profits is estimated for Pakistan since they will affect investment behaviour only if they are not trivial. In sect. 3 the impact of overinvoicing profits is expressed alternatively as the effective exchange rate for capital imports that includes both tariffs and the subsidy of overinvoicing profits. Finally, sects. 4, 5 and 6 consider the price distortions that overinvoicing creates among capital goods and what these imply for industrial development and performance, for foreign-capital intensity, capital utilization and employment and output growth.

The facts and estimates in this paper are Pakistani, but the forces described apply to any underdeveloped country with an overvalued domestic currency. Overvaluation creates the incentives to overinvoicing capital imports and competition among foreign-equipment suppliers assures dissemination of the techniques of overinvoicing. So misallocation of investment due to overinvoicing of capital imports is one among the many development problems of distorted industrial incentives created by an artificial exchange rate (Bhagwati, 1968; Bruton, 1970; Power, 1966).

2. The foreign-exchange profits of overinvoicing

In overinvoicing, a real transaction (the purchase of equipment[2]) is used as the vehicle for a financial transaction (the purchase of cheap dollars for resale in the black market). These are two sides of the same coin, of course, but it is helpful at first to separate them and look *only* at the financial transaction – at the profit earned through the foreign-exchange purchase and sale. It is important to note that we are completely disregarding any profit the industrialist may expect to earn on products made by the equipment. In order to see the magnitude and

[2] Equipment is used to emphasize that the analysis deals with real capital investments. But it applies equally to nontangible imports of services that go into an investment budget – consultant and engineering services being the most obvious.

effects of the financial incentives alone, we are explicitly ignoring what is usually taken to be the *only* reason for importing capital equipment – expected operating profits[3].

The amount of financial profit (in rupees) from an overinvoiced capital-goods import is simply what the industrialist earns by selling his Swiss bank deposit on the black market, less what he paid for it. So

$$\Pi^r = E_b(C_i^\$ - C_a^\$) - (1 + t)E_o(C_i^\$ - C_a^\$), \tag{1}$$

where the first term is proceeds (the amount earned by selling the overinvoiced dollars $C_i^\$ - C_a^\$$ at the black-market exchange rate, E_b) and the second term is costs (the amount paid to buy $C_i^\$ - C_a^\$$ of dollars at the official exchange rate, E_o, given that he has to pay the tariff, t, on the fictitious part of the import too[4]). The invoiced value of the import is $C_i^\$$ while the amount actually paid to the supplier is $C_a^\$$, so the difference is the number of dollars accumulated through overinvoicing[5]. Superscripts indicate dollars ($) or rupees (r). If the amount of

[3] A more general analysis of allocational distortions of overinvoicing would have to recognize, in addition to financial profits and operating profits, the trading profits possible from reselling licence-restricted imports at a domestic price higher than landed costs plus tariff (Lewis and Guisinger, 1968; Pal, 1970). If trading profits were sufficiently large and licences were issued for a limited total value of imports, there would be an incentive to *under*invoice the imports and *buy* black-market foreign exchange to pay the excess of actual overinvoiced value (Bhagwati, 1967). The reason for ignoring this possibility here is simply that a small part of industrial investment in Pakistan can be resold, hence trading profits do not figure prominently in investment-allocation decisions.

[4] For some imports, Pakistan uses a system of bonus vouchers (Bruton and Swadesh, 1963) to achieve a partial devaluation. Its application to capital-goods imports would modify (1) to the extent of

$$\Pi^r = E_b(C_i^\$ - C_a^\$) - (1 + t + bv)E_o(C_i^\$ - C_a^\$), \tag{1'}$$

where v is the premium paid for dollars bought with bonus vouchers and b is the proportion of the invoice value that must be paid in those dollars (currently 0, $\frac{1}{2}$ or 1 for different imports). Since $0 \leqslant b \leqslant 1$ and $0 \leqslant v$, profits from overinvoicing would be reduced by an increase in the bonus-voucher premium and/or the proportion of invoice value for which bonus dollars must be bought – an effective devaluation. These complications have been ignored in the text simply because most new capital equipment is imported outside the bonus-voucher system ($b = 0$) and the system applies almost exclusively to spare parts, maintenance and balancing equipment compounding the skewing of prices discussed in detail in sect. 6. In considering corrective policies, of course, 'devaluation' should be read to include *de facto* devaluation through sufficient increases in b and v applicable to all capital goods.

[5] Interest payments do not appear in these costs – despite the fact that the industrialist must pay interest on a loan for capital imports – because their relevance depends on the particular time pattern of costs and payments from overinvoicing. To the extent that the two parts of the transaction (commitment of rupees and acquisition of dollars) are separated by a short time, any interest charges paid to borrow rupees are offset by the interest earned on the dollar deposits. Only in the interim period when rupees have been committed but dollars are not yet secured is the interest rate relevant and there is no evidence that this period is considerable (or even that it exists).

overinvoicing is expressed as a fraction of the invoice value, we can deal with

$$\phi = (C_i^\$ - C_a^\$)/C_i^\$,$$

and in these terms, financial profits can be expressed simply as

$$\Pi^r = \phi\, C_i^\$[E_b - (1 + t)E_o],$$

or in rupees

$$\Pi^r = \phi\, C_i^r[E_b/E_o - (1 + t)]. \quad (2)$$

This is a most useful result. The industrialist's profit depends (quite sensibly) on the fraction of the invoice that is fictitious, on the size of the equipment order, on tariffs and on the spread between black-market and official rates of exchange. Notice that if the government did not maintain an artificial exchange rate, overinvoicing profits would be eliminated – an official exchange rate within $1 + t$ of the black-market rate (so $E_b = (1 + t)E_o$) would make eq. (2) equal zero.

Profits affect behaviour and it is unimportant to the analysis of overinvoicing whether industrialists in an underdeveloped country 'maximize' profits in some purists' sense. What is important is that the promise of higher profits creates incentives, pressures, to which some industrialists may well respond all the time and all industrialists will respond some of the time. We can understand important, perhaps dominant, pressures on industrialists' investment behaviour if we understand what influences profits. Among the determinants of profits, we shall discuss, some apply to areas within the firm's discretion; some apply to industry as a whole; some work only through government policy and the incentive of the industrialist is to influence that policy.

2.1. *Profit incentives*

On the simplified level represented by eq. (2), the drive for profits through overinvoicing creates among industrialists incentives for the following behaviour. Industrialists will try to:

(1) *Make the amount of sanctioned industrial investment* C_i^r *as large as possible.* This has two corollaries:

(a) *encourage inflows of foreign aid, discounting its high social cost,* since these largely determine the amount of total industrial capital imports; and

(b) for any one individual or firm, *increase his share of sanctioned investment* from a given amount of foreign aid.

(2) *Increase the fraction of overinvoicing* ϕ *on capital imports.* Even if we assume that this fraction is determined by 'common business practices' and is constant

between different kinds of capital imports (an assumption examined below), there is still an incentive to increase the overinvoiced proportion over time. Competition among suppliers will contribute to this.

(3) *Maintain or increase the disparity between the official and black-market rates of exchange* E_b/E_o. This has two elements:

(a) *devaluation should be resisted* by whatever argument has political appeal (national pride (Bhagwati, 1968), threat to industrial development, inflation[6]); and

(b) *the black-market price should be maintained or increased by encouraging enforcement of foreign-exchange controls* on other suppliers of black-market dollars[7].

(4) *Discourage tariffs on capital imports* since they directly reduce financial profits by increasing the cost of getting dollars through overinvoicing. The most persuasive argument within the compass of the industrialists would be that there is a severe limit on the ability to create projects that will use available foreign exchange – an 'absorptive capacity limit' – so that higher tariffs would radically reduce industrial development.

2.2. *Estimated profits*

Just how strong these pressures are likely to be on the typical Pakistani industrialist depends on how much these variables affect actual profits, quantities have to be substituted for the symbols of eq. (2). We can estimate two figures: the rate of profit that business overinvoicing practices created in Pakistan four years ago (1966); and the rate of profit that business practices now generate (1970).

(a) The typical magnitude of overinvoicing ϕ that prevailed in 1966 was 10% of the invoice price, the black market rate of exchange E_b was about 10 rupees to the dollar for these highly liquid funds[8], and the official exchange rate E_o was 4.75 rupees. The average tariff rate on capital-equipment imports was 34% (Lewis, 1970). Substituting these values into eq. (2), the rate of purely financial

[6] For a highly imaginative (if not always consistent) list of reasons to resist devaluation, see National Institute of Social and Economic Research (1970).

[7] How this works depends on the interaction between official and black markets – whether the total supply of dollars is fixed or whether the black market itself leads to price elasticity (Bhagwati, 1967). If the supply of available foreign exchange is increased by increased black-market activity, then 'too much' black-market activity will lower the profit of overinvoicing. There is always an 'optimum degree of enforcement' for the law-breaking firm (Shelling, 1967).

[8] Which sell in large amounts, are untraceable, and are not subject to any national capital-flow restrictions. So they are more valuable than London or New York dollars.

profit on a capital import in 1966 was 5.8%[9]. This is solely profit from overinvoicing and foreign-exchange market manipulation. On the import of an invoiced 1 000 000 rupees of foreign capital equipment, the financial profit earned by an industrialist taking advantage of overinvoicing was 76 514 rupees. An investment worth 1 340 000 rupees would be recorded officially as $(1 + t)C_i^r$ but it would represent an actual import of 900 000 rupees of equipment.

(b) In 1970, both the typical level of overinvoicing and the black-market rate for highly liquid dollars has increased significantly. Estimates of 20% overinvoicing ϕ and a free-market exchange rate of 15 rupees to the dollar E_b are not extreme[10]. The official exchange rate E_o still stands at 4.75 rupees. Average tariffs on capital imports have risen to about 40%[11]. Substituting these values into eq. (2), the rate of financial profit from overinvoicing becomes a remarkable 25.1%. Now importing 1 000 000 rupees of invoiced capital goods earns a financial profit of 351 540 rupees. The investment worth 1 400 000 rupees in the official record represents capital goods with an actual pre-tariff value of 800 000 rupees.

These estimates of overinvoicing profits suggest that opportunities for overinvoicing capital goods may be terribly important in underdeveloped countries in creating conflicts of interest, political pressures and incentives that lower the price of industrial capital, systematically affecting its allocation and encouraging its waste. We shall return to this below.

3. The effective exchange rate for capital imports

An alternative way to describe the distorting effect of overinvoicing is through the

[9] It is not clear what the denominator of a profit rate from overinvoicing should be. The absolute amount of profit is as stated in eq. (2), but should this be measured against the actual value of the capital (C_a^r), against the invoiced value (C_i^r), or against the total resources the industrialist has to commit to the transaction including invoice payment and tariffs on it all $[(1 + t)C_i^r]$. The estimates in the text are conservative; they are based on the largest of these defensible denominators (the last) so the reader who would choose a different base for calculating profit rates will increase the estimates (significantly).

[10] It can be questioned whether 15 rupees to the dollar is a reasonable black market rate for even these highly liquid funds. In fact, it does not matter much to the argument whether it is. An estimate of 13 rupees gives a 1970-overinvoicing profit rate of 19% and an effective exchange rate for capital imports of 5.06 rupees to the dollar, both of which still give dramatic evidence of the incentive effect of overinvoicing. The reader who would try the impact of other black market rates of exchange can readily do so. In table 1, a column has been added to show the effect of a black market rate of 13 rupees in 1970.

[11] There have been no careful estimates of the average tariff on capital goods since those for 1966. The rate on most capital goods has risen since then from a nominal 40% to a nominal 50% at the same time that the number of exceptions for which a 30% rate applies (largely to spread regional distribution of investment) has increased. The net effect of these contradictory movements is estimated as 6%, raising average tariffs on capital-goods imports to about 40%.

implicit exchange rate that applies to imports of capital goods when overinvoicing profits reduce the real rupee costs of capital. Tariffs increase the implicit exchange rate; overinvoicing profits reduce it. The real rupee cost of imported capital is

$$C_f^r = (1 + t)\, E_o\, C_a^\$ - [E_b(C_i^\$ - C_a^\$) - (1 + t)\, E_o(C_i^\$ - C_a^\$)]. \qquad (3)$$

The first term describes the gross costs of the real transaction (buying the equipment) while the second, bracketed, term describes the (offsetting) financial profits. Simplifying this expression gives

$$C_f^r = C_a^\$[(1 + t)\, E_o - \phi E_b]/(1 - \phi) \qquad (4)$$

as the real rupee cost of capital to the industrialist.

The implicit exchange rate for capital imports is derived simply by dividing the real rupee cost by the actual dollar cost of the same equipment, so

$$C_f^r/C_a^\$ = \{(1 + t)\, E_o - \phi E_b\}/(1 - \phi) \qquad (5)$$

is the effective exchange rate for capital imports that should be compared to other exchange rates in the economy (those applying to consumption goods and raw materials) and to other prices (labour, domestic materials) to judge the relative price of foreign capital. Notice again that in the absence of an artificial exchange rate, $(1 + t)E_o = E_b$ and the right-hand side of eq. (5) reduces to $(1 + t)E_o$, making the implicit exchange rate the same as the official exchange rate plus tariff. The overinvoicing distortion (and incentive) vanishes.

3.1. Estimated effective exchange rate for capital imports

As with financial profits, two sets of estimates of the effective exchange rate are possible; one for 1966 the other for 1970:

(a) Using the figures that describe 1966 business practices, eq. (5) gives an effective exchange rate of 5.96 rupees per dollar. So the industrialist taking advantage of overinvoicing in 1966 paid for imported capital at an exchange rate lower than the one derived from tariffs alone; 6.37 rupees was used by Lewis (1970).

(b) But using figures describing 1970 practices, the effective exchange rate for capital goods falls to 4.56 rupees per dollar and this of course includes the 40% average tariff rate. So despite tariffs, the effective exchange rate for capital-goods imports in Pakistan appears to be below the official rate. The subsidy effect of overinvoicing is larger than the tariff; the net 'tariff' is −4%.

Because devaluation is an obvious way to eliminate overinvoicing profits (directly or through bonus generalization), it is interesting to ask what amount of devaluation is implied by these estimates. Mechanically applying the conditions of 1970 to eq. (2), a devaluation to 10.71 rupees would eliminate the profits from capital overinvoicing. But this is probably a slight overestimate of the required devaluation for two reasons: (i) the existing black market rate is likely higher, given restrictions on exchange transactions, than an 'equilibrium rate' would be; and (ii) there are administrative costs of overinvoicing that we have (properly) ignored.

These estimates of sects. 2 and 3 are summarized in table 1 for an import of 1 000 000 rupees of invoiced value.

Table 1.
The impact of overinvoicing on the cost of capital-goods imports (for Rs. 1 000 000 of imports).

	1966	1970	1970[a]
1. Invoiced value C_i^r	1 000 000	1 000 000	1 000 000
2. Nominal cost $(1 + t)C_i^r$	1 340 000	1 400 000	1 400 000
3. Financial profit from overinvoicing Π^r	76 514	351 540	267 400
4. Payment to supplier C_a^r (rupees)	900 000	800 000	800 000
5. Payment to supplier $C_a^\$$ (dollars)	189 474	168 421	168 421
6. Real rupee cost C_f^r	1 129 265	768 000	852 631
7. Effective exchange rate $C_f^r/C_a^\$$ (rupees per dollar)	5.96	4.56	5.06
8. Tariff (+) or subsidy (−) re. official exchange rate	+25.5%	−4.0%	+6.6%

[a] The impact of overinvoicing profits in 1970, if 13 rupees is assumed to be the black market rate of exchange. See footnote 10.

4. The effect on the choice between imported and domestic capital goods

Not all capital is imported, of course, and the industrialist always has some choice in the import content of his investments, either through choosing the way a product is made or, if not there, simply in the choice of which products to make[12]. Using the subscript d to indicate domestically supplied capital, the total nominal cost of an investment project (or a group of investments making up an investment (budget)) with both foreign and domestic component is

$$C^r = C_d^r + (1 + t)C_i^r.$$

If we describe the choice between imported and domestic capital goods by the relative size of the imported component of investment

[12] The usually weak assertion that there is no choice of import coefficients in industrial development is indefensible unless all industries have fixed coefficients, all coefficients are identical, and all industries operate at the same level of utilization (Khan, 1970; Winston, 1973).

$$f = C_i^r / C_d^r,$$

then

$$C^r = C_i^r[(1 + t) + 1/f]. \tag{6}$$

Earlier we showed profits as a function of the nominal value of foreign capital, C_i^r (among other things) so we can solve that earlier eq. (2) for C_i^r and substitute the result into eq. (6) to get a total investment cost of

$$C^r = \Pi^r[(1 + t) + 1/f]/\phi[E_b/E_o - (1 + t)]. \tag{7}$$

This, in turn, can be solved for Π^r so that total financial profit from overinvoicing becomes

$$\Pi^r = \frac{C^r\phi[E_b/E_o - (1 + t)]}{(1 + t) + 1/f}. \tag{8}$$

It is clear that total profits depend, as before, on the size of the investment budget, on tariffs, on the amount of overinvoicing and on the black market rate of exchange relative to the official market rate. What is added by eq. (8) is that profits depend, too, on the amount of imported capital. For any given investment budget, the industrialist's profit is higher the larger the proportion of imported capital used, i.e. the less is the use of domestically produced capital goods.

4.1. Incentives

In addition to the profit incentives described in sect. 2, industrialists will try to:

(5) *Increase their use of imported capital equipment* which can be done both by

(a) *selecting foreign capital-intensive techniques of production*; and

(b) *investing in those industries that use much foreign capital* at the expense of those that use little.

4.2. Estimates

For the second-plan period (1960–1965), Naqvi (1973) has collected data on total sanctioned private investment and the amount of it that was made up of foreign capital. So from these, f can be computed for eq. (8) as well as the effect on profits of changes in f. It should be remembered that the same rupee profits that were earlier expressed as a percentage of the cost of foreign capital alone (see footnote 9) are now expressed as a percentage of total capital cost, so the percentage on this larger base must necessarily be smaller.

Using the value for 1970, the rate of overinvoicing profit on total investment is 16.4% for West Pakistan and 15.4 for East Pakistan. The sensitivity of these profit rates to changes in the proportion of foreign capital is illustrated if we assume a change from half imported capital/half domestic ($f = 1$) to two-thirds imported/one-third domestic ($f = 2$)[13]. Such an increase in imported capital would cause the rate of financial profit on total investment to rise from 14.65 to 18.51%. So in this range, doubling the proportion of imported capital increases the financial profit rate by 3.9 percentage points. Profits are 26% higher[14].

5. The effect on the choice between expanding capital or utilizing existing capital

The last steps in the analysis recognize that the amount of overinvoicing depends on what kind of capital equipment the industrialist imports. Earlier, we dealt with the fact that this fraction ϕ changes over time; now we consider different fractions of overinvoicing among different classes of equipment at one point in time. The fictitious portion of an invoice will vary because of differences in bargaining power between buyer and seller for different goods and because of differences in the effectiveness of surveillance by the foreign-exchange control authorities between different capital goods. The first of these is treated here; the second in sect. 6.

Capital equipment can be bought either to build new plants or, alternatively, to maintain and balance existing plants increasing the level of their utilization. For any industrialist (beyond the neophyte with his first investment) there is a choice to be made in dividing an investment budget C^r between expansion C^r_e and utilization C^r_u,

$$C^r = C^r_e + C^r_u.$$

The result of the investment allocation can be described by the size of investment spending on utilization relative to spending for expansion

$$u = C^r_u/C^r_e,$$

so that

$$C^r = C^r_e(1 + u) = C^r_u(1 + 1/u). \tag{9}$$

13 These bracket the values of f from Naqvi's figures which are 1.35 for West Pakistan and 1.13 for East Pakistan.

14 Since the elasticity of the profit rate with respect to f is $1/\{(1 + t)f + 1\}$, the sensitivity of profits to f declines as tariffs rise and as the proportion of foreign capital increases. 'Early' increases in the import coefficient of investment, therefore, are more powerful than the same proportional increases from a larger base.

These two types of capital goods should be treated differently as regards overinvoicing profits because of the very different competitive position of the industrialist *vis-à-vis* the equipment seller in the two purchases. A new investment is typically self-contained, technically independent of existing capital except through product flows. If these are pretty much the same from different brands and configurations of equipment, the industrialist is free to choose among suppliers and this freedom will lead to competition among suppliers that appears in part in the amount of overinvoicing. In contrast, the industrialist seeking balancing equipment has less freedom since the equipment must fit into an existing plant, maintenance organization and parts inventory and this relative absence of competitive flexibility to choose among suppliers will show up in lower overinvoicing. So the overinvoicing that can be had on new capital is likely to be greater than that which can be had on capital to increase utilization of existing plant, or formally

$$\phi_e \geqslant \phi_u. \tag{10}$$

An industrialist's financial profits from overinvoicing will thus be a weighted average of the profits from each kind of investment spending, the weights depending on the relative rates of overinvoicing on expansion capital ϕ_e and maintenance-balancing capital ϕ_u and on the distribution of investment between these two u. Substituting from eq. (9) into eq. (8) for each type of capital investment separately and adding them together gives overinvoicing profits of

$$\Pi^r = \left[\frac{1}{1+u}\phi_e + \frac{u}{1+u}\phi_u\right]\frac{C^r[E_b/E_o - (1+t)]}{(1+t) + 1/f}. \tag{11}$$

Despite the cumbersome appearance of eq. (11), it is clear that if the rate of overinvoicing is higher for new expansion investment, profits are increased by decreasing the allocation of investment for *using* the existing capital stock.

5.1. Incentives

Industrialists will try to:

(6) *Devote as much investment as possible to new equipment to expand the capital stock* and, *as a* concomitant, *as little as possible to maintenance and balancing equipment to increase the utilization of existing capital.* In fact, incentives in this direction are even stronger than implied, since in Pakistan some spare parts are imported on bonus vouchers, increasing effective tariffs and likely eliminating most prospects of overinvoicing profits from these imports while leaving expansion investment largely unaffected.

5.2. Estimates

If we assume, arbitrarily, that new capital can be overinvoiced by 20% while maintenance and balancing capital is overinvoiced at 10% under the conditions assumed for 1970, the rate of profit would be 25.11% for the imported new investment and 12.6% for maintenance and balancing investment. If all other factors were comparable, an industrialist who spent nothing out of 1 000 000 rupees of capital imports for maintenance and balancing $u = 0$ would earn 251 100 rupees on overinvoicing profits while another who spent half his investment budget on increasing utilization of existing capital $u = 1$ would earn only 188 250 rupees. These are suggestive of the price incentives that induce firms to expand industrial capacity rather than increase its utilization.

Such price incentives – along with the general cheapness of capital we have described – may go far to explain why, in capital-scarce West Pakistan, existing industrial capital is used 14% of the time, in the capital-rich United States, it is used almost twice as much[15]. Where capital is scarce, it is wasted; where it is abundant, it is conserved. This is a paradox of no small significance for a poor developing country.

6. The effect on capital complexity, industrial employment and output growth

Overinvoicing operates despite surveillance by the foreign-exchange authorities. In Pakistan, engineering-price committees serve in the major agencies involved in capital-import transactions[16] to scrutinize capital invoices and challenge the validity of those considered suspicious. If surveillance fell with an absolutely even hand on all capital imports, it would concern us only as part of the optimum enforcement of exchange-control laws. But it cannot. These agencies have limited resources and must concentrate their efforts where they are most effective. This means that surveillance is heaviest where overinvoicing is most likely to be discovered and this inevitably is on imports of standardized kinds of capital equipment for which there is a well-established world market. Surveillance is least effective on highly complex modern plants that are tailored to a specific installation and user. For these, the task of accurately validating capital prices is beyond the competence of even the best-intentioned price-surveillance group[17]. What gives

[15] Based on Foss's estimates of capital use in the US (Foss, 1963) and mine in Pakistan (Winston, 1971), made comparable as described in Winston (1973).

[16] Which are Customs, Pakistan Industrial Credit and Investment Corporation (PICIC) and the Industrial Development Bank of Pakistan (IDBP).

[17] And scholars. Engineering complexity of capital imports combines with illegality to make

this economic significance is that the complexity of equipment that makes surveillance of capital imports more difficult involves a high proportion of capital relative to labour and relative to output and, in all likelihood, a bias toward large-scale installations. So the overinvoicing attainable on new equipment imports ϕ_e increases as the capital–labour ratio, the capital–output ratio and project size increase[18].

6.1. Incentives

Industrialists will tend to:

(7) *Select investment projects and sectors that are as complex as possible* though this typically involves *more capital per labourer and per unit of output*. Overinvoicing profit incentives thereby *reduce employment creation and output growth* in industry.

7. The implications for industrial development

Of the many ramifications of overinvoicing for economic development, three seem of central importance.

(a) *The structure and growth of industry* is affected seriously by the lowered general price of scarce capital equipment and by the distortions of relative prices among types and uses of capital[19].

it impossible to verify or deny the parameters of overinvoicing reported off the record by industrialists, bankers, foreign-exchange authorities, aid officials and others. Bhagwati's experience in investigating faked invoices in Turkey and India was much the same as mine in Pakistan though his concern with balance-of-payments aspects of faking allowed him one independent rough measure of total magnitudes (Bhagwati, 1967, p. 66).

[18] This bias in favour of large, complex, capital-using, labour-saving technologies and sectors can be represented by substituting

$$\phi_e = g(K/L+, K/Y+, P+)$$

into the earlier statement of overinvoicing profits to get

$$\Pi^r = \left[\frac{1}{1+u}\, g(K/L+, K/Y+, P+) + \frac{u}{1+u}\,\phi_u\right] \frac{C^r[E_b/E_o - (1+t)]}{(1+t) + 1/f}, \quad (12)$$

which is as detailed a formal representation of overinvoicing as we shall attempt.

[19] There is a third statistical distortion in the overstatement of industrial investment that overinvoicing produces. This is significant when overinvoicing practices change as in Pakistan between 1966 and 1970.

The problems created by *generally* low capital prices in poor, capital-scarce countries have worried some economists for a long time and they are only compounded by overinvoicing. They rest on the fact that capital with a too low price relative to its scarcity is wasted, it is used in place of abundant factors (notably labour), it is left idle too much of the time, and it makes the wrong products appear profitable. To this, analysis of overinvoicing adds a better sense of just how low capital prices really are, and a sense of how tariffs can effectively be circumvented by changing the practices of overinvoicing (as in the estimate that overinvoicing in Pakistan more than offsets the existing tariffs on capital imports providing a 4% subsidy to foreign capital at the official exchange rate). Capital appears to be a good deal cheaper to the industrialist than we had thought.

Using the 1970 estimates, the price actually paid for imported capital by Pakistan industrialists was 45% *below* the price implied by the official record[20]. Analyses of response to 'the price of capital' that disregard the effects of overinvoicing – for instance in estimating elasticities of factor substitution – may therefore be seriously mistaken. In terms of 'factor price distortions', *per se*, the firms' price for imported capital was more than 60% below its shadow price, assuming a scarcity value of 10 rupees to the dollar but tariffs on capital reduced by half.

The distortions *among* capital prices that are created by overinvoicing are interesting both because they have not previously been identified and because they appear in part to explain patterns of industrial growth that are increasingly disturbing. Among capital goods, overinvoicing tends to raise the relative price and discourage the use of domestically produced capital; of capital that increases the utilization of existing plant and equipment; and of capital that creates employment.

To the extent that the profit incentives of overinvoicing influence investment decisions, they will create or compound a set of familiar and disturbing problems in economic development:

(i) by discouraging the growth of a domestic capital-goods industry since it must compete with an effectively subsidized import. In Pakistan, domestic producers must compete with foreign capital goods at 4.56 rupees to the dollar, but with foreign consumption goods at rates as high as 22.00 rupees to the dollar (Thomas, 1967). This clearly compounds the bias of cascaded protection under import-substitution policies (Bruton, 1970; Power, 1966);
(ii) by creating industry that is unnecessarily foreign-capital intensive in its techniques and sectors of production and by perpetuating that pattern so that growth remains heavily dependent on foreign capital (Winston, 1972);

[20] From table 1, col. 2: 1 400 000 rupees is the implicit domestic price of the bundle of capital that actually costs the firm 768 000 rupees.

(iii) by discouraging the *use* of existing plant and equipment in favour of adding new capital with consequent reduction in both the level and growth of consumption and employment (Winston, 1971); and

(iv) by discouraging industrial employment both through reduced capital utilization and through selection of complex, labour-saving and capital-using techniques and products (Winston, 1972).

(b) *The distribution of income* is affected by overinvoicing on both ends of the income scale. Investment in employment-denying techniques and sectors reduces potential earnings of the unemployed and underemployed at the same time that profits accruing to the already privileged industrialists are increased.

(c) *The external effects of overinvoicing* on the growth of the economy may be among its most costly consequences. The very real pressures and temptations faced by individuals in sanctioning agencies who have something very valuable to give away tends to redistribute overinvoicing profits from industrialists to agency employees, spreading corruption and raising 'the cost of doing business'. And whatever economic criteria these agencies may have applied to investment decisions[21] will tend to get lost under mutual political and financial payoffs that have nothing to do with economic development objectives. By a sort of Gresham's law of honesty, bad intentions drive out good as a rising cost of doing business forces corruption on even the reluctant businessman. This is a major source of concern about the increase in overinvoicing in Pakistan over the past four years; that it is increasingly difficult for businessmen to choose not to overinvoice.

Finally, corruption increases the demands on industrialists' energies at the same time that it restricts the number of persons who can be trusted to share management's (often illegal) decisions. Industrial corruption not only diverts limited entrepreneurial talents from production, innovation, market and employment concerns and toward illicit financial intricacies, but its illegality also restricts – often to family members – the number who can be trusted to know of a firm's methods of operation.

Four alternatives appear open to a government faced with large-scale over-

[21] Quite apart from individuals' temptations to ignore overinvoicing, note that the agencies mainly responsible for the surveillance of overinvoicing are semi-private investment loan organizations and as such they have an inherent conflict between their interest in honesty and economic development on the one hand and their interest as a bank in the volume of loans and the financial solidity of their borrowers on the other. Overinvoicing gives foreign-exchange market profits to their borrowers, increasing their financial resources (if profits are kept within the company) and the loans made by the agency thereby become more secure. Even without this added protection to already well-secured loans, a policy of tolerance increases loans outstanding and, therefore, profits to the lending agency. Ethics and economic development aside, there is a clear motive for these agencies to wink at overinvoicing of capital-goods imports. Even if they do not succumb to this temptation, it can certainly be doubted that they should have the major role in policing overinvoicing.

invoicing of capital imports and its destructive effects on development:

(a) *inaction*, with continued opportunities for overinvoicing profits;

(b) *increased surveillance* to try to reduce overinvoicing. But regardless of the sincerity of efforts, it is virtually impossible to control overinvoicing considering the myriad ways it can, in fact, be done (misstatement of invoice value, shortages in actual shipments, substitution of old machinery for new, substitution of cheap models for expensive, omission of invoiced spare parts, etc.). What is more, to the extent that control is effective, it is possible that increased enforcement would increase overinvoicing profits by reducing the supply of dollars and raising the black-market rate of exchange. This is the problem of 'optimal enforcement';

(c) *detailed specification of allowable industrial capital imports* so that only specified plant configurations with detailed equipment lists are importable. This would not only run into the same problems as any other increase in surveillance, but to the extent that it worked, it would introduce further rigidities and compound the problems of inappropriate technology created by overinvoicing; and

(d) *devaluation* to remove the primary incentive to overinvoicing. As I have shown, an adequate effective devaluation would both remove the incentive to overinvoicing and remove the biases among various types of capital goods. It is important that effective devaluation can be accomplished by (i) a change in the official exchange rate; (ii) an increase in the general tariff on all capital imports; or (iii) an extension of the bonus system through an increase in coverage and premium.

References

Bhagwati, J., 1967, Fiscal policies, the faking of foreign trade declarations, and the balance of payments, Bulletin of the Oxford University Institute of Economics and Statistics 29, No. 1, February.

Bhagwati, J., 1968, The Theory and Practice of Commercial Policy (Princeton University Press, Princeton).

Bruton, H. J., 1970, The import-substitution strategy of economic development: A Survey, Pakistan Development Review X, No. 2, Summer.

Bruton, H. J. and R. B. Swadesh, 1963, The Pakistan export bonus scheme, Monographs in the Economics of Development, No. 11 (Pakistan Institute of Development Economics, Karachi).

Foss, M. F., 1963, The utilization of capital equipment: postwar compared with prewar, Survey of Current Business, June.

Khan, A. R., 1970, Capital-intensity and the efficiency of factor use – a comparative study of the observed capital–labour ratios of Pakistani industries, Pakistan Development Review X, No. 2, Summer.

Lewis, S. R., Jr., 1970, Pakistan: Industrialization and Trade Policies (Oxford University Press for the Organization for Economic Development and Cooperation, London).

Lewis, S. R., Jr. and S. E. Guisinger, 1968, Measuring protection in a developing country: the case of Pakistan, Journal of Political Economy, November-December.

Naqvi, S. N. H., 1973, Investment Licensing in Pakistan.
National Institute of Social and Economic Research, 1970, Devaluation Debate NISER (Karachi).
Pal, M. L., 1970, The determinants of domestic prices of imports, in: Islam, N., ed., Studies on Commercial Policy and Economic Growth (Pakistan Institute of Development Economics, Karachi).
Power, J. H., 1966. Import substitution as an industrialization strategy, Philippine Economic Journal, Second Semester.
Shelling, T. C., 1967, Economic analysis of organized crime, in the President's Commission on Law Enforcement and Administration of Justice, Task Force Report: Organized Crime (Washington).
Thomas, P. S., 1967, Effective Exchange Rates in Pakistan, Mimeographed.
Winston, G. C., 1971, Capital utilization in economic development, The Economic Journal, March.
Winston, G. C., 1973, A comparison of capital utilization in the United States and Pakistan, in: Singer, H. et al., Readings in Employment and Economic Development (Penguin).
Winston, G. C., 1972, On the inevitability of factor substitution, Williams College Research Memorandum, No. 46, April.

Chapter 6

FISCAL POLICIES, THE FAKING OF FOREIGN TRADE DECLARATIONS, AND THE BALANCE OF PAYMENTS

Jagdish N. BHAGWATI

1. Introduction

The interaction between fiscal and monetary policies, including foreign and domestic taxation measures, and the balance of payments has been analysed at several levels by trade theorists. The effects of changes in interest rates on the current and capital accounts are, for example, very much at the core of the classical analysis of balance of payments adjustment. So also the macro-analysis of fiscal policy, via budgetary surplus and deficit changes, has now been integrated into the recent absorption approach to balance of payments analysis[1]. Recently, there have also been attempts to analyse the effects of certain domestic taxes (such as the value added tax, the corporation tax, etc.) for balance of payments behaviour via their effects on costs and prices. (Two recent contributions of interest are Musgrave (1964) and Salant (1964).)

However, there is a curious absence of systematic analysis of the effects that fiscal policies, in the nature of export and import duties and/or subsidies, have on the balance of payments via the incentives they often create for faking customs declarations. These effects are important to comprehend for making policy decisions arising from balance of payments changes.

In an earlier statistical exercise (Bhagwati, 1964), I attempted to demonstrate that import tariffs had resulted in the underinvoicing of Turkish imports. The present paper goes beyond that limited treatment of the problem of faked declarations to offer more systematic treatment of *alternative* possibilities of faking transactions and to extend the analysis to cover the question of the economic, essentially *balance of payments effects* of such faking. More specifically, the paper:

[1] Numerous references could be cited in support of these statements; the following, however, are quite sufficient: Johnson (1958), for the absorption approach and macro-fiscal policies; and Meade (1955), for the classical analysis of the balance of payments.

(1) restates more tightly the reasons for which *trade* tariffs and subsidies can lead to faked trade declarations;

(2) discusses the techniques of examining empirically the phenomenon of faking, now stating their limitations more clearly; and

(3) examines the implications of such faking of trade data for economic analysis and policy with respect to the balance of payments.

A further section explores similar issues from the point of view of *internal* levies and subsidies.

2. Trade tariffs and subsidies

2.1. Theoretical analysis

The presence of tariffs and subsidies on international trade transactions generally creates immediately an incentive to overinvoice or underinvoice the value of the transactions. Which of these two possibilities obtains will depend not merely on the rate of the tariff or subsidy but also on the premium or discount at which the incremental foreign exchange, so required or acquired, is bought or sold in the foreign exchange market.

For example, if an *ad valorem* export subsidy is available and there is no exchange control so that all exchange transactions take place only within the insignificant range legally permitted around the parity value, there will immediately be an incentive to overinvoice exports. The exporter who does overinvoice will enjoy a profit of $tx\%$ on the *actual* export value, where t is the *ad valorem* subsidy rate and x the percentage by which exports are overinvoiced. Where, however, there is exchange control, and the exporter must surrender to the exchange authorities the full, *declared* value of exports, the exporter will have to purchase illegal foreign exchange in the black market to the amount of the excess of declared over actual value of exports. In this case, if the black market premium on foreign exchange is $P\%$, the incentive to overinvoice will exist only if $t > P$.[2] In practice, of course, the overinvoicing, in view of the illegality entailed both in faking the declaration and in the purchase of foreign exchange in the black market (in case of exchange control), will be practised only when t exceeds P significantly enough to outweigh the risks ensuing from the illegal transactions. Where t

[2] Note that the formula applies equally to the case where there is no exchange control, as in the preceding case. In that case, $P = 0$ and therefore t, which is positive, will exceed P, creating an incentive to overinvoice exports. The phenomenon of faked trade declarations has thus nothing to do with whether there is exchange control or not. This point was slurred over, and the argument presented only in terms of the premium on illegal exchange as present in Turkey, in my earlier paper on Turkish imports (Bhagwati, 1964), reprinted as ch. 9 in this volume.

happens to be below P, further, the incentive will be to underinvoice exports. This will be the case, for example, when there is a tariff on exports; in this case the exporter makes a profit, via underinvoicing, both by avoiding tariff and by earning a premium on the sale of illegally acquired foreign exchange. But such underinvoicing will occur even when there is an export subsidy (at rate t) and $t < P$.

Correspondingly, on the *import* side, a similar analysis holds. If t now stands for an import tariff (rate), and P again for the premium on illegal foreign exchange, there will be an incentive to underinvoice imports when $t > P$ and to overinvoice imports when $t < P$. For example, where there is an import subsidy and no exchange control or a net premium on illegal exchange the incentive will clearly be to overinvoice imports; and where there is a tariff and there is no exchange control (so that $P = 0$), the incentive will clearly be to underinvoice imports.

Where there is overinvoicing of exports or underinvoicing of imports, the transaction will create a net *demand* for illegal foreign exchange (in exchange-control economies); where there is underinvoicing of exports or overinvoicing of imports, the transaction will create a net *supply* of illegal foreign exchange. In the former case, the effect will be to increase the black market premium on foreign exchange; in the latter case, to reduce it.

2.2. Possibility of empirical analysis

Whereas it is easy to establish the conditions under which the faking of trade values, as argued above, will occur, it is in practice extremely difficult to set about determining whether such faking is *actually* occurring. It is further *impossible* to find out *how much* faking is going on.

One method, traditionally used by economists and now more or less out of favour, is to ask those engaged in the actual transactions whether such faking occurs and, if so, in what direction. This method *can* work to some extent, especially if the interviewees confess to themselves having indulged in these 'malpractices'. Rare, however, are such instances; the business ethos does not permit the admission of such behaviour. It is much easier, in fact, to get such admissions in respect of *other* firms in the industry; the interviewees are readier to accuse then to confess[3]!

One would thus like to supplement such 'evidence' with analysis based on 'cold facts'. There *is*, in fact, a method which I have found useful and which is generally applicable to the analysis of overinvoiced exports and underinvoiced imports (although, with slight amendment, it can be extended to the analysis of

[3] This statement is based on my experience with Indian exporters, several of whom were interviewed by me during June 1965 on the question of overinvoicing in their field.

underinvoiced exports and overinvoiced exports as well). It is *not* free from certain methodological limitations; but it seems to me to possess a fair degree of power in furnishing 'reasonable' evidence of overinvoicing or underinvoicing of trade figures. The method rests essentially on comparing partner-country trade data.

It is well known that, with a few exceptions, import data are published at c.i.f. value and export data at f.o.b. value. As a consequence most teachers of international economics are likely, at some stage or other, to have been confronted by a research student who has looked at international trade statistics and 'discovered' that the world as a whole has a deficit in its balance of trade! Now, one would normally expect partner-country statistics to show an excess of c.i.f. import values over corresponding f.o.b. export values (relating to the *same* trade flows). If, therefore, the observed discrepancy between these data is in the 'perverse' direction, one may conclude that there is a *prima facie* evidence for *either* overinvoiced exports or underinvoiced imports (or both, of course).

Of course, either of these phenomena may obtain without being large enough to reverse the 'normal' excess of import over (partner) export values, in which case the present statistical technique will not be useful (*unless* the insurance and freight element can be reasonably approximated and adjusted for). Again, the method will not be available when one is looking for overinvoicing of imports or underinvoicing of exports (*unless* again the insurance and freight margins can be reasonably adjusted for), because these would merely reinforce, rather than reverse, the 'normal' excess of c.i.f. import over (partner-country) f.o.b. export values. A further and yet more serious limitation of the method arises from the fact that it presumes the faking of invoices to occur only at one end, *or* that the incentive to fake runs in contrary directions at the two ends (so that the exporter, for example, wishes to overinvoice and the importer to underinvoice). In such cases, the invoices surrendered to partner countries, by corresponding nationals, will be different and, since no international cross-check by customs authorities is practised, the discrepancy will arise and remain unchecked. Where, however, the incentive to fake as also the direction of this faking are common to both parties – as when, for example, the exporter wishes to overinvoice in view of remunerative subsidies and the importer *also* wishes to overinvoice to export unauthorised capital to the exporter's country, as seems to be the case with some recent overinvoicing of exports in India – the proposed statistical technique for detecting faked invoicing would normally break down.

But even where the method is *prima facie* usable, there are, of course, difficulties in using it for our purpose. In fact, the statisticians have long observed *both* discrepancies in partner-country data and the occasional 'perversity' of these discrepancies[4]. And their traditional observations on these 'inconsistencies' provide clues to the possible *alternative* explanation of the perverse discrepancies. It is only when these alternative explanations have been examined and dismissed as inapplicable to the specific empirical analysis, and the relative magnitudes of the premium on the black market for foreign exchange and the import tariff (or export subsidy) on the items where the 'perverse' discrepancies have been observed are such as to indicate an incentive for underinvoicing of imports (or overinvoicing of exports) that we can consider having produced 'reasonable' evidence in support of the hypothesis of underinvoicing of imports (or overinvoicing of exports). And even then, it is always possible to raise the methodological objection that one may have overlooked either some evidence in support of the alternative explanations examined and dismissed or, more pointedly still, an alternative explanation itself. 'Proof' is thus impossible; only 'plausibility' can be procured by the method proposed.

What are these alternative, possible explanations of 'perverse' discrepancies between partner-country, export and import statistics? Several exist:

(1) There can be 'misallocations' of the same traded item, by both Standard International Trade Classification (SITC) category and by country. If inconsistencies obtain between partner countries on either score, then a comparison of c.i.f. import and f.o.b. export values of the two countries with each other, by SITC categories, could well show 'perverse' discrepancies. These inconsistencies can arise from both genuine customs' mistakes and differences in conventions adopted (chiefly with respect to questions of origin and transit). An example from actual trade data is provided by the fact that Malayan exports of rubber to Turkey are attributed in Turkish import statistics to the United Kingdom because an English exporter is handling the transaction, whereas United Kingdom export statistics do not register the transaction, thus leading to a discrepancy in the partner-country statistics of United Kingdom and Turkey but *not* if the exercise of comparisons is extended to include Malaya as well.

Cross-checking with other SITC categories for the *same* pair of countries (to

[4] Any random reference to a statistical publication containing data on exports, according to category and destination and a patient preparation of partner-country tables, will demonstrate this point effectively if one is not satisfied by the testimony of those who compile or use international trade statistics. Refer also to Allen (1960), for a statistical examination of discrepancies in the partner-country data for the following countries: Soviet Union, India, France, Italy, Japan, Sweden, Switzerland, United Kingdom, United States and West Germany, for the year 1956. Allen's objective is to examine whether the discrepancies for the Soviet Union are any larger than those to be found for every country, whether communist or not. No attention is paid by him, however, to the *direction* of these discrepancies.

Another important reference which has come to my attention on this question is Morgenstern (1965), which is a scholarly account of the statistical literature on discrepancies in partner-country trade data, relating, however, to *totals* of exports and imports and to balances of trade.

discover possible misallocations by category) and with similar comparisons for *other pairs of countries* is essential before one can rule out statistical misallocations as an explanation of any observed 'perversity' in discrepancies. That this may well be an important point to remember is illustrated by the fact that, in a previous study on underinvoicing of Turkish imports, I found that, for petroleum products, the large 'perverse' discrepancies with France and Italy nearly cancelled out with 'normal' discrepancies with the United Kingdom and the United States, the discrepancies having arisen from international differences in treatment of the question of refinery ownership. (For details see Bhagwati (1964, pp. 391, 396–397).)

(2) The discrepancies can arise also from the lag between shipment and arrival in the importing country. If the average lag remains unchanged, and the level of export values is not changing, there would of course be no discrepancy between export and import statistics from this source: the excess of import over exports owing to the preceding year's carry-over would offset the deficit owing to this year's carry-forward. Where, however, exports are rising, and the lag is unchanged, there *would* result an excess of recorded exports over imports[5].

(3) Some observed discrepancies are also to be attributed to inaccuracies arising from conversion calculations. More important, however, may be the general customs practice of scaling down or up the invoices presented to them. This practice itself originates from the suspicion of the genuineness of the presented invoices. Where the scaling down takes place when overinvoicing of exports is suspected *and* is actually taking place, there is no complication from this source; nor does it matter when the scaling up occurs when underinvoicing of imports is suspected *and* is actually being attempted. Where, however, the enforced revisions occur in the opposite directions, such that scaling down for example is undertaken for fear of overinvoicing of imports when in fact the invoice is correct, the 'perverse' discrepancy can arise from the customs revisions rather than from genuine faking of invoices!

This rather long analysis of alternative, possible explanations of perverse discrepancies shows how difficult it is, in practice, to use the statistical technique of partner-country data comparisons for reaching any conclusions about faking of trade invoices and the direction of such faking.

However, it is interesting to note that, in an attempt at empirical use of this technique on Turkish statistics for 1960 and 1961, briefly reported at an earlier date (Bhagwati, 1964) I did manage to convince myself that there was quite

[5] This is unlikely, however, to be significant in normal cases. Even if trade grows at 10% – which is quite a generous assumption for most countries – and the carry-forward applies to a three-month period, the resulting discrepancy as a percentage of the recorded trade cannot be more than about 3%, unless unusual and contrasting bunching of trade is assumed for the preceding and the present years.

reasonable evidence of underinvoicing of imports. Partner-country comparisons with the major industrial partners of Turkey showed that, despite checks for other possible explanations, there seemed to be several 'perverse' discrepancies in a significant number of SITC categories which therefore seemed to be accountable, *prima facie*, only by an underinvoicing-of-imports hypothesis. Further investigation strengthened the plausibility of this conclusion by showing that:

(a) these SITC categories consisted overwhelmingly of manufactures, and largely of capital goods of one kind or another – where it is relatively easy to overstate or understate invoices because several quality differences foul up the concept of an 'international' standard price and frequently goods are even made to order, so that the customs authorities cannot really use a reliable yardstick to avoid faking of invoices except outside very wide limits; and

(b) the large majority of these items carried import duties which were in excess of the black market premium on foreign exchange, thus carrying an incentive to understate import values.

Whereas the Turkish case yielded an interesting 'confirmation' of the usefulness of the proposed technique for inferring the faking of trade invoices and hence trade data, my attempt at inferring overinvoicing of exports in the Indian context has had to bypass this technique for reasons which throw the limitations of this technique into sharp focus. There are two fairly strong reasons for believing that a segment of Indian exports has been recently overinvoiced.

(a) There has been *de facto* subsidisation of several new exports, via a form of 'import entitlement' (similar to 'exchange retention') schemes, and there has been general admission, by business houses and official export-promoting agencies, of the overinvoicing that has prevailed; and

(b) An examination of the premium on the (transferable) import entitlements, and the relationship of the entitlements to the export values, shows a subsidy which exceeds the black market discount on the Indian rupee, both for currency rates and for illegal transfers, at most of the principal centres (Hong Kong, Nairobi, Mombasa, Aden and Berne), so that the incentive to overinvoice has been considerable[6].

However, the applicability of the proposed statistical technique breaks down in certain significant ways, all of some interest.

(1) The SITC data required for such analysis are not available except for the

[6] The statement on the *de facto* subsidies, resulting from the import entitlement schemes, is based on information gathered from interviews which I had with export houses and manufacturer-exporters, during June 1965. The information on the black market discount on the rupee is regularly received officially by the central banking authorities from the different centres via 'contacts'; the information for Hong Kong is, in any case, regularly listed on the back pages of the *Far Eastern Economic Review*.

Organisation for Economic Cooperation and Development (OECD) countries (with insignificant exceptions) so that the technique cannot even be a starter on much of India's exports of the incentive-covered items outside the Soviet bloc.

(2) The application of the technique to the OECD countries shows, in fact, that there are excessive 'normal' discrepancies which may *either* imply under-invoicing of exports (as it well may, since the items in which the serious differences occur are where there are no significant subsidies at all) *or* be a result of different conventions (which may be the case with imports of Indian goods by certain Western European countries via the Soviet bloc, these being classified by the former as imports from India but by India as exports to the Soviet bloc). Where there seems to be some slender evidence for the latter explanation, in the form of complaints by Indian exporters that Indian goods purchased by the Soviet bloc under bilateral agreements are being resold at 'dumped' prices in India's traditional markets, it is not possible to cross-check for this 'misallocation' in trade statistics by using independent Soviet bloc data on direction-cum-SITC-categories trade because these data are not available[7]. Nor is it possible to check whether the large excesses of European Economic Community (EEC) c.i.f. import values over Indian f.o.b. export data are not due to misallocations with yet other countries for whom no direction-cum-categories data are available.

(3) Further, the overinvoicing of Indian exports is suspected to have occurred largely with respect to exports to certain 'free ports' such as Hong Kong, Aden and Panama, where the 'partner-country-comparison' technique is inapplicable owing to lack of data.

(4) Finally, much overinvoicing has also allegedly taken place with East Africa and Malaysia. There, the 'Indians' are aiming to pull out capital, in violation of exchange control on capital movement. They are thus happy to fake the value of their imports, in collaboration with the Indian exporters. The resulting difference from the normal overinvoicing is that *both* import and (corresponding) export invoices are faked upwards. This being the case, the statistical technique of partner-country comparisons breaks down as an aid to empirical analysis.

The usability of the statistical technique suggested here is thus dependent on several favourable circumstances. In other cases, the analyst will have to rely on word-of-mouth assurances subjected only to two 'indirect' tests:

(a) Are the items on which the faking of invoices is allegedly practised of a kind where such faking is possible in teeth of customs' checks?

[7] It is possible, however, to go *some* way towards a cross-check, by examining whether the SITC groups in which the excessive discrepancies obtain with EEC countries are also the groups where India's exports to the Soviet bloc are reasonably commensurate. If not, clearly the explanation of 're-sale' by the Soviet bloc will not hold. Indeed, such a check shows that the 're-sale' explanation cannot explain more than a limited fraction of the excessively large 'normal' discrepancies in EEC–India trade data.

(b) Are the magnitudes of the black market premium on foreign exchange and the subsidy or tariff rates on trade transactions such as to provide a significant incentive for the alleged faking of invoices?

For most purposes, these two tests ought to provide a fairly strong indication of some (though indeterminate) amount of faking of invoices in external transactions.

2.3. Economic implications

Whereas, however, it is difficult to secure objective and strong evidence on the prevalence of faked invoicing in foreign trade declarations, these practices frequently obtain when fiscal and exchange policies combine to make them worthwhile. The economic implications of these practices are thus important to analyse. It will be useful to distinguish, for this purpose, among: (a) overinvoicing of exports; (b) underinvoicing of imports; (c) underinvoicing of exports; and (d) overinvoicing of imports.

Since the analysis can be readily adapted for the remaining phenomena, overinvoicing of exports alone is subjected to detailed analysis.

Further, the following analysis begins with (1) the impact on the balance of payments, distinguishing between the 'official' and the 'real' balance, and then extends the argument to the effect of overinvoicing of exports (2) on individual items in the balance of payments and via that on other variables and (3) on the time-lag between exports and receipts.

(1) The analysis of the impact on the *balance of payments* at any point of time (and thus abstracting from long-run effects) must distinguish between what may be described as the *real* position and the *official*, recorded position. The official balance of payments record need not necessarily reflect the real foreign exchange position and generally will not do so when faking is occurring. This real position is given by net availability of foreign exchange for use by the country *after* adjusting for all leakages into prohibited uses resulting in loss of foreign exchange to the country, these leakages being unauthorized remittances and transfers of capital abroad and tourist expenditure in foreign countries (as also possible, unauthorised import expenditure via smuggling).

Assume initially then that the export *volume* and *unfaked value* as well as *authorised* import *expenditure* are given. The illegal foreign exchange market is being fed by supplies from overinvoicing of imports, underinvoicing of exports, diverted remittances and foreign-tourist expenditure and foreign flight of capital. The demands for black exchange come from underinvoicing of imports, illegal tourist expenditure and transfers of capital and remittances abroad, and overinvoicing of exports. Assume further that:

(a) the flight of foreign capital is channelled in through the overinvoicing of exports; and

(b) all illegal demands respond inversely to changes in the premium on black market exchange and all illegal supplies respond directly to such changes.

Effect on 'real' balance of payments. The effect of any increase in overinvoicing of exports on the *real* balance of payments is then measured by the impact change in the total foreign supply of remittances, capital transfers and tourist expenditure (insofar as they respond to the increase in over-invoicing of exports) *plus* any change in the leakage into illegal transfers of capital and remittances to foreign countries and unauthorised tourist expenditure abroad. The change in this measures the net increment or reduction in foreign exchange availability for authorised uses. In the following analysis, two principal varieties of increments in the overinvoicing of exports are discussed:

(a) where the cause is net increase in subsidisation of exports; and

(b) where the cause is an autonomous, illegal transfer of foreign capital via the overinvoicing of exports.

(i) It will be clear that any increase in overinvoicing of exports which reflects a policy change such as the expansion of the export-subsidisation programme, will lead to an increase in the black market premium and thus have two favourable effects:

(a) it will cut into the illegal leakages into capital and remittance transfers abroad and also into unauthorised expenditure on foreign travel; and

(b) it will induce an increase in the *overall* inflow of remittances, funds transfers and foreign tourist expenditure insofar as these are price-elastic.

Note that if we were to assume away these effects, such that these illegal leakages and also the overall inflows of remittances, etc. are now assumed not to respond to increase in the premium, then the incremental overinvoicing of exports will create a demand for black market exchange that will necessarily involve a diversion from official channels. This can take different forms, among them a diversion from official receipts or a stimulation of overinvoicing of imports (owing to the rise in the black market premium). In none of these cases, however, will the real balance of payments be affected.

Thus, consider the case where the incremental, overinvoiced exports are 'financed' by diversion of official remittances. In this case, the diverted remittances *in any case* wind up eventually with the exchange authorities. [This is *not* to argue, of course, that there would be no economic 'loss' at all. For example, if an *ad valorem*, *cash* subsidy is given on exports, this diversion leads to an 'unnecessary' subsidy transfer, which may jeopardise some economic objective, especially if there is a political constraint on the revenues that can be raised; or, for example, if the subsidisation takes the form of *exchange retention* by exporters, overinvoicing will bias the allocation of foreign exchange earnings towards the exporters and thereby possibly distort the priorities in allocation that may have been laid down by the authorities[8].]

Alternatively, consider the other case where the illegal overinvoiced amount of foreign exchange is secured, not by diversion from 'normal' inflow of receipts (such as remittances, tourist expenditure), but by the stimulation of faking on the import side: for example, through the overinvoicing of imports which yields the illegal supply of exchange. In this case, part of the official, foreign exchange allocation for imports, in the first round, will be used up in 'financing' the over-invoiced part of imports; it will then leak into the illegal market for 'financing' overinvoicing of exports; it will therewith return to the exchange authorities and then be re-allocated to the users of foreign exchange. Once again, therefore, there is no adverse effect on the real balance of payments. [The allocation of available exchange *will*, however, be affected, thereby affecting any priorities that the authorities may have concerning the use of foreign exchange.] Thus, in these and similar cases, the effect on the real balance of payments position will be neutral (although, as already discussed, *other* economic effects cannot be ruled out).

Hence, the overall effect on the real balance of payments position, when the increment in overinvoicing of exports follows upon an expanded subsidy programme, will be:

(a) favourable whenever illegal leakages and/or overall inflow of remittances, transfers and foreign-tourist expenditures are responsive to changes in the black market premium on foreign exchange; and

(b) neutral when these effects are assumed away[9].

In either case, internal economic effects will undoubtedly follow, which may well be adverse.

(ii) On the other hand, insofar as the increase in overinvoicing merely reflects an illegal inflow of foreign capital, the overinvoicing creates its own, *net* source of foreign exchange supply and no increment in the premium need therefore be expected so that none of the favourable effects considered so far will follow. However, the illegal inflow of foreign capital *itself* will, of course, represent a *net* gain to the real balance of payments position. This phenomenon occurs, for example, when a Malaysian trader, wishing to pull capital out of Malaysia in contravention of the exchange control rules, overinvoices his imports from India, matched by overinvoiced exports from India, and the capital thus flows from

[8] This may well be considered a significant effect, especially by governments which opt for strong ordering of priorities.

[9] There *is* one important exception, which follows from the effect of overinvoicing on the lag between exports and export receipts. This is considered later in the text.

Malaysia to India. To consider this net inflow of capital into India, where exports are overinvoiced, a net gain to the real balance of payments position in India would naturally involve an implicit, though normally legitimate, assumption that the capital export would not otherwise have been feasible.

Effect on official balance of payments. While therefore the *real* balance of payments will generally improve, and at worst may remain unaffected, following upon an increase in the overinvoicing of exports, the *official* balance of payments position will also generally look better – provided the illegal loss of exchange responds to the increment in the black market premium when the overinvoicing of exports increases in response to a subsidy programme (see Appendix). Where the incremental overinvoicing of exports elicits its own net inflow of capital, further, this itself constitutes the full measure of the improvement in the official balance of payments position.

Hence (under the assumptions so far made) overinvoicing of exports, though widely condemned as a malpractice, is from both the real and the official points of view as considered in this paper, advantageous to a country's overall balance of payments position[10]. The conclusion is merely reinforced if we bring in the possibility of unauthorised import expenditure (on smuggled goods and gold) being reduced as the black market premium on exchange rises. Nor does the conclusion alter if we assume that the authorised import quantities rather than authorised import expenditure are fixed (see Appendix).

(2) On the other hand, the implication for *individual*, recorded entries in the balance of payments is not necessarily advantageous. The fact remains that the *composition* of the balance of payments will look different from its 'actual' position. The question then is whether this can have any adverse or favourable effects, in turn, aside from the obvious misleading effect on economic policy based on balance of payments analysis. At least one important implication does, in fact, follow and needs to be spelled out. Aid inflow is frequently conditional upon the trends in the balance of payments. At the consortium (or aid club) meetings, the recipient country's foreign exchange performance becomes usually the focal point of overall evaluation, the discussion frequently turning on whether the recipient country is likely to be able to earn enough foreign exchange to become

[10] Note that we have so far not made any allowance for the fact that there may be 'secondary' effects on the balance of payments, arising from (alternative) ways in which any 'improvements' in the payments position are 'disposed of'. Also there may be 'indirect' effects on the balance of payments; for example, with exchange authorisation for imports taken as fixed and overinvoicing of imports increasing and underinvoicing decreasing, the *quantum* of imports will fall and this itself may have expenditure effects affecting the balance of payments currently; or, via shift in pattern of availabilities, there may be effects on the future balance of payments.

eventually 'viable', i.e. presumably to meet her debt servicing requirements plus the 'normal' import requirements[11].

In a country where a good (visible) export performance does make a considerable difference and serves to impress the possibility of long-run 'viability' on the aid-givers (as, for example, in the case of India), inflation of export values is a psychological booster to *easier*, maybe even bigger, aid-flow. But where the overinvoicing springs from diverted supplies of exchange from remittances, tourist earnings, etc. and the aid-givers are relying upon performance in *these* areas of invisible earnings for signs of the possibility of long-run viability (as, for example, in Turkey), the net effect may be unfavourable rather than favourable.

(3) There is yet another significant way in which overinvoicing of exports can affect the balance of payments behaviour and which must be discussed here. All countries, which have exchange control on capital movements, impose a time limit on the (possible) *lag* between exports and the surrender of the exchange earned therefrom; for example, with insignificant exceptions for certain capital goods, the permitted lag in India is currently six months. *Within* this permissible limit, exporters have the choice of either keeping their earnings abroad or remitting them home. The former will take usually the shape of a trade credit or may even be an explicit, short-term investment. In either case, the basic choice will be determined by the factors governing the rates of return on either option. These rates of return are supposed to be a reflection largely of respective short-term interest rates and it seems sensible to argue, at the least, that a widening of the difference between foreign and domestic short-term interest rates, in favour of the former, will tend to lengthen the average lag between exports and export receipts.

The overinvoicing of exports will also generally lengthen this lag. The overinvoiced part of the declared value has to be secured from illegal sources; this is likely to take time if the exporter wishes to find out the cheapest source for illegal purchase of foreign exchange. More important, the exporter can avoid altogether any interest charge on the cost (equivalent to the premium on illegal foreign exchange) incurred by the purchase of illegal foreign exchange, by putting it off till the very end of the permissible period. Hence, he has a definite incentive, as long as the interest rate is positive, to defer (as long as possible) the return of the overinvoiced part of the export 'earnings'. This will, therefore, increase the *average*

[11] This appears to be valid certainly, in my experience, for Turkey and India. Of course, the cynics may argue that economic arguments are only a cloak for what are really hard, political factors governing the level of aid given, and that a reduction in aid, for example, will follow from political considerations rather than because viability seems dubious at higher aid levels. On the other hand, it certainly makes it *easier* to reduce aid, if convenient economic 'excuses' can be found to do so, so that there may well be a relationship between economic arguments and the level of aid inflow.

lag on total export 'earnings' insofar as such overinvoicing is a new, or an increasing, phenomenon[12]. Insofar as this happens, further, the time-profile of receipts of foreign exchange will undoubtedly be affected, and the result may well be, after taking into account the source from which the illegal exchange comes to 'finance' the overinvoicing, a net deterioration in the *immediate* availability of foreign exchange to the country.

Similar arguments can be applied, *mutatis mutandis*, to the other varieties of faked, trade declarations. For those who attach any weight to the *political* aspects of economic policy, it is further pertinent to note the corruption which both follows, and later prevents the elimination of, the fiscal policies that lead to such faking of trade declarations.

Acknowledgements

I should like to thank V. K. Ramaswami, T. N. Srinivasan, and A. Vaidyanathan for their helpful comments on an early draft of this paper.

Appendix

The arguments in the text concerning the implications for the balance of payments of the overinvoicing of exports can be readily supported by extremely elementary mathematical analysis.

Take the following system:

$$S = S_1 + S_2 + S_3 + S_4 + S_5, \tag{1}$$

where S is the total supply of illegal foreign exchange, S_1 the supply from overinvoicing of imports, S_2 the supply from underinvoicing of exports, S_3 the supply from diverted remittances, S_4 the supply from diverted expenditure of foreign tourists and S_5 the supply from flight of foreign capital (coming into this country via overinvoiced exports from this country to the foreign countries from where capital is illegally being taken out and via matching overinvoicing of corresponding imports in these foreign countries).

[12] This is likely to have happened in the case of India during the fiscal year 1964–1965 when a very large excess of recorded exports over export earnings developed along with an intensification of the export promotion drive. For details, see Bhagwati (1965). For an illuminating theoretical analysis of the effect of an extended lag between exports and receipts, on the time-profile of the difference between the two, Hansen (1961) remains the standard work so far.

$$S_1 = S_1(P) \qquad (S_1' > 0), \tag{2}$$

such that S_1 is an increasing function of the premium (P) on foreign exchange. Similarly,

$$S_2 = S_2(P) \qquad (S_2' > 0), \tag{3}$$
$$S_3 = S_3(P) \qquad (S_3' > 0), \tag{4}$$
$$S_4 = S_4(P) \qquad (S_4' > 0). \tag{5}$$

Moreover,

$$S_3 + S_3^{\circ} = \bar{S}_3, \tag{6}$$

where $\bar{S}_3$ is the *given*, total supply of remittances from abroad to this country, with S_3° the *official* inflow and S_3 the *illegal* inflow; and similarly

$$S_4 + S_4^{\circ} = \bar{S}_4, \tag{7}$$

where $\bar{S}_4$ is the fixed, *total* foreign-tourist expenditure in this country, of which S_4° is the legal, *official* receipts.

Further,

$$D = D_1 + D_2 + D_3 + D_4 + D_5, \tag{8}$$

where D is the total demand for illegal foreign exchange, D_1 the demand from underinvoicing of imports, D_2 the demand from illegal tourist expenditure in foreign countries, D_3 the demand from illegal capital transfers to foreign countries, and finally D_4 and D_5 are the demands from overinvoicing of exports where D_5 is that part which is related to the illegal transfer of capital from abroad.

$$D_1 = D_1(P) \qquad (D_1' < 0), \tag{9}$$
$$D_2 = D_2(P) \qquad (D_2' < 0), \tag{10}$$
$$D_3 = D_3(P) \qquad (D_3' < 0), \tag{11}$$
$$D_4 = D_4(P, r) \tag{12}$$

(where $\partial D_4/\partial P < 0$ and $\partial D_4/\partial r > 0$ and r is the subsidy rate on the subsidised exports), and

$$D_5 = S_5, \tag{13}$$

such that it is assumed that the illegal transfer of capital from abroad to this country takes the form, and elicits an *equal* amount, of overinvoicing of exports (as in the example of overinvoiced Indian exports to East Africa and Malaysia in the text).

Finally,

$$S = D. \tag{14}$$

Altogether, therefore, the system has 14 equations, and provided r and S_5 are specified, 14 unknowns: S, D, D_1, D_2, D_3, D_4, D_5, S_1, S_2, S_3, S_4, S_3^o, S_4^o and P. By differentiating the system with respect to r, therefore, the effect of the resulting increase in overinvoicing of exports can be readily investigated.

First, examine the impact on the *official* balance of payments. This is measured by

$$\mathrm{d}\left(\frac{S_3^o + S_4^o + D_4 + D_5 - S_2}{\mathrm{d}r}\right),$$

because S_3^o represents the official remittances, S_4^o the official receipts from foreign tourist expenditure, D_4 and D_5 represent the overinvoiced part of export receipts, and S_2 represents the underinvoiced part of (other) export receipts. It is assumed that the total allocation for *imports* remains unchanged, regardless of faking.

$$\begin{aligned}\frac{\mathrm{d}S}{\mathrm{d}r} &= \frac{\mathrm{d}S_1}{\mathrm{d}r} + \frac{\mathrm{d}S_2}{\mathrm{d}r} + \frac{\mathrm{d}S_3}{\mathrm{d}r} + \frac{\mathrm{d}S_4}{\mathrm{d}r} \\ &= (S_1' + S_2' + S_3' + S_4')\,(\mathrm{d}P/\mathrm{d}r),\end{aligned} \tag{15}$$

and

$$\begin{aligned}\frac{\mathrm{d}D}{\mathrm{d}r} &= \frac{\mathrm{d}D_1}{\mathrm{d}r} + \frac{\mathrm{d}D_2}{\mathrm{d}r} + \frac{\mathrm{d}D_3}{\mathrm{d}r} + \frac{\mathrm{d}D_4}{\mathrm{d}r} \\ &= (D_1' + D_2' + D_3' + D_{4P}')\,\mathrm{d}P/\mathrm{d}r + D_{4r}',\end{aligned}$$

where

$$D_{4P}' = \partial D_4/\partial P \quad \text{and} \quad D_{4r}' = \partial D_4/\partial r. \tag{16}$$

Therefore, since $\mathrm{d}S/\mathrm{d}r = \mathrm{d}D/\mathrm{d}r$ from eq. (14), we have

$$\frac{\mathrm{d}P}{\mathrm{d}r} = \frac{D_{4r}'}{S_1' + S_2' + S_3' + S_4' - (D_1' + D_2' + D_3' + D_{4P}')}, \tag{17}$$

and therefore

$$\frac{\mathrm{d}(S_3^o + S_4^o + D_4 + D_5 - S_2)}{\mathrm{d}r} = D_{4r}'\,\frac{S_1' - (D_1' + D_2' + D_3')}{S_1' + S_2' + S_3' + S_4' - (D_1' + D_2' + D_3' + D_{4P}')} > 0. \tag{18}$$

The *official* balance of payments will thus necessarily improve, under the assumption made.

The impact on the *real* balance of payments may, however, be defined as the impact on the net accrual of all foreign exchange (legal and illegal) to the country after adjusting for leakages into unauthorised and wasteful uses such as illegal transfers of capital and tourist expenditure abroad. In this case, we wish to find out

$$\frac{\mathrm{d}(\bar{S}_3 + \bar{S}_4 + S_5 - D_2 - D_3)}{\mathrm{d}r}.$$

This reduces to

$$\frac{\mathrm{d}(-D_2 - D_3)}{\mathrm{d}r} = \frac{(-D_2' - D_3')D_{4r}'}{S_1' + S_2' + S_3' + S_4' - (D_1' + D_2' + D_3' + D_{4P}')} > 0. \tag{19}$$

Thus the *real* balance of payments will necessarily improve, under the assumptions made. Note further that it will improve more, the larger the size of the reduction in leakage of foreign exchange into illegal capital transfers and unauthorised expenditure abroad, i.e. of D_2' and D_3'. Therefore both the official and the 'real' balance of payments situations will improve following upon an increase in the export subsidy programme and hence in export-overinvoicing.

These conclusions are further *strengthened* if we assume the *total* inflow of remittances ($\bar{S}_3$) and tourist expenditure ($\bar{S}_4$) to be not fixed but themselves positively responsive to higher return, i.e. $\mathrm{d}\bar{S}_3/\mathrm{d}P > 0$ and $\mathrm{d}\bar{S}_4/\mathrm{d}P > 0$. So will any (autonomous) change in S_5 and D_5 only improve (and by the same amount) the official and 'real' balance of payments positions[13].

A change in the assumption of *fixed*, authorised import expenditure will also not impair the (directional) conclusions reached if we assume, for example, that the authorised import *quantities* are fixed instead. In this case, the authorised, official allocations for imports will vary with the overinvoicing and underinvoicing of imports. But neither the official[14] nor the real balance of payments[15] will worsen, as a result of this.

Note finally that *individual* balance of payments entries, such as official remittances, will undoubtedly be affected and may, in turn, have economic implica-

[13] This is obvious because S_5 and D_5 represent respectively the flight of capital from foreign countries and the overinvoicing of exports in this country (matched by overinvoicing of corresponding imports in these foreign countries) which permits this flight and canalises it to itself. Since S_5 and D_5 are identically equal, there will be no effect on the premium or any other magnitude.

[14] The change in the official balance of payments will now be

$$D_{4r}' \frac{-(D_2' + D_3')}{S_1' + S_2' + S_3' + S_4' - (D_1' + D_2' + D_3' + D_{4P}')}, \tag{20}$$

which is greater than zero.

[15] This change in the real balance of payments will remain as in eq. (19).

tions insofar as they are treated by influential commentators, such as aid-giving agencies, as significant indicators of health in the balance of payments[16].

References

Allen, L., 1960, Soviet Economic Warfare (Public Affairs Press, Washington, D.C.), 268, 284–291.
Bhagwati, J., 1964, On the under-invoicing of imports, Bulletin 26, November.
Bhagwati, J., 1965, Why export receipts lag behind exports, Economic Weekly 27, July.
Hansen, B., 1961, Foreign Trade Credits and Exchange Reserves (North-Holland Publishing Co., Amsterdam).
Johnson, H. G., 1958, International Trade and Economic Growth (George Allen and Unwin Ltd., London), ch. 6.
Meade, J. E., 1955, The balance of payments, The Theory of International Economic Policy I (Oxford University Press, Oxford).
Morgenstern, O., 1965, On the Accuracy of Economic Observations (Princeton University Press), ch. 9.
Musgrave, R. A., 1964, Tax policy, Review of Economics and Statistics 46 (2), May.
Salant, W. B., 1964, The balance-of-payments deficit and the tax structure, Review of Economics and Statistics, May.

16 The analysis above has ignored the complications arising from swings in the trade credits as overinvoicing of exports increases. Yet other qualifications have been noted in the text. It would be useful also to add that, as Peter Oppenheimer has pointed out to me, the definition of the 'real' balance of payments adopted in this paper is a 'resource-allocational' one, appropriate to a planning authority examining the availability of foreign exchange for its authorised uses, and ought not to be confused with the traditional formulations of balance of payments 'imbalance' or 'disequilibrium'.

PART III

PARTNER-COUNTRY DATA COMPARISONS AND FAKED INVOICING

Chapter 7

ON THE ACCURACY OF ECONOMIC OBSERVATIONS: FOREIGN TRADE STATISTICS*

Oskar MORGENSTERN

1. Introductory remarks

The following discussion bears mainly on the difficulties of ascertaining the quality of foreign trade statistics, whether they be used for relatively detailed business information or for the study of the overall trade among nations. The quality of these statistics also presents an interesting problem in the relation between data and theory. It will be seen that statistics on foreign trade and gold movements are exceedingly poor, and as a result large parts of the theory of international trade are open to doubt. This presents a real dilemma: economic theory has unquestionably postulated a fine structure in the international field; yet we cannot describe this structure adequately by relying on the data with which we are confronted[1]. This dilemma will be made amply clear by the examples to be discussed. The problem is, of course, not restricted to foreign transactions, but the general accessibility of foreign trade statistics makes this field particularly attractive. Extensive accounts of nearly identical events are given by observers in slightly different positions in time and space: those recording the physical quantity and the value of an *exported* commodity and those recording both again as an *import*. Such double reporting is not normally available for purely domestic economic activities, although most transactions could, of course, be recorded both as a sale and as a purchase.

* Editor's note: This reprint of ch. IX of Morgenstern's work *On the Accuracy of Economic Observations* omits the first three paragraphs. Figure and table numbers have been re-numbered to conform to the style of this volume. However, the original numbers are given below each table or figure to facilitate reference to the original volume.

[1] For example, in our study (Morgenstern, 1959, ch. V, pp. 565–579), we found that the assertions, made mostly in the 1930s, that the gold standard mechanism imposed a rigid behavior upon the countries adhering to it, were not borne out by the facts as described by the data. So either the theory is at fault, or the data are inadequate (assuming that their confrontation was done correctly).

Foreign trade is therefore a well-defined area in which to study discrepancies in reports. The problem is to differentiate between true discrepancies of reporting, see Graham (1942)[2], and the influence of such items as import duties, transportation charges, time lags, classification of commodities, deliberate falsification for political reasons, etc. The separation of these factors is exceedingly difficult and will succeed only occasionally. When that is not the case, possibly big gaps remain in the respective reports.

The need for studies of this type has been noted by many writers over a long period of time. One of the earliest writers on this subject was the Italian economist, C. F. Ferraris, who developed (for gold movements) a test which did cast grave doubts on the validity of official returns[3]. Ferraris measured the movement of gold from France to Great Britain for the periods 1876–1880 and 1881–1884, using the statistical sources of both countries. This showed, see table 1, large discrepancies (even after making allowance for transport costs, tariff duties, etc.).

Table 1.
Gold imports in Britain (in millions of francs).

	According to French export statistics	According to British import statistics
1876–1880	41.5	94.4
1881–1884	52.9	112.2

These differences are appalling and show that one is dealing with far from trivial troubles. Even if they were much smaller, they would call for study and remedial action. As we shall see, little has been accomplished, though the matter has been observed from time to time.

2 'Much confusion arises from the fact that only a varying part of the total exports or imports of any given country is recorded in the statistics ordinarily published . . . Official statistics, in fact, merely show the results of that portion of foreign commerce which happens to be easy of surveillance, or they reflect the statistical whims of legislatures.' Yet Graham did not draw further consequences from this correct evaluation.

3 See his almost totally neglected work (Ferraris, 1885) and also another contribution (Ferraris, 1899–1900). Another writer of note is Bodio (1896) who had also treated this problem earlier in 1865; and an important piece was written by Ricci (1914). A more recent work is the paper by Gini (1928) where criticisms directed against Italian foreign trade statistics by Mortara and others are discussed. There have undoubtedly been similar studies made in other countries and on other occasions. In particular reference is made to the paper by Bowley (1928). He has shown wide discrepancies in the transit trade of Scandinavian countries. (I owe my acquaintance with this paper to C. Clark.)

The long history of efforts on the part of various international organizations to standardize the classifications of commodities moving in international trade might lead eventually to increased validity at least as far as matching statistics is concerned. The reliability of data will depend on intensive analysis – perhaps by commodities – into the data. Recently the Inter-American Statistical Institute (1955) has made some preliminary investigations along these lines. We will have more to say on this subject in sect. 3 below.

The most important causes for disparities between statistics of exporting and importing countries are the differences in:

(a) Coverage of the statistics and definitions of commodities.

(b) The methods adopted for showing 'provenance' of imports and destination of exports.

(c) Detailed definitions used in connection with a given method.

(d) Methods of valuation and exchange conversion.

(e) Inability (or unwillingness) of importers and especially exporters to furnish accurate information; it is usually more difficult to furnish correct data as to destination of exports than as to provenance of imports (Allen and Ely, 1953).

In the following pages we shall first take up gold movements, partly for their intrinsic interest and the great role they have always played as a critical component in the items that make up the balance of payments, and partly because gold offers the simplest and most standardized of all cases where commodity movements are to be recorded. Then we shall examine some cases of commodity statistics other than gold.

2. Statistics of gold movements

2.1. Introduction

In this section we will examine statistics of international gold movements for their reliability and usefulness[4]. An investigation of this kind is justified for the light

[4] This section is based, for the most part, on my monograph (Morgenstern, 1955a), to which the reader is referred for more detail. That paper grew out of the work involved in a larger investigation undertaken for the National Bureau of Economic Research (Morgenstern, 1959). In the course of this investigation, gold movements, gold points, their relations to exchange rates, etc. had to be examined. It was hoped that significant correlations could be computed on the basis of monthly data for exchange rates and gold movements for the important countries of the world during a period from approximately 1870 to 1939. However, studies by other writers of these relationships had already shown that it was very difficult, if at all possible, to obtain intelligible and significant relationships. The question therefore arose whether there might be troubles with the basic statistics themselves. Few difficulties are to be expected or found in the

it may shed on the problem of the analysis of economic data in general, and, specifically, because gold movements are important in the study of international trade, especially in the behavior of exchange rates and capital movements. Gold movements are of particular significance for our understanding of the period of the gold standard, but they are also important for any other monetary system. The accuracy of the statistics on gold movements should probably be the least questionable of all the components of balance of payments statistics, certainly not to be compared with such items as security movements, the pure (and usually wild) estimates of tourists' expenditures, and immigrants' remittances[5]. It is therefore of singular importance to determine their worth. In the absence of fortuitously offsetting errors, the aggregate, formed of parts of widely diverse quality, cannot be better than the best part; in fact, it will in almost all cases be considerably below that standard.

In the case of gold, one is dealing with a clearly defined commodity of great significance. There are no technological changes in the product considered, and there is no serious problem of classification; it is easy to ascertain what constitutes gold, though not necessarily monetary gold. The statistics of gold movements have been and are being used by hosts of writers in their analyses of the conditions in various countries, in the studies of balance of payments, and for the verification and development of the theory of money and international trade. Most observations regarding gold in the field of the theory of international balances ultimately rely on information that can be culled only from gold movement statistics. Consequently, a test of the value and the significance of these statistics is of considerable interest and serves as an example for the statistics of foreign trade.

The 'test' described in the next pages is entirely on a common-sense basis. The fact that no high-powered statistical procedures are used is explained by the peculiar circumstance that, as already commented on earlier, no techniques specifically appropriate for the subsequently shown situation exist, the tremendous development of statistics during the last decades notwithstanding.

In order to determine the value of statistics of gold movements, it is necessary to establish a standard of accuracy. This standard, by common scientific practice, can be derived only from the uses to which the data are to be put. The uses are, of course, governed by the 'theories' for which the data are needed. If no theories

statistics of exchange rates. Statistics of gold points were non-existent; a collection of all accessible information about gold points for New York, London, Paris, and Berlin from 1870 to 1938 is given in my book (Morgenstern, 1955a, ch. V). The plentiful statistics of gold movements lent themselves to an investigation of their accuracy.

[5] The very great difficulties in obtaining reasonably reliable migration statistics are described by Linder (1959). Migration is a world-wide phenomenon, affecting international transactions, the labor market, etc. Yet the coverage is only for about 32% of the world population and differs widely even among countries having such statistics at all.

existed, it would be impossible to say what 'accuracy' of measurement of these quantities means. It will be seen in the following, however, that even for ordinary description, which is in itself not intended to be an application of high-powered economic theory, the statistics are so grossly bad that for most purposes they must be rejected.

Data on international gold movements are used not only for purposes of description and analysis, but also for policy guidance. The rates of interest of central banks, for example, frequently have been changed because of reported gold flows between countries. Such changes were justified by data which are of highly questionable character.

2.2. Uses of gold movement statistics

The statistics of international gold movements are used primarily for two general purposes: (1) broad observations of long-run behavior of, say, gold and prices, using years as the minimum unit; and (2) the study of the fine structure of international economic interaction, as described, for example, by the variants of the theory of the gold standard and various theories of adjustment of balances of payments for which monthly data are indispensable. Obviously, the criteria of the usefulness of the data must be taken from the maximal requirements to be made for them.

We are concerned here only with gold movements across national borders. The separation of monetary gold and non-monetary gold used for industrial purposes, is neither simple nor conclusive[6], although it would be desirable since the indirect effects of gold as an industrial commodity upon the price system and upon the international accounts are less important and direct than its monetary effects.

Gold statistics are derived from the statistics of monetary gold movements plus those of some gold stocks (in banks and treasuries). Important judgments hinge on them, including the nature and extent of the 'gaps' in the balance of payments. Information about gold in possession of central and commercial banks and of treasuries is generally made available not only in the usual trade statistics but also in special reports. Nonetheless, such information is seldom trustworthy. At any rate, none of the available statistics shows the variations in the possessions of banks and treasuries as originating from contact with specific single countries (see footnote 16); they are thus only useful for more limited investigations than those now under discussion.

[6] Some of the problems arising in this area are discussed by Gardner (1953). For some comments on this work, see Morgenstern (1955b).

A simple test of the data on official records of gold movements (as well as for other items in foreign trade) is the one developed (for gold) by Ferraris (1885), mentioned earlier. The following test uses Ferraris' principle and consists in taking A's exports to B according to A's export statistics and B's import statistics and B's exports to A according to B's export statistics and A's import statistics. Each of these two sets should agree within certain bounds that are set by such items as freight, insurance, and duties. To these some other factors may have to be added, mostly in the nature of lags; a reasonable allowance for clerical and printing errors must also be made.

2.3. *The test of validity*

The problem may be broken down into four parts: (1) the formulation of the underlying hypothesis; (2) the description of the sample and the results; (3) the explanation of the failure of the statistics to confirm the hypothesis and a discussion of certain difficulties even if it had been confirmed; and (4) the consequences of (2) and (3).

2.3.1. *Formulation of the hypothesis*

The observations of gold movements from country A to country B are made in A's export and in B's import statistics. The two should coincide. In neighboring countries such factors as transportation costs and time lags virtually disappear; in countries more distant from each other, a time lag may have to be considered. Costs of transportation, insurance, handling charges, and so on, which all enter significantly into the determination of gold points, play no appreciable role here. Gold is so valuable that these costs all but disappear from the statistics, as is evident from the value of these items relative to the value of gold shipments[7]. Nevertheless, we shall not expect 100% agreement between the two statistics describing the same foreign trade operation, but will accept 'reasonable' deviations. However, differences also due to other causes should be random. If they are not, there exists probably a special factor or bias that should be accounted for separately.

Thus, the expectation of practical identity of the two sets of data for neighboring countries, after allowing for a possible, but not necessary, time lag for others, constitutes the hypothesis of the following test.

[7] This does not contradict the fact that the profitability of shipments depends on very small changes of transportation cost, interest rates, etc.

2.3.2. Description of the sample test and its results

(i) The data used are the official statistics of imports and exports of gold, gold coin, bullion, leaf, etc. Sterling was chosen as the unit of measurement because most references to gold movements are in sterling, although the test, determining the ratio between the two observations, is independent of units and could have been made in any currency[8].

(ii) Fig. 3 shows two monthly time series over longer consecutive periods than were used for the sample in order to demonstrate that the choice of one source rather than of another, presumably equivalent, leads to widely different results concerning cycle turning points and the duration of cycles, the cycles merely determined in the conventional, intuitive manner of the National Bureau of Economic Research.

For each year, monthly data were assembled from both sources in a total of eight directions for the United Kingdom, the United States, Germany, and France. Canada was introduced only in her relations with the United Kingdom and the United States. This gives six pairs of countries plus two pairs involving Canada. Since each country's export and import statistics were examined and compared with the import and export statistics of each other country for the four years, there are 1536 possible monthly observations[9]. However, since only the differences between the reports enter into our subsequent computations, the number is cut to one-half, or 768 months. Quarterly and yearly values were obtained by summation from the monthly data. The monthly statistics are summarized in table 2 in annual form[10].

Table 2 gives exports and imports of gold in £1000 units from both sources, where available. There is also shown the ratio between the statistics from the two sources. If both sets of data were accurate, the ratios should be unity or very near to unity. But, the ratios do not cluster closely around 1; indeed, quite absurd and fantastic values occur. The spread, as is to be expected, was even greater for the quarterly than for the yearly data, and would be still larger for monthly data were they shown.

An even more comprehensive picture is obtained from fig. 1, which is, essentially, a frequency distribution. On the horizontal axis the ratios are shown and on the vertical axis the values of the transactions (using log-scale) are shown in £1000,

[8] The period covered by the sample includes the years 1900, 1907, 1928, and 1935.

[9] There were, in fact, somewhat fewer entries, inasmuch as data were not available for each country for every month.

[10] Monthly data are not shown because of their bulk and in order to avoid any impression of erratic behavior of the sample. See, however, the monthly data of net movements in fig. 4. The quarterly data are reproduced in full in table 2 in my monograph (Morgenstern, 1955a, pp. 14–17).

the value taken from the first named country in each case[11].

An additional hypothesis is suggested by fig. 1: When gold movements are large the ratio will improve[12], perhaps because greater care in reporting might usually be taken by both sides in such cases. Whatever the reason, the noted relation seems to be borne out by the yearly data. But it is noteworthy that the four largest values occur for 1935, and the really interesting gold standard period (pre-World War I) again fares badly. Even more noteworthy is the fact that the second largest movement, involving not less than £85 million of shipment between the United States and the United Kingdom, was, according to the statistics of the latter, only 75% of that which the United States reported for the same time – hardly a reliable piece of information!

2.3.3. Failure of the statistics

The charts of quarterly data, see Morgenstern (1955a, pp. 20, 22), are even more revealing, showing departures from unity larger than would be admissible for reliable data. Even for 1900 and 1907, the years of the classical gold standard, the results were catastrophic. There was no recognizable tendency or systematic bias of any sort. The statistics were simply contradictory. Although the quarterly sums for the period after World War I fared somewhat better (there were fewer entries), they are useless for purposes of more intricate economic reasoning. Nonetheless, they were used in thousands of publications, scientific and political, with all kinds of delicate 'inferences' drawn.

If the monthly data of gold movements were correlated month for month with movements in exchange rates, short-term interest rates, and short-term interest rate differentials on the basis of the data included in our sample, or with any other available gold movement data, especially for the classical time of the gold standard before World War I, the results would be very poor almost without exception. Correlations are not observed where they are expected, and in this case there are no potent reasons for permitting the lack of correlations to override the expecta-

[11] Fig. 1 shows the frequency distribution of the ratios of table 2 in the following manner: To take an example, in fig. 1, U.K. 35 U.S. at • means that the statistics of the United Kingdom indicate a gold movement to the United States in 1935 (summed over the whole year). The dot shows (from the legend in fig. 1) that the United Kingdom statistics were used to determine the ordinate, i.e. in this case the placement of the dot tells us that the cumulative amount transacted was given as £85 883 000. The ratio at the bottom of the chart is taken from table 2; that is, in the numerator are the data of the country whose statistics were not used for the determination of the ordinate (in this case the United States), and in the denominator are the data of the other country (in this case the United Kingdom). In the case of U.K. 35 U.S. the ratio was 0.75, as table 2 shows, and to this corresponds the abscissa of the dot • on fig. 1. The other points on the chart should be interpreted in the same way.

[12] The chart omits the extreme ratios altogether for reasons of difficulty in plotting, but they can be seen in table 2.

Table 2.
Comparison of annual gold movements and ratio of pairs of statistics for selected countries for 1900, 1907, 1928, and 1935[a]. (Unit: £1000.)

		U.K.–Germany	Germany–U.K.	Ratio Germany–U.K.[c]	U.K.–France	France–U.K.	Ratio France–U.K.	U.K.–U.S.	U.S.–U.K.	Ratio U.S.–U.K.	Germany–U.S.	U.S.–Germany	Ratio U.S.–Germany
1900	Exports[b]	4 903	2 065	1.12	2 360	671	1.76	1 082	3 896	0.68	—	1 052	—
	Imports	2 544	5 490	0.81	2 154	4 165	0.31	5 872	738	0.66	804	776	1.31
1907	Exports	3 162	7 176	1.25	7 208	3 224	0.92	18 354	898	0.99	210	558	2.25
	Imports	7 760	3 947	0.93	5 204	6 590	0.62	652	18 104	1.38	—	473	—
1928	Exports	21 047	116	—	19 969	—	0.01	6 602	6 684	1.17	19	5 913	—
	Imports	52	—	2.22[d]	187	285	—	6 684	7 708	1.00	—	—	—
1935	Exports	1 373	149	—	49 845	77 164	1.00	85 883	117	0.75	10	36	0.80
	Imports	454	—	0.33	81 000	49 631	0.95	168	64 485	0.70	—	8	—

(contd.)

Table 2 (contd.)

		Germany–France	France–Germany	Ratio France–Germany	U.S.–France	France–U.S.	Ratio France–U.S.	U.K.–Canada[e]	Canada–U.K.	Ratio Canada–U.K.	U.S.–Canada	Canada–U.S.	Ratio Canada–U.S.
1900	Exports	16	—	*28.1*	3 527	185	0.47	—	—	—	645	204	0.87
	Imports	130	450	—	368	1 667	0.50	—	21	—	1 387	558	0.15
1907	Exports	481	—	1.22	5 197	422	0.94	—	1	—	2 795	3 955	0.47
	Imports	641	589	—	1 035	4 879	0.41	—	135	—	5 197	1 309	0.76
1928	Exports	—	—	—	63 296	—	—	—	1 958	—	4 653	21 323	1.04
	Imports	—	—	—	31	—	—	1 958	1 014	1.00	21 038	4 854	1.01
1935	Exports	18	1 832	*15.4*	12	186 791	*84.91*	—	2 164	—	15	17 466	*11.20*
	Imports	—	277	—	192 005	1 019	0.97	2 174	1	0.99	19 573	168	0.89

This was originally table 5 in Morgenstern (1965).

[a] The figures are those of the first named country for each pair. In some instances the sum of the monthly figures does not add up to the annual total given in the trade statistics. When this occurs the final figure reported, that is, the annual total, is used here. A dash means negligible amounts. For sources and further notes see Morgenstern (1955b, Appendix).

[b] The figures should be compared on the diagonal for each pair.

[c] The ratio is the proportion of imports from A to B to exports from A to B, e.g. $\frac{\text{B's imports from A in B's figures}}{\text{A's exports to B in A's figures}}$.

[d] Pairs of data with italicized ratios are excluded from the charts due to the smallness of the original figures or to the large size of the ratio.

[e] The pairs including Canada cover only July–December for 1900.

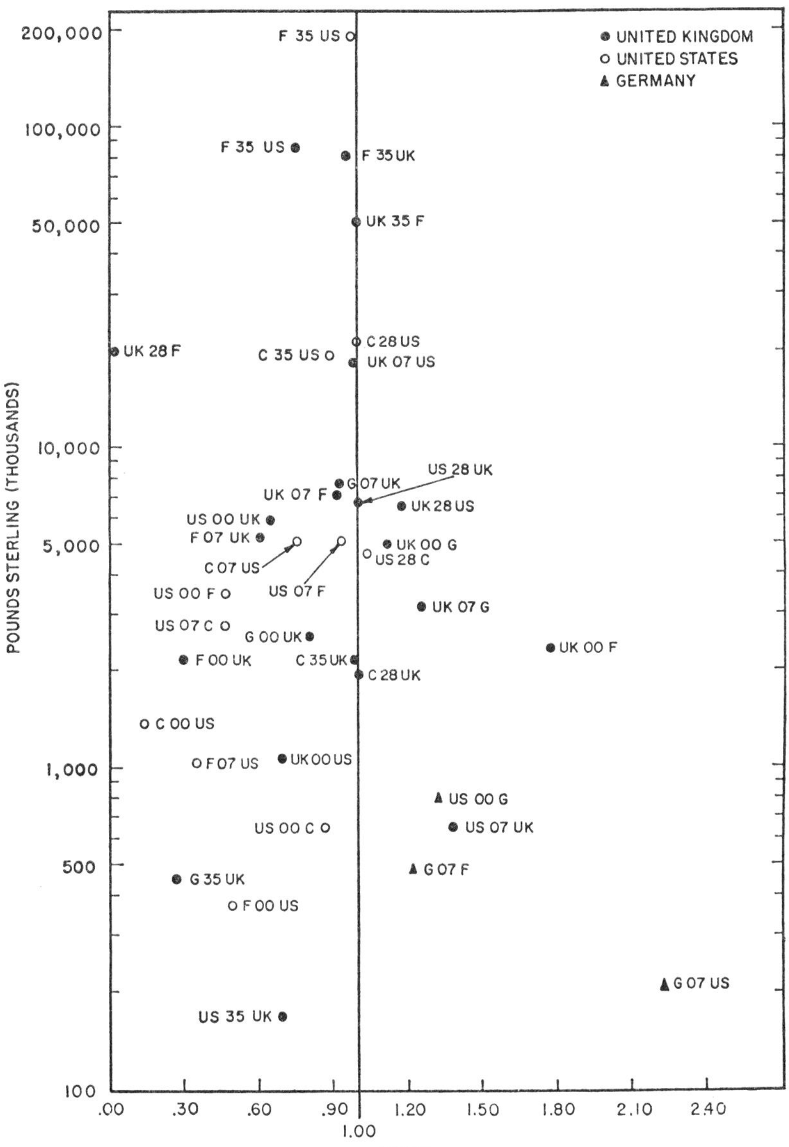

Fig. 1. Ratio and magnitude of gold movement statistics of pairs of countries, yearly sums. (Originally fig. 5 in Morgenstern (1965).)

tions. Furthermore, the results differ depending on which set of statistics is used, and there is no reason to prefer one set of these statistics over the others.

These observations apply even if the cycle turning points are determined only for gold movements and exchange rates or the other series referred to, or if the correlations are time series correlations involving all consecutive values. Since this is a question of application of series and is not directly connected with the test of the validity of the statistics, the material on which these remarks are based is not published in this book.

Further information about the inner nature of the discrepancies is highlighted in fig. 2 which shows, for some randomly chosen cases, cumulative sums of monthly data from two sources. It is surprising that the statistics involving Canada and the United States are among the most unreliable; this is especially the case because of the shift of the discrepancy first from one, then to the other. We have no way of telling whether the Canadian or the United States statistics, or both, have to be rejected. The differences are particularly notable for the United States exports to Canada for 1907. But the other pairs of countries do not fare much better. They do have one thing in common: when differences exist, very frequently they persist for many months in succession and often are not removed. This means that there are, apparently, at best no self-correcting forces at work making themselves swiftly felt[13]. In general, even if the direction of movement should be the same, the great *absolute* differences make it impossible to use these statistics for purposes of determining, for reasonably short intervals, the amounts of gold shipped and, possibly, of capital transfers. They can only be used for the crudest kinds of estimates and can play no major role in the fine-structured theory of international trade.

2.3.4. Further explorations

Since most writers on international trade are particularly concerned with net movements, we insert a chart showing the net movement of gold from the United Kingdom to Germany for the periods from 1900 to 1913 and 1931 to 1936 on a monthly basis. The statistics are made up from the two possible sources: United Kingdom figures and German figures. In fig. 3, the two lines would coincide if the data were accurate, but this is the case only in rare instances. Anyone interested in the cyclical aspects of gold movements would be in a considerable quandary in trying to determine where the cycles are, what the amplitudes are, and into which particular month the peaks and troughs of the cycles fall.

The confusion of the statistics between the two European countries is much

[13] There is a *lag* in several cases and there may be transit movements, as already mentioned. Elaborate statistical operations on these data may be indicated in order to discover lags, especially when more than two countries are simultaneously considered.

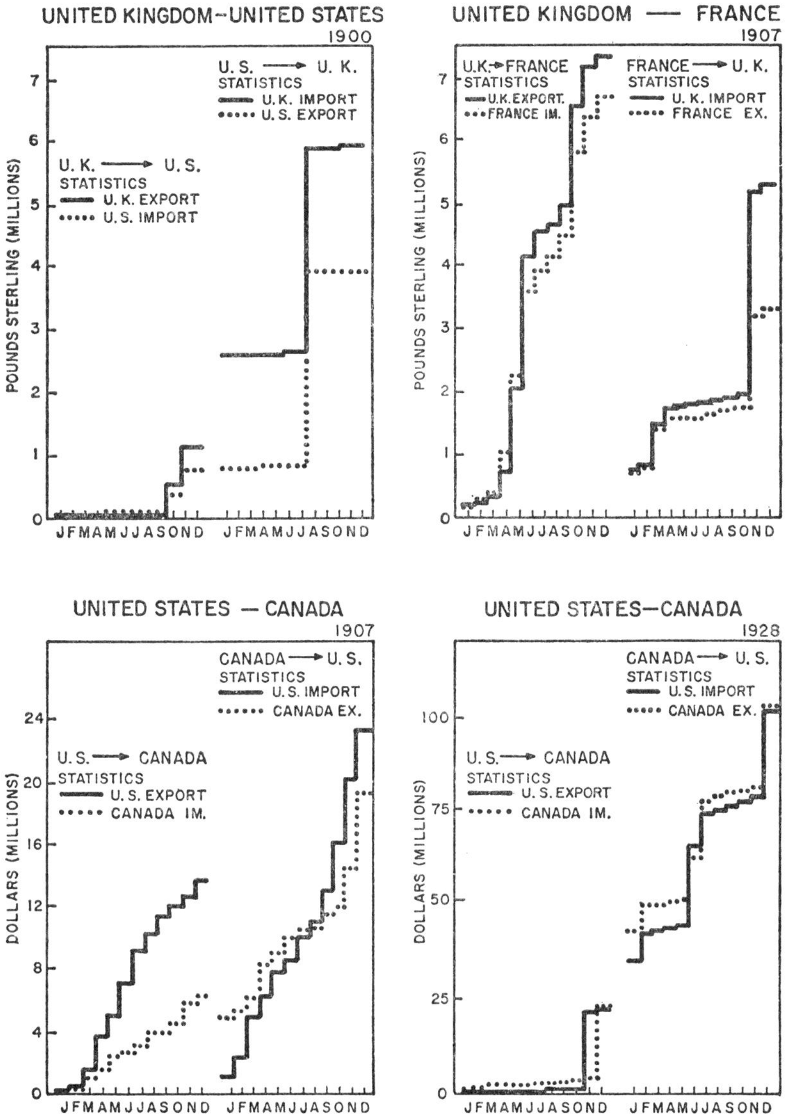

Fig. 2. Cumulative monthly gold movement statistics for pairs of countries from respective sources 1900, 1907, 1928. (Originally fig. 6 in Morgenstern (1965).)

greater for the time before World War I than it is in the early 1930s, but it is worth recalling that this latter period coincides with a time in which exchange control was applied quite strictly by Germany and so it would be expected that more accurate records would be kept[14].

In order to facilitate the evaluation of the information contained in fig. 3, we have cumulated quarterly the discrepancies in the reported net gold movements for both cases. Fig. 4 shows the quarterly cumulative values as well as the percentage of the cumulative discrepancies. Any one point of the series indicates how much gold is cumulatively unaccounted for from the beginning of this series up to that particular point of time. From January 1900 to July 1900 the cumulative net movement was from Germany to the United Kingdom. Germany then reported a net movement £310 000 *less* than the United Kingdom reported. From July 1900 on, the cumulative net gold movement was in the other direction (from the United Kingdom to Germany). From January 1900 to October 1907, for example, Germany reported a cumulative net gold movement to Germany of £29 million in excess of that reported by the United Kingdom. This £29 million discrepancy is 156% of the cumulative amount reported by the United Kingdom. Any other parts of the chart may be interpreted similarly.

The reader may judge for himself whether differences of these orders of magnitude mean anything. At any rate, what has happened in these arbitrarily chosen, short time intervals may easily have happened for other countries and for other intervals. For some purposes, the discrepancies may not matter, but if they do not, then it is because economic reasoning in these fields cannot be as sharp as it is often assumed to be.

The arguments used so far in evaluating the statistics were mostly qualitative because the lack of statistical theory makes the desired quantitative expression at present impossible. But in order at least to describe the data along statistically conventional lines, the significance of algebraic differences of the quarterly statistics of gold shipments between pairs of countries is shown in table 3. The data used here include quarterly statistics of gold movements between all possible pairs, covering trade of the United States, Germany, France, the United Kingdom, and Canada for the years 1900, 1907, 1928, and 1935. Silver transactions between the United States and the United Kingdom are also included in order to provide at least one comparison of the two precious metals.

[14] A somewhat laborious extension of our procedures suggests itself: instead of forming cumulative sums (gross or net) merely for significant pairs of countries, all countries, or at least the most important, could be taken together and an overall total of imports and of exports could be formed. It might be hoped that in this way all major discrepancies would disappear. But even if a favorable result should be obtained, it is difficult to see how the all-important country-to-country data could be corrected.

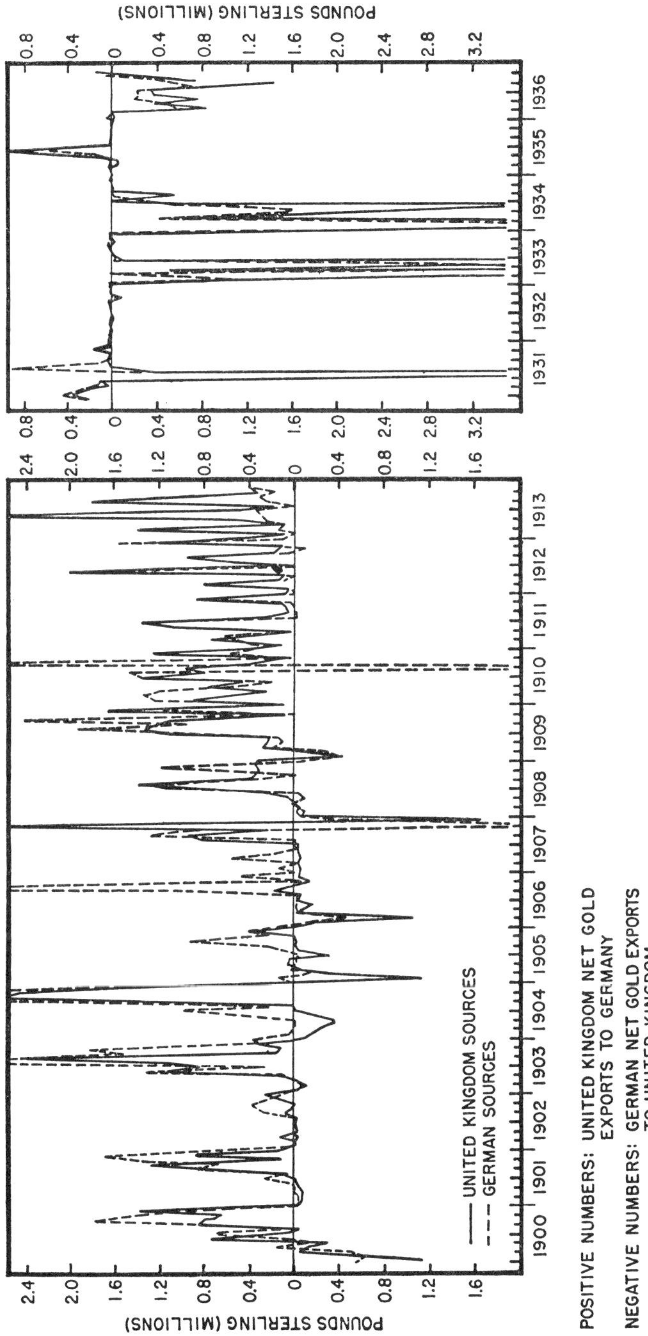

Fig. 3. Comparison of statistics of monthly net gold movements between the United Kingdom and Germany, 1900–1913, 1931–1936. (Originally fig. 7 in Morgenstern (1965).)

Table 3.
Test of quarterly gold statistics (1900, 1907, 1928, 1935).

Pairs of countries[b]		Algebraic differences[a] between pairs of countries and a test of their significance: Average differences[c] (1)	Standard deviation[d] (2)	n (3)	Standard deviation of sample mean $\sigma/\sqrt{n}$ (4)
United Kingdom–	I	1 741.7	3 466	12	1 000.55
United States	II	168.5	600	10	189.74
United Kingdom–	I	1 696.6	5 230	12	1 509.77
France	II	727.0	2 302	8	813.88
United Kingdom–	I	−171.5	652	8	230.52
Germany	II	81.6	94	16	23.50
Germany–France	I	−45.1	109	8	38.54
Germany–United States	I	−67.5	83	4	41.50
United States–	I	38.4	2 458	5	1 099.37
France	II	832.4	2 326	7	876.85
United States–	I	97.7	272	13	75.43
Canada	II	303.4	912	14	243.75
Silver					
United Kingdom–	I	−13 810.3	27 959	14	7 556.48
United States	II	−6 426.8	4 854.1	12	1 402.92

Originally table 6 in Morgenstern (1965).

[a] For each pair of countries there are four possible differences for each year of every series. There are four countries and six possible pairs of differences between them. In addition, the difference between Canada and the United States is introduced; and for silver the difference between the United Kingdom and the United States is examined.

[b] The series of differences in observations between each pair of countries is divided into two parts:

I. The difference between the observations of A and B with regard to the gold flow from A to B, i.e. the exports of A minus the imports of B.
II. The difference between the observations of A and B with regard to the gold flow from B to A, i.e. the imports of A minus the exports of B.

[c] Statistics of first country minus those of second. These algebraic differences are then summed and divided by their total number. In some pairs of countries, data are not reported for all years. This diminishes the number of differences to less than 16 (quarterly figures taken for four years) since years for which no data are reported are excluded.

[d] The computation of the standard deviation of the sample mean is sometimes conventionally restricted to $n \geqq 10$. We nevertheless include the values for smaller n since the tendency of the different computations appears to agree in all relevant aspects.

In this table, the first column shows the average differences with regard to the two directions of the gold flow between two countries. The second column shows the standard deviations of the population, the third the size of the sample, and the last gives $\sigma/\sqrt{n}$ the standard deviation of the sample mean. For the rationale of

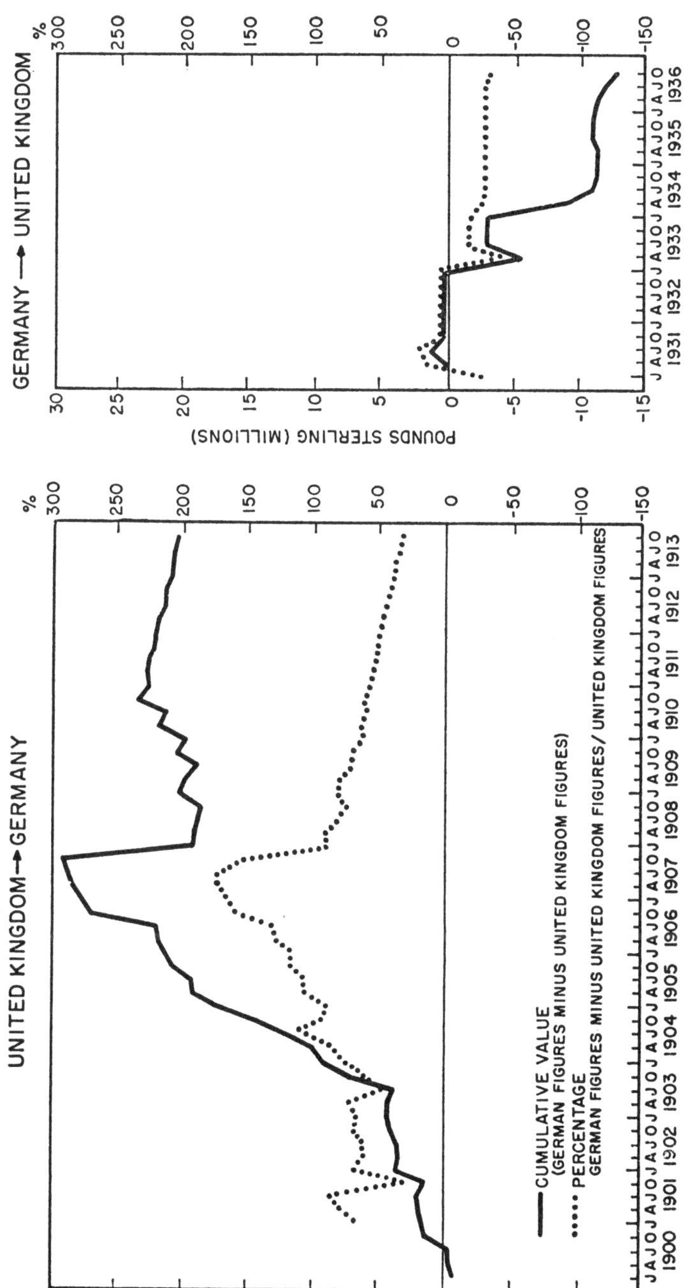

Fig. 4. Cumulative discrepancies in reported net gold movements between United Kingdom and Germany, 1900–1913, 1931–1936 (cumulative values and percentages). (Originally fig. 8 in Morgenstern (1965).)

the calculations, see, for example, Cramér (1946), Mood (1950), or Wilks (1962). Inspection of the first column of the table shows that the average differences between reports are much larger than can be explained by the known factors of freight, insurance charges, and the like. This indicates faulty statistics. One might take a general point of view that all measurements are subject to error and that the discrepancies indicated are natural consequences of this phenomenon; but, in terms of a simple theory of errors, the possibility of a bias is still present.

The result of the computations is clearly this: the statistics are so bad that a finer test is not warranted. The standard deviations of the sample mean show this directly. A reasonable interpretation of the situation is that it is impossible to determine what bias exists, which is to say that the reliable and the faulty statistics cannot be identified. This agrees entirely with what common sense has indicated. It may be possible to develop another approach to the problem of error and bias for the present case, but the explanation of the discrepancies, given in the following section, seems valid in any case.

2.3.5. Explanation of the differences and further difficulties

What are the factors explaining these differences? We see here the consequences of the fact that economic statistics are in the rarest instances the result of scientific observations. They are usually only a by-product of other activities. There is also the difference in the position of the 'observers'; this consists, for gold, mostly in the time interval which occurs when recording an export and when recording the corresponding import. When 'lags' appear, they are not stable, sometimes going in one direction, sometimes in the other. Besides the genuine time lag due to transportation between distant countries, there are others that are (a) spurious and due to inaccuracy, and (b) due to transit. Most likely, (a) holds more frequently.

All differences due to prices, freights, insurance, duty (zero!), exchange rates (except for Germany which, in 1935, had a variety of exchange rates) can be neglected. They are more or less known and trifling.

So there remain the 'true' causes. We leave open whether the statistics were often, occasionally, or never deliberately falsified. Since we are dealing with gold transactions, in which a great deal of secrecy often prevailed, it is not impossible that such manipulation occurred. Inaccuracy as a consequence of privilege is a frequent occurrence; central banks, and sometimes even private banks, often could remove gold from ships in a great hurry, and the statistical records may then have suffered even unintentionally. Furthermore, the high value of the metal is not a sufficient cause for accurate entries, especially when the customs officials had no interest whatsoever in the valuation of gold. They may indeed have been under orders *not* to report.

There are even explanations arising from differences in classification, which, of course, become really troublesome with ordinary commodities (see p. 111). Gold and silver were often thrown together in the same cases and shipments, and frequently in such instances there were false declarations on the part of the shippers. Freight and insurance were cheaper on a 'mixture' of gold and silver, and it was often easy to add a piece of silver to a gold bar in order to get a 'mixture'. In one country the mixture might leave as 'silver' and arrive as 'gold' in the other, and vice versa[15]. Besides savings in freight and insurance there was also the desire for secrecy as to shipments when private and commercial banks were involved and were assuming the risks.

Coverage of all gold movements by the statistics was unquestionably incomplete because of secrecy, the removal of gold at arrival in port before customs, and so on. There are, furthermore, the not negligible gold movements in the form of gold carried by travelers during the periods of gold coin circulation. While the amounts were large, they were neglected in *all* the statistics and would not, therefore, even if included, have closed the differences in reporting shown in this study. The discovery of the origin and destination of gold shipments probably offers as great an objective difficulty as for all other commodities. In different countries different practices exist as to how to enter amounts of gold ('specie') into the statistics when the gold is reported by a country other than the sending or receiving country. Sometimes gold would travel through several countries in transit status.

Among a host of other difficulties, the earmarking of gold, needs attention, for difficulties arise even when the statistics are accurate. The question of accuracy must be directed to the central banks in this case, rather than to the authorities responsible for foreign trade statistics. Earmarking became widespread from the late 1920s, and central banks do not as a rule say for whom they hold earmarked gold and sometimes do not say whether they hold it at all. There may thus be many changes in the composition of ownership of an otherwise unchanged total held in a given country. This makes a correction of the foreign trade figures impossible.

There remains the question of substitute statistics from which pairwise gold movements might be deduced. On that basis, in turn, inferences about capital movements could be made. This gives an uncomfortably long chain of deduction and there are no substitutes. Statistics of gold movements represent at best only a small part of capital movements. The published central bank figures do not

15 Table 3 includes a separate row for silver. The results are no better for this metal, as further checks have revealed. Nor does a total of gold and silver give better results, which shows the absence of any self-correcting elements in the statistics. Silver is, of course, more in the nature of a commercial commodity than gold. This gives some idea of what to expect from tests of foreign commodity trade statistics.

inform us about pairwise movements, nor can it be expected that pairwise gold transactions could still be uncovered from the unpublished records. Furthermore, it is impossible to reconstruct transactions from the records of commercial and private banks which often put the larger part of gold into the open market. For general economic histories, especially those dealing with large international crises, a combination of foreign trade and central bank statistics may roughly suffice; but for purposes of finer detail of economic theory such is not the case. Moreover, a careful test of the accuracy of central bank figures would also be necessary[16]. They are sometimes deliberately falsified by combining data on gold and silver and by reporting bullion gold or foreign coins under 'other assets', a common practice in the period between the two world wars. Finally, there is the general secrecy regarding operations of exchange stabilization funds whose gold operations overshadowed those of the central banks. Such irregular accounting practices were also common in the nineteenth century, but economists have paid only scant attention to them.

Our discussion of gold movements has been in terms of pairwise trade between countries. This is unquestionably the basic information needed when variations in exchange rates are considered and when general trade with another country is studied. One may also be interested in the aggregate position of the balance of payments of a country. In that case, the total net gold movement is of interest. It is clear, however, that this figure is ultimately based upon those pertaining to the pairwise relationships which we have found to be very defective. If it could be proved that the aggregation has some self-correcting feature, such that the errors in the individual components of the aggregate tend to cancel out, the total would be more valuable than the parts. Yet there appears to be nothing that would allow us to draw this comforting conclusion, though it is a frequent argument whenever grave faults in economic statistics are pointed out. No self-corrections can be observed.

The net gold position of a country is thus only inadequately known. It is, however, theoretically possible to check the movement data from the changes in the position of the gold stocks in a country. This is not too difficult in those countries where strict controls exist – at least as far as monetary gold is concerned. But it is a virtual impossibility for the period of the classical gold standard, where bullion and gold coins could be in anyone's possession and where neither commercial

[16] I have also attempted to break up gold transactions of central banks according to countries in order that such time series might be used as substitutes for those derived from foreign trade statistics. This idea was kindly tested for me for 1898 and 1907 by the Bank of England, but the results were entirely negative. They disclosed that private gold shipments were very large, if the customs figures can be accepted. However, even if such series were constructed, they would not form the desired substitute.

banks nor the central bank made correct and complete disclosures of their assets, not to mention the movements in and out of industrial gold.

Considerations of this kind are of interest when the gold movements from the United States to Europe during the last few years are studied. The weekly published figures show that the United States has consistently seemed to lose gold in round numbers. One week the gold outflow would be reported as $100 million, the next three weeks it would amount to exactly nothing; in effect a monthly series accurate to one digit results.

Even if the reported figures were accurate, their meaning should be questioned. Gold is purchased, usually in lump-sums, by countries who have built up their dollar balances beyond their requirements. Since most of these countries (including the United Kingdom) report gold flows monthly, gold will tend to be purchased at monthly intervals.

It may therefore be argued that week-to-week changes are really misleading and that a longer time interval should be looked at regarding the significance of gold flows, and that we need not report the figures more than monthly. The weekly reporting which distorts only the short-run picture might therefore be completely harmless. Yet this sidesteps the issue. If a series is reported on a weekly basis, then it should be significant to the best of the knowledge of the compilers, on a weekly basis. If only a monthly series is desired, then only a monthly series should be published. The present state of affairs must leave the analyst of short-term international financial movements with a considerable and unnecessary burden of uncertainty.

2.3.6. Summary and conclusions

The regrettable lack of trustworthy gold statistics deprives the study of international trade and business cycles of one of its most important means of analysis. The effects are felt not only in the inability to make reliable correlations between gold movements and other time series[17], but also in respect to further exploitation of statistics which make essential use of the information on gold movements. This matter is particularly relevant with respect to balance-of-payment statistics which abound with fanciful estimates covering large percentage of the total balances.

The question arises whether gold movement statistics are better or worse than others, especially in the field of international commodity trade.

What should be done about this situation? It requires a great deal of strength *not* to use ready-made and commonly available statistics, dealing with important events, when there are no substitutes. But great as the temptation may be to

[17] When such correlations have been made, they have failed to show any relations that could be interpreted with our present knowledge.

continue as if everything were in tolerable shape, a greater service is rendered to economics by insisting that a good theory cannot be built on shaky data.

3. Statistics of foreign commodity trade

The gold statistics discussed above *in extenso* are a special case of the far more voluminous figures on foreign commodity trade. The problem arises whether these large aggregates are less subject to doubt, for example, because of compensation of errors (or at least, differences in reports). As will be seen, this is not the case.

In this sector, we rely on the apparently wholly neglected work of Zuckermann (1920), who compared, in the manner of Ferraris, the statistics of trade between

Table 4.
Total world trade (billion U.S. dollars).

Year	Imports c.i.f.	Exports f.o.b.	$M - X$	$\frac{M-X}{X} \times 100$
1938	23.7	21.1	2.6	12.3
1947	50.1	46.9	3.2	6.8
1948	59.7	53.6	6.1	11.4
1949	58.5	53.7	4.8	8.9
1950	59.0	56.3	2.7	4.8
1951	80.9	76.1	4.8	6.3
1952	79.6	72.3	7.3	10.1
1953	75.9	74.1	1.8	2.4
1954	79.2	76.9	2.3	3.0
1955	88.6	83.7	4.9	5.9
1956	97.4	93.0	4.4	4.7
1957	107.2	99.8	7.4	7.4
1958	100.0	95.2	4.8	5.0
1959	105.6	100.9	4.7	4.7
1960	118.3	112.6	5.7	5.1

Originally table 7 in Morgenstern (1965).

Excluding Albania, Bulgaria, Mainland China, Czechoslovakia, East Germany (beginning 1948), Hungary, North Korea (beginning 1948), North Vietnam (beginning 1955), Poland, Rumania, U.S.S.R. (A set of supplementary tables is published by the United Nations for the Soviet area.)

Source: 1953–1960, United Nations (1962).
1938,
1947–1952, United Nations (1960).

Note: All exports are valued f.o.b.; imports are c.i.f. except for U.S. and Canada, which are f.o.b.

many pairs of countries for the years 1909–1913[18], the League of Nations fundamental study on world trade for the period 1928–1938 (Hilgert, 1942), and the United Nations' compilations of trade statistics.

In 1928 it was reported that imports were $35.5 billion and exports $32.6 billion for total world trade (a difference of 8.9%). In 1938 it was reported that imports were $24.6 billion and exports were $21.9 billion (a difference of 12.3%). Table 4 shows world trade for 1938–1960 (note, however, the countries omitted for lack of comparable data!). It appears that for some years, e.g. 1953 and 1954 (during the Korean War), correspondence was very good, only to drop again. It will be seen from tables 5–10, that for pairs of individual countries correspondences are as a rule very poor, so it remains a puzzle how the aggregate could be better.

The disparities in statistics of importing and exporting countries are due to the inclusion in imports of transport charges between frontiers (or ports) of the importing and exporting countries, which amounted to about 9% of the world's exports in 1928, and 12% in 1938 (Hilgert, 1942). In addition, because of the increase in the number of countries, the additional possibilities of difficulties in recording value, of diversion *en route*, re-export, time lag, differences in classification of commodities, differences in valuation, existence of multiple exchange rates, and differences in quality[19], it will be more difficult here than in the case of gold (in fact it is impossible) *to separate actual errors in reporting from mere differences in emphasis and definition*, when sets of statistics are compared. The conversion of statistics to a common unit, mostly the United States dollar, though needed, is one of the prime sources of trouble and not permissible when there are no truly convertible currencies. When exchange control and multiple rates exist on either one or both sides of a pair of countries, the quoted figures are mostly meaningless since it is impossible to know at which rate which imports and which exports were computed, and for what reason. All this was commented on briefly above (p. 106), but it is imperative to bring up the issue at this crucial point. The remark

[18] I owe the acquaintance with this work to the late Professor V. Furlan of Basel, Switzerland. (The author of this atlas of world trade is not to be confused with Sir Solly Zuckerman, who in *Foreign Affairs* (January 1962) published the grossest misunderstandings of the theory of games noted so far, while at the same time acknowledging that he did not understand its mathematical and logical content.)

[19] Each of these factors would deserve a lengthy treatment of its own. Space forbids this. But the reader who wishes to study further any of these points will quickly confirm the seriousness of the situation. The book by Allen and Ely (1953), contains numerous, excellent contributions which are relevant in this connection. This important work shows many of the tremendous difficulties of obtaining correct foreign trade statistics, but it offers no method for the numerical estimation of the errors. The book contains detailed references to numerous specific studies of these issues, showing the great efforts that have been made over the decades in many countries to arrive at better information and to estimate the value of the data on hand. Of the literature that has followed this book, I especially mention Ely (1961).

applies to the 1930s and to the time after the end of World War II to the present. Even in 1962 there are still many countries which have multiple exchange rates.

When reporting *values*, differences arise due to the factors mentioned above. It is therefore important to point out that enormous discrepancies in foreign trade statistics (sometimes up to 100%) also occur when *physical quantities* are considered. This was found to be the case, for example, before World War II for the carload shipments of coal from Czechoslovakia to neighboring Austria. It is well known that the quantities of grain shipped undergo great changes because of destruction *en route*, etc. But there are also great differences in the reports of shipments of coal and other bulk transports, even when no transit is involved. These differences cannot be explained except as faults of the reporting of one or of both countries or because of different methods of attribution; differences in definition play a minor role with these types of standard and bulky commodities.

Since the price of gold is constant within each of the years investigated (relative to the gross nature of foreign trade statistics given in millions of $, £, etc.) and other charges are minimal, gold value figures are an indication of what can be expected from the comparison of physical quantities. Therefore they have a wider interest here than merely as statistics of *values* of gold shipments[20]. In the following, we restrict ourselves to the statistics of *values*[21].

In what follows, we deal with the existing statistics, though we have pointed out that arriving at 'values' by the different statistical offices is far from being a simple matter. Even when there are no doubts about exchange rates, there is the possibility that the invoices accompanying the commodities are not properly made out, are falsified, that values are hard to attribute to the right categories of commodities, etc., all of which give rise to variations. Often the imported commodities are not followed or preceded by bills and invoices, which is why price estimation plays such a big role in this area of making statistical reports. Special experts for valuation have to be called in and trained, and practices vary widely from one country to another, all of which bespeaks of the great uncertainties prevailing in this area[22].

Before proceeding, we shall point out one of the principal difficulties in foreign

[20] It must be observed, however, that another difficulty arises: While there is no doubt what constitutes the commodity 'gold', and while the fineness of the bars is attested, gold shippers have or had (during the gold standard) an interest in declaring gold wrongly (e.g. as silver or as mixtures of gold and silver – obtained by adding a small silver coin to the gold bar) in order to keep shipments secret or to save costs and insurance. This is, therefore, also an instance of deliberate lying, a phenomenon discussed in Morgenstern (1965, ch. II, sect. 2).

[21] Concerning the influence of fluctuating *exchange rates* upon these values, see p. 119, where also the obscuring influence of exchange controls is noted.

[22] In 1831, values of imports to England were arrived at officially on prices prevailing in 1690! See Young (1936).

trade statistics: *the classification of commodities.* The enormous importance of forming acceptable aggregates in economics was mentioned above (Morgenstern, 1965, ch. II, sect. 5), but the difficulties are nowhere as clear as in this area, where they are perhaps the main source of the confused state of information. In the previous discussion the chief difficulty alluded to was the identification and classification of commodities (i.e. 'is this object a natural fiber, a synthetic fiber, a plastic material; is it spun glass, or is it . . ., etc.?'). Now we have this problem *plus* that of grouping many items into more comprehensive categories. Since literally millions of different things are being produced, of which undoubtedly at least hundreds of thousands cross national borders in trade transactions, it is clear that the grouping problem is a big one. Full detail being out of the question, only a small, comprehensive listing is possible. What the best listing is, how large it should be, what to do when new commodities appear (as is the case with ever increasing frequency), how often to change the listing, etc. – all this has for a long time been of great concern to those in charge of foreign trade statistics.

Numerous international conferences were held to arrive at a Standard International Trade Classification (SITC), see the work by Allen and Ely (1953). The first conference was held as early as 1853 in Brussels; eventually a first international convention was signed in 1913 by 29 countries. An improved minimum list was published by the League of Nations in 1938; it had 17 major sections, divided into 50 chapters, summarizing the 456 items on the list. The current SITC, first published in 1950, has 10 major sections, divided into 52 divisions, subdivided into 150 groups, which in turn are divided into 570 commodity items. According to the United Nations, by 1960 governments of countries accounting for about 80% of world trade were compiling trade-by-commodity data according to the 1950 SITC, and the major international agencies had adopted it as a basis for the reporting of trade statistics. The SITC has recently been revised and has 1312 basic items: 10 sections, 56 divisions, 177 groups, and 625 subgroups, with 257 of the subgroups divided into 944 subsidiary headings (United Nations, 1950; United Nations, 1961). The task is clearly an unending one and will never be settled to every country's satisfaction. Nor will the scientific user ever be accommodated according to his wishes because of the immense expense that would be connected with any rearrangement according to varying scientific needs.

The *de facto* situation is that a few countries report only principal exports (Brazil, Egypt, Indonesia, etc.); the rest report for all groups of the SITC, although some without analyses of provenance and destination. Even among those countries conforming to the overall scheme the differences in classification are enormous. France, for example, has 6500 classifications, but the United States export list contains less than half this many, only 2600 items, though obviously United States' exports do not contain fewer commodities than French exports! In general, large trading nations provide statistical information on two to three thousand items in the export and import trade. For smaller, or less developed countries, the number of commodities runs only to a few hundred, as for Turkey, which has a list of 300. It is obvious that an item exported from the United States to Turkey will be grouped together with many more items (of probably great diversity) than if the same item is exported to France, which indicates the reason for the confusion attendant upon interpreting the 'meaning' of such transactions! Considering that there are 104 countries in the United Nations alone, making up a very large network of trade (though not all trade with each other), one gets an idea of the tremendous complexity of the statistics of total world trade.

In this light one should doubt that the differences shown on table 4 can actually be as small as reported, especially when the subsequent tables show very large discrepancies for the pairwise trade. Table 4 is only a statement of the difference between imports and exports. It is built up on figures which will be seen to be of very doubtful value. This is demonstrated in tables 5–10. These summarize in part the work done by Zuckermann for the period 1909–1913, and by the League of Nations for 1929, 1935, and 1938. The data for more recent years are from various United Nations' documents based upon the original sources. The tables compare the trade transactions between pairs of countries A and B as described by the separate statistics of each country. The first col. in each case gives the percentage differences between the estimates of A's imports and B's exports; the second col. gives the percentage differences between the estimates of A's exports and B's imports; and the last col. describes the differences in percentages between the estimates of the balance of trade. (These last are included in order to show how smaller errors in the import and export statistics may be *magnified* in balance of trade statistics. We shall not make full use of these balance of trade data, however, since this would require a separate study.)

Five main cases have to be distinguished:

Case I: Positive values for cols. (1) and (2) in all cases. This may indicate that the first country overstates its foreign trade statistics in both directions, or that the second country understates its foreign trade in both directions.

Case II: Positive values for all cases in col. (1). Negative values for all cases in col. (2). This may indicate that imports are overstated in both countries or that exports are understated in both countries. A possible reason could be that duties and transportation charges are usually paid by the importing country, are sizeable, and have been included in the statistics of the importing nations.

Case III: Negative values for all cases in col. (1). Positive values for all cases in col. (2). This may indicate that exports are overstated in both countries or that imports are understated in both countries.

Case IV: Negative values for all cases in cols. (1) and (2). This may indicate

Key to tables 5–10. (Originally tables 8–13, respectively, in Morgenstern (1965).)

The subscripts 1 and 2 denote the country. In tables 5–9, 1 indicates the United States; 2 indicates the other country. In table 10, 1 refers to the country listed first and 2 to the country listed second.

I_1 = { Imports of country 1 according to 1's statistics; Exports of country 2 according to 1's statistics }

I_2 = { Imports of 2 according to 2; Exports of 1 according to 2 }

E_1 = { Exports of 1 according to 1; Imports of 2 according to 1 }

E_2 = { Exports of 2 according to 2; Imports of 1 according to 2 }

b_1 = Balance of trade of 1 according to 1

b_2 = Balance of trade of 1 according to 2

Sources for tables 5–10:

Period A: Zuckermann (1921).

Period B: Hilgert (1942).

Period C: United Nations, *Direction of International Trade*, several issues.

Table 5.
United States–France
Comparison of American and French statistics describing trade with each other.

Year	(1) $\frac{I_1 - E_2}{I_1}$ (%)	(2) $\frac{E_1 - I_2}{E_1}$ (%)	(3) $\frac{b_1 - b_2}{b_1}$ (%)
A. 1909	+30.7	−11.2	+ 972.3
1910	+27.8	− 2.4	+ 597.4
1911	+39.8	−24.4	−1220.4
1912	+37.8	−10.7	− 316.4
1913	+41.3	−12.0	− 492.8
Average: 1909–1913	+35.6	−12.2	−1013.1
B. 1928	+25.3	− 1.0	− 52.2
1935	+15.5	− 1.7	− 18.6
1938	+ 9.3	−13.4	− 28.8
C. 1948	+15.4	− 0.1	− 2.4
1952	+ 5.6	−25.5	− 51.8
1956	+ 4.1	−21.3	− 39.8
1960	− 1.4	−29.5	− 90.9

Table 6.
United States–Germany
Comparison of American and German statistics describing trade with each other.

Year	(1) $\frac{I_1 - E_2}{I_1}$ (%)	(2) $\frac{E_1 - I_2}{E_1}$ (%)	(3) $\frac{b_1 - b_2}{b_1}$ (%)
A. 1909	+10.8	−21.7	− 83.3
1910	+ 9.4	− 9.6	− 44.1
1911	+ 7.9	− 8.1	− 29.8
1912	+10.6	−14.4	− 46.7
1913	+ 7.7	−15.9	− 41.9
Average: 1909–1913	+ 9.0	−14.1	− 46.5
B. 1928	+14.6	− 3.3	− 19.5
1935	+11.5	− 6.5	−107.1
1938	+ 4.8	−55.2	−145.2
C. 1948	− 4.9	− 4.3	− 4.3
1952[a]	−17.8	−33.9	− 48.6
1956	− 0.6	−21.3	− 56.4
1960	[b]	−33.7	−213.9

[a] After 1948 figures are trade of German Federal Republic, including the American, British, and French sectors of Berlin.
[b] Less than 0.1.

Table 7.
United States–Great Britain
Comparison of American and British statistics describing trade with each other.

Year	(1) $\frac{I_1 - E_2}{I_1}$ (%)	(2) $\frac{E_1 - I_2}{E_1}$ (%)	(3) $\frac{b_1 - b_2}{b_1}$ (%)
A. 1909	+41.5	− 2.1	− 41.4
1910	+43.5	+ 6.1	− 30.1
1911	+46.4	− 0.1	− 40.4
1912	+53.2	+ 1.0	− 54.6
1913	+47.6	− 7.8	− 55.4
Average: 1909–1913	+46.7	− 0.6	− 44.7
B. 1928[a]	+34.6	− 2.2	− 27.9
1935	+26.5	+ 7.4	− 3.2
1938	+14.4	− 5.2	− 10.9
C. 1948[a]	+ 2.1	−14.7	− 28.5
1952	− 4.1	−31.7	−103.2
1956	+ 6.1	−25.8	−207.7
1960	+ 3.3	−12.7	− 50.6

[a] Periods B and C represent trade of the United States and the United Kingdom.

Table 8.
United States–Canada
Comparison of American and Canadian statistics describing trade with each other.

Year	(1) $\frac{I_1 - E_2}{I_1}$ (%)	(2) $\frac{E_1 - I_2}{E_1}$ (%)	(3) $\frac{b_1 - b_2}{b_1}$ (%)
A. 1909	−19.3	−19.1	−18.8
1910	− 0.8	−40.0	−80.2
1911	− 8.6	−19.1	−23.9
1912	−15.6	−17.6	−18.5
1913	−15.0	− 1.8	+ 5.3
Average: 1909–1913	−12.1	−16.9	−19.7
B. 1928	− 3.4	+ 9.6	+24.5
1935	+ 3.8	+ 3.1	− 2.7
1938	− 3.8	+ 9.6	+27.5
C. 1948	+ 2.1	+ 4.8	+17.4
1952	− 0.6	− 9.1	−61.0
1956	− 1.2	− 5.5	−17.1
1960	− 7.1	− 2.2	+16.0

Table 9.
United States–Belgium
Comparison of American and Belgian statistics describing trade with each other.

Year	(1) $\frac{I_1 - E_2}{I_1}$ (%)	(2) $\frac{E_1 - I_2}{E_1}$ (%)	(3) $\frac{b_1 - b_2}{b_1}$ (%)
A. 1909	+43.0	−20.3	− 298.5
1910	+39.8	−14.5	−1459.7
1911	+41.1	−31.8	− 246.4
1912	+34.3	−27.7	− 160.6
1913	+50.3	−26.2	− 164.1
Average: 1909–1913	+41.6	−24.9	− 224.1
B. 1928[a]	+ 9.4	+22.8	+ 50.0
1935	+ 5.0	+19.0	+ 50.0
1938	−23.8	−10.4	+ 5.7
C. 1948[a]	+ 4.7	−15.3	− 25.8
1952	+ 1.4	−24.0	− 71.4
1956	− 0.1	+ 6.2	+ 20.6
1960	+ 1.8	−10.0	+ 52.5

[a] Belgium–Luxembourg, 1928–1960.

Table 10.
Comparison of averages[a] in pairs of countries for periods A, B, and C.

Pairs of countries		(1) $\frac{I_1 - E_2}{I_1}$ (%)	(2) $\frac{E_1 - I_2}{E_1}$ (%)	(3) $\frac{b_1 - b_2}{b_2}$ (%)
United States–France	A	+35.6	−12.2	−1013.1
	B	+21.5	− 3.6	− 38.3
	C	+ 2.9	−18.3	− 33.4
United States–Germany	A	+ 9.0	−14.1	− 46.5
	B	+13.0	− 9.1	− 33.3
	C	− 2.6	−22.6	− 44.1
United States–Great Britain	A	+46.7	− 0.6	− 44.7
	B	+30.4	− 1.1	− 18.9
	C	+ 2.6	−19.8	− 72.0
United States–Canada	A	−12.1	−16.9	− 19.7
	B	− 2.5	+ 8.7	+ 24.7
	C	− 2.3	− 3.7	− 9.2
United States–Belgium	A	+41.6	−24.9	− 224.1
	B	+ 1.9	+14.2	− 36.5
	C	+ 1.5	− 3.2	− 12.0
Germany–France	A	−22.4	−20.3	− 6.6
	B	+ 4.1	− 3.9	−4100.0
	C	− 0.6	0.0	+ 3.2
Germany–Great Britain	A	+ 3.6	−10.2	− 40.4
	B	+ 7.5	− 3.0	− 34.6
	C	−10.1	− 4.8	+ 41.7
Great Britain–France	A	−34.4	−60.0	+ 10.5
	B	− 8.1	−51.2	+ 41.6
	C	+10.7	+23.8	− 61.8
Canada–Great Britain	A	+16.0	+22.7	+ 41.5
	B	+11.0	+23.8	+ 32.4
	C	− 1.2	−16.8	− 35.4
Canada–France	A	+63.4	+12.1	+ 76.9
	B	+ 5.1	−95.1	+ 233.3
	C	+ 4.6	− 2.4	− 7.6
Canada–Germany	A	+ 8.8	−166.7	+ 68.9
	B	+14.8	−90.8	− 220.5
	C	+ 3.3	−16.8	− 43.6
Belgium–France	A	−81.2	+18.3	+1123.0
	B	−45.8	−11.4	− 159.3
	C	+ 7.7	+ 8.5	+ 4.7
Belgium–Germany	A	+13.4	+53.9	+ 145.5
	B	− 4.2	+ 7.8	− 525.0
	C	− 1.7	+ 4.5	− 25.9
Belgium–Great Britain	A	+34.0	− 1.5	− 288.0
	B	+20.6	−19.9	− 92.9
	C	+21.8	− 1.6	+ 191.2

[a] Averages were computed from the original trade data.

that the second country overstates its foreign trade statistics in both directions or that the first country understates its foreign trade statistics in both directions.

Case V: The third column is chiefly interesting as expressing the balance of trade between the two countries. The signs here indicate that the balance of the second country is larger than the balance of the first, if the sign is *negative.* The converse is the case if the sign is *positive.*

3.1. Examples

(1) The comparisons of the United States and France (table 5) are an example of case II. This may be partly explained by import duties and transportation charges paid by the importer.

(2) The United States–Germany example (table 6) also belongs, up to 1938, to case II, probably for similar reasons. However, in both cases the irregularity of the percentage deviations must be noted. This betrays faulty reporting since transportation costs and other charges cannot possibly have varied to this extent. After World War II, case IV becomes applicable, but it is doubtful that this should be interpreted as a change in making the statistics.

(3) The United States–Great Britain example (table 7) shows that there were several changes over the period. This does not fit into any of the simple cases discussed above. Here col. (1), referring to United States imports and British exports, shows that the United States' import figures were higher throughout both periods. Until 1913, the United States had several tariffs on British imports; transportation was mostly in British bottoms. This meant that British exports to the United States were valued at a higher rate by the United States (for they included the tariffs) than by Britain. After 1914, there were smaller differences between the statistics of American imports and of British exports (although American import figures were still higher than British export figures), a fact that may be due to shifting of American imports away from taxable items, to avoid the very high American tariffs.

In col. (2) of table 7 we see no definite tendency. In more than half of the cases British imports were stated to be higher than American exports. Until 1913, the British had only a small revenue tax. This may account for the slight excess in the British import statistics over American exports. In the later period, 1928–1938, nothing conclusive can be said about the influence of tariffs in producing discrepancies between the two reports. The devaluations of sterling and the dollar in 1931 and 1933, respectively, also fall in this period. A noteworthy jump occurs in 1948–1960, when the negative entries in col. (2) are multiples of those for the earlier years and the reverse for col. (1). It should be noted that the figures in *all* these tables do not record what actually happened, but only examine the character of the statistics. The above changes describe, therefore, quality and recording characteristics, not the simultaneous changes in trade structure, post-war aid, currency troubles, etc. These latter may very well have contributed to the observed variations, but there is not only no need for these effects to have occurred, rather they should not have shown up at all, since the ideal difference for all columns is zero, no matter what the volume, structure, direction, or rate of change of the trade.

(4) In the instance of the United States' trade with Canada (table 8), we have an example of case IV for the earlier period and something similar to case III for the second period. For 1909–1913, Canada consistently *over*stated both its imports and exports to the United States, as compared with American statements. (Or did the United States consistently *under*state imports?) In 1928, 1935, and 1938, American exports were stated to be larger than Canadian imports. But during these same years American imports were reported as smaller than the corresponding Canadian exports! For 1952, 1956, and 1960, we revert to the pattern of period A. No firm conclusions can be drawn[23] since no definite patterns appear and no other knowledge can be brought into play allowing the determination of the errors.

(5) Comparison of American and Belgian statistics (table 9) indicates an example of case II for the period 1909–1913. American imports were stated on the average to be about 40% higher than Belgian exports. Belgian imports, on the other hand, are stated to be about 25% higher on the average than American exports. The large discrepancy in the former case would have to be explained by factors other than tariffs and transportation. In the periods 1928–1938 and 1948–1960, no definite tendency is indicated.

We have mainly discussed discrepancy of signs so far, and have said little about magnitudes. Signs might differ, but the differences in amounts might be slight. But in fact, the quantities are large, sometimes even grotesquely so. To probe into the reasons for such magnitudes would require a detailed study of tariffs and transportation charges (Karreman, 1961)[24], in order to state conclusively what part of the differences was due to error in the comparisons examined. It must be emphasized again that these differences due to error would still not yield margins

[23] Canadian wheat exported to Europe via the United States appears to have been a particularly disturbing factor. Though we can mention it and may be told to consider its influence (as the transit trade of any country, e.g. Belgium), the brutal fact still is that the statistics do not agree, that the reader does not know how to disentangle these influences, and if he knew how, would require an incredibly large machinery which no one has at his disposal. Therefore we have here a particularly good illustration that it is one thing to state a probable source of trouble (or error?) and a very different one to assess quantitatively its influence upon the final figure.

[24] This study not only shows the great difficulties of arriving at reliable information but also illustrates the nature of one of the principal gaps in balance of payment statistics of all principal nations. The variations in transportation costs among countries is discussed also in Moneta (1959).

of error for *either* of the statistics concerned. We are only attempting to indicate a *method* whereby statistics could be tested for error, but we do not come to definite conclusions about the size of errors, although we feel confident enough to state that they are very large.

In table 10, a summary is given of the averages found in the previous tables. Also included are averages (but not the basic data) of several other pairs of countries.

An average is taken for each of the three periods for each column in the original tables. Although an average for a single period is not very significant, because the years are scattered, few, and fairly unrelated, it does give some indication of the order of magnitude of divergency. The totals for the three columns show that in some periods there was slightly less discrepancy between estimates than in others. Is this an indication that perhaps international conventions and agreements about uniformity of statistics did have some effect on foreign trade observations, even though they did not eliminate the wide margins? On the other hand, violent fluctuations in exchange rates occurred and exchange controls involving multiple rates were introduced which greatly obscured the valuation of goods moved across national borders. The decreasing importance of import duties and their substitution by complicated licensing systems strengthens the tendencies toward more numerous and probably larger errors in foreign trade statistics.

Examining this table in more detail, we find that there are some pairs of countries that reflect close agreement in their statistics (if we take a divergence of 25% in all cases in cols. (1) and (2) as a 'good' result!): Germany–France, United States–Germany, Canada–Great Britain, United States–Canada, and Germany–Great Britain, with the last two combinations producing the closest agreement. In three of these pairs the countries border on each other or are close to each other. However, proximity has not counted heavily in other pairs of countries, e.g. pairs of European countries such as Belgium–Germany, Belgium–France, and Great Britain–France. Thus, there must be other more important factors to produce these wide discrepancies.

The obviously bad results obtained in the cases of Canada–France, Great Britain–France, Canada–Germany, and Belgium–France are difficult to explain in terms of tariffs and transportation costs alone. It would require a much fuller treatment of this subject to decide whether the discrepancies are significant and due to differences for these more valid reasons, or to errors in the reports of one or both of the parties. The published material of either country does not make this possible. The books are forever closed. However, we can state intuitively and with confidence that discrepancies of the order of 50–60% are not solely attributable to an inadequate consideration of tariffs and transportation costs.

Although the columns on the balance of trade are included in tables 5–10, we forego a thorough discussion. The reader will have no difficulty interpreting the figures and convincing himself of the highly doubtful value of statements about trade balances. The quantitative differences reported are so large as to limit the use of these statistics severely. They cannot be used for 'fine-structured' arguments; they are at best suitable for broad overall statements and observations. The size of foreign trade differs widely from one country to another. Even though we are just discussing the unreliability of foreign trade statistics and shall find similar results regarding national income, there is no doubt that foreign trade is a far larger percentage of the latter in Belgium, Holland, Norway, Germany, Japan, etc. than in the United States. Thus the observations in this section have different relevance for the various types of countries. But for all it can be stated safely that we have here another indication that our picture of the various economies is far more vague and hazy than the pretended sharpness of the figures would make us believe.

It is easy to arrive, if one wishes, at diametrically opposed conclusions, based on 'the facts', by merely making a suitable and just as reasonable choice of the statistic[25]. Beyond this, however, it is necessary to understand that the sum total of commodities included in trade statistics, as already stated earlier, is only an arbitrarily cut-off segment of all items making up the balance of payments. This segment of 'visible' commodities has only very limited value for the analysis of the foreign trade of a nation, even if the information should be excellent. This does not preclude that commodity by commodity studies have good meaning, provided, of course, that the statistics for individual commodities are reliable in the particular case and circumstance. As was shown, the chances that this is the case often enough are slim. The *statistical accident* of which aggregate of items is chosen to represent *all* transactions between countries is hardly of much economic significance, although economists usually attribute to this truncated information a deeper economic meaning.

4. Concluding remarks

Further investigations of this nature must be undertaken to decide whether foreign trade statistics can be trusted in proving fine theoretical points and in formulating policy. Their great role in the estimation of national income is obvious, and their influence upon the construction of adequate input–output tables is also evident.

[25] However, if we had to choose in describing, say, American–Chinese trade, we would probably take the statistics from the former source. We would be governed by a generally higher confidence, although a large error, resting in the United States' statistics, would still remain unknown.

We have not tested the foreign trade statistics by more elaborate and sophisticated tests, but there is no doubt that the situation is not better; it is bound to be worse. Economists should carefully consider what the implications are: The theory of international trade with all its fine points of delicate changes in the 'terms of trade', 'comparative costs', etc. rests, *at best*, on this type of information. There is no other information. So do further theorems derived with the aid of these concepts. Comparisons of foreign trade fluctuations with business cycles, exchange rates, etc. by necessity requiring high detail and precision, are likewise adversely affected.

The *balance of payments* is estimated with such figures included in the total, to which are added pure guesses of the most doubtful character. Yet, consider its immense practical significance, involving the gift of billions of dollars to foreign countries on the basis of allegedly scientific, accurate, and reliable information!

We have not even discussed the making of statistics of the 'invisible' items in the balance of payments. There the gaps are enormous and the methods for closing them fall far short of the needs. It appears to be *a priori* certain that the 'invisible' items cannot be *better* known than the visible ones. Yet statistics of the latter are found to be of poor and uncertain quality, even in their best appearance – gold.

It is perhaps possible to estimate from the movement of the exchange rates (provided there is an absolute free market!) whether the balance is 'active' or 'passive'. But it would be naive to think that one could determine the movements from the component statistic[26]. Sampling is sometimes used conscientiously to ascertain emigrant remittances, tourist expenditures, medical services used abroad, etc. and this is a sound procedure. Nevertheless the results are in grave doubt, largely because of the lie-component, strongly at work because of fear from income tax involvement. Anyone who has ever sat through meetings (as the author has) in which final balance of payment figures for most invisible items were put together, can only marvel at the naiveté with which these products of fantasy, policy, and imagination, combined with figures diligently arrived at, are gravely used in subsequent publications. Even if the practices are fairly good in one country, recall that there are at present 104 United Nations members, and that statistical and political standards differ widely.

Writers on all phases of foreign trade will have to assume the burden of proof that the figures on commodity movements are good enough to warrant the manipulation and the reasoning to which they are customarily subject.

[26] Noteworthy are the recent differences between European observers of the difficulties of the American balance of payments and the United States Treasury. In 1961, the Europeans believed that the Treasury (i.e. American statistics) overstated the United States' deficit, which was promptly denied by the Secretary of the Treasury. This is a nice illustration for the presence of a strong policy-making and political factor in what under other circumstances purports to be a strictly scientific matter.

References

Allen, R. G. D. and J. E. Ely, eds., 1953, International Trade Statistics (John Wiley, New York), 117–118.

Bodio, L., 1896, Sulle discordanze che si osservano fra le statistiche commerciali dei vari Stati, Biblioteca dell'Economista, ser. IV, vol. I, part I, 77.

Bowley, Sir Arthur, 1928, Some tests of the trustworthiness of public statistics, Economica 8, 253–278.

Cramér, H., 1946, Mathematical Methods of Statistics (Princeton University Press), 345.

Ely, J. E., 1961, Variations between U.S. and its trading partner import and export statistics, The American Statistician 15, No. 2, April, 23–26.

Ferraris, C. F., 1885, La Statistica del Movimento dei Metalli Preziosi fra l'Italia e l'Estero (Rome).

Ferraris, C. F., 1899–1900, Bulletin de l'Institut International de Statistique 11, 12, especially 12, 338–340.

Gardner, W. R., 1953, Merchandise trade in the balance of payments, in: International Trade Statistics (John Wiley, New York).

Gini, C., 1928, Le statistiche delle esportazioni, Rivista di Politica Economica V.

Graham, F. D., 1942, Protective Tariffs (Princeton University Press), 28, footnote.

Hilgert, F., 1942, Network of World Trade (League of Nations, Geneva).

Inter-American Statistical Institute, 1955, Discrepancies in Foreign Trade Statistical Data as Reported by Trading Partners, prepared for the Third Inter-American Statistical Conference (Brazil), reference document 3225a (mimeographed), June.

Karreman, H. F., 1961, Methods for improving world transportation accounts, applied to 1950–1953, National Bureau of Economic Research, Technical Paper 15, chs. 1, 2.

Linder, F. E., 1959, World Demographic Data, in: Hauser, P. M. and O. D. Duncan, eds., The Study of Population (Chicago), 321–360.

Moneta, C., 1959, The estimation of transportation costs in international trade, The Journal of Political Economy LXVII, February, 41–58.

Mood, A. M., 1950, Introduction to the Theory of Statistics (New York), 133.

Morgenstern, O., 1955a, review in: Econometrica 23, 105.

Morgenstern, O., 1955b, The validity of international gold movement statistics, Special Papers in International Economics, No. 2 (International Finance Section, Princeton University), November.

Morgenstern, O., 1959, International Financial Transactions and Business Cycles (Princeton University Press).

Morgenstern, O., 1965, On the Accuracy of Economic Observations (Princeton University Press), ch. II, sect. 2.

Ricci, U., 1914, Sulle Divergence fra Statistiche del Movimento Commerciale (Turin).

United Nations, 1950, Standard International Trade Classification (SITC), Statistical Papers, ser. M, no. 10 (New York), September.

United Nations, 1960, Yearbook of International Trade Statistics 1 (New York), 12–13.

United Nations, 1961, Standard International Trade Classification, Revised, Statistical Papers, ser. M, no. 34 (New York).

United Nations Statistical Office, 1962, Monthly Bulletin of Statistics XVI, no. 1, January, 86–87.

United Nations, International Monetary Fund and International Bank for Reconstruction and Development, Direction of International Trade, Series T.

Wilks, S. S., 1962, Mathematical Statistics (New York), 198–199.

Young, G. M., 1936, Victorian England, Portrait of an Age (London), 32.

Zuckermann, S., 1920, Statistischer Atlas zum Welthandel (Berlin).

Zuckermann, S., 1921, Statistischer Atlas zum Welthandel II (Berlin).

Chapter 8

THE ACCURACY OF INTERNATIONAL TRADE DATA: THE CASE OF SOUTHEAST ASIAN COUNTRIES*

Seiji NAYA and Theodore MORGAN

1. Introduction

The empirically oriented economist is regularly handicapped by 'inadequacy', as measured by availability and reliability of economic data from less developed countries. At the same time, the need for empirical studies for these countries has become acute, owing to their importance in the formulation of specific development policies, general national plans, regional cooperation, and like activities.

Evaluating the problem of 'inadequacy' and checking accuracy of data should be an automatic part of any such empirical study. The primary burden falls on the original investigator whose figures and findings are often used by others unable to check the quality of the data.

Unfortunately, checking the reliability of data and the extent of error is not easy since the sources of error are many, ranging from difficulties of collection and organization to plain falsification. The latter is a problem peculiar to the social sciences: the physical and biological sciences face the chance of blunders, but seldom of intent, and error. Morgenstern (1963) comments: 'The undeniable existence of an unknown but undoubtedly substantial amount of deliberately falsified information presents a unique feature for the theoretical social sciences . . .'

Trade data from less developed countries (LDCs) are available and relatively abundant. By no coincidence, studies related to some aspect of trade are conspicuously popular. In many instances, trade data serve as a substitute for data on domestic economic activities, especially when the latter are not available. The trade–income ratio of many LDCs is high, and economic structure and the pattern of economic development are often inferred from the pattern and composition of foreign trade. Also, with the recent rising expectations of regional cooperation, a better grasp of trade relationships among groups of countries has become

* Editor's note: Sects. 3 and 4 from the original article have been omitted here.

especially important. The impact of research effort into LDC trade data is likely to continue to be large.

For a number of reasons, trade statistics are considered to be, among various LDC economic data, the most reliable. Firstly, foreign trade is a well-defined area in which goods move under the noses of customs officers. Goods are supposedly counted and/or measured systematically for such purposes as the imposition of tariffs, subsidies and other regulations. In LDCs where foreign exchange is scarce, particular attention is focused on the trade sector, the single largest source of demand and supply of foreign exchange. Secondly, a check on accuracy is presented by the records kept by both trading partners, which can be compared side by side. Comparable double accounts are not usually available for domestic economic transactions.

Conceptually, one country's exports to another country should be identical in value and type with the imports of the receiving country. But in practice there can be differences due to transport and other service charges, timing lags, differences and inconsistencies of classification, and transit trading[1]. The amounts of these causes of divergence, however, are rarely measured quantitatively. Rather, any differences in two records are usually assumed away or considered to be caused by these obvious factors, especially the transport margin (c.i.f. imports and f.o.b. exports). For example, in the regional model in a trade projection study made by ECAFE, adjustment is made for the difference between values of intra-regional exports and imports by attributing the difference to shipping and insurance charges between the region and outside (United Nations, 1964a). The freight and insurance accounts in the balance of payments of a given country are often derived simply by taking some percentage margin of imports, e.g., Malaya has used 8.9% and 6.5% of the c.i.f. imports from sterling and non-sterling areas, respectively (Department of Statistics, States of Malaya, 1963).

In examining the quality of Southeast Asian trade statistics, the following countries have been selected for this paper: Burma, Ceylon, Indonesia, the Federation of Malaysia (Malaysia hereafter), the Philippines, Singapore, and Thailand. For each of these countries, the following two ratios are first computed:

(1) M_{ij} (*i*'s imports from *j*) to X_{ji} (*j*'s export to *i*),

(2) M_{ji} (*j*'s imports from *i*) to X_{ij} (*i*'s exports to *j*),

where *j* is a given Southeast Asian country and *i* is *j*'s trading partner. The trading partner countries include both Asian and developed Western countries (approximately 30 in all). (1) and (2) are defined respectively as export and import ratios of *j* country. For most of these bilateral or pairwise comparisons, the average

[1] See Allen and Ely (1953) for detailed appraisal of international trade statistics and definitions, and also Lichtenberg (1959).

value of 1962 and 1963 trade figures is used in order to minimize differences that can result from time lags in the reportings of any two trading countries[2]. For Indonesia's exports (import figures not available) and some minor cases of other Southeast Asian countries, one-year figures are used, due to the lack of suitable figures and comparable data.

In sect. 2 averages, standard errors, and '*t*' statistics are first presented using export and import ratios of each *j* country. Then '*F*' statistics are calculated to ascertain whether or not there exists a significant difference between the variances of *j*'s intra-regional trade ratios and that of its trade ratios with developed countries (DCs). Also the rank correlation is computed to examine the association between the height of the trade ratios and the size of corresponding trade values.

2. Errors in corresponding trade data

The ratios of all pairs of recordings for every Southeast Asian country's exports (M_{ij}/X_{ji}) and imports (M_{ji}/X_{ij}) are given in Appendix table A1[3]. If bilateral pairs of recordings of trade are accurate, then the ratios should be close to or slightly above the value of 1.0 since imports are typically recorded at c.i.f. The diversion of the ratios from 1.0 measures the influences of obvious causes such as transportation and other charges, and of uncertain factors, such as errors and deliberate falsification.

Conspicuous in both ratios, especially for exports, are the wide dispersion and variation of the ratios. The transport margin alone does not adequately explain the wide variation and height of many of the ratios. Many ratios demonstrate flagrant discrepancy, with the higher figure of a pair 100% or more above the value of 1.0. Ratios for Indonesia reach as high as 4800! A surprising number of ratios fall well below 1.0 – a deviation in the reverse direction from what the transport cost margin could explain. The number of the ratios below 1.0 varies widely from country to country. For the region as a whole, almost one-third of the total are below 1.0. The discrepancy in these pair records that have ratios less than 1.0 is larger than it appears. The overstatement of X_{ji} (or X_{ij}) in relation to M_{ij} (or M_{ji}) is proportional to the reciprocal of ratios of M_{ij}/X_{ji} (or M_{ji}/X_{ij}) between 1.0 and 0.

Most of Singapore's M_{ij}/X_{ji} ratios can be plausibly explained. Out of 25 ratios,

[2] The trade data are taken primarily from United Nations (1962, 1963); and United Nations (1965, 1966).

[3] Export and import values on which these ratios are based can be obtained from the authors by request.

22 are below 1.0. The qualitative implication of these low ratios is difference in labels, not statistical error. Singapore's entrepôt trade is large, and much of such exports are not recorded as being from Singapore by her trading partners. Similarly, Singapore's import ratios M_{ji}/X_{ij} are generally much greater than 1.0, suggesting that countries exporting via Singapore as entrepôt often list those exports as going to the ultimate destination, while Singapore customs enter the goods simply as an import (only 2 out of 26 ratios fall below 1.0).

A 10% margin is often used to convert the value of imports from a c.i.f. to f.o.b. basis[4]. If we tolerate this 10% margin, that is, if ratio 1.10 is accepted as reasonable, a significance test (the 't' test) can be applied to judge whether or not the average ratio of each Southeast Asian country can be explained by normal statistical error. Data for each country j were evaluated separately since there is considerable variation from country to country. In assigning equal weight to ratios of all paired recordings, however, we have excluded ratios involving absolute values less than $20 000 in either X or M on the grounds that small absolute errors can, in these cases, lead to large proportionate errors. These exclusions have eliminated most of the extreme ratios. Results of the significance test are given in tables 1 and 2 for exports and imports respectively.

A survey of col. 2 in both tables 1 and 2 reveals that the average ratios of M_{ij}/X_{ji} and M_{ji}/X_{ij} usually differ considerably from the assumed norm ratio of 1.10. According to the values of 't' (col. 5 in both tables), about one-half the cases in each table meet the test: 't' is adequately low, using the 5% criterion of significance as the watershed; and the other half fail the criterion. Even for the former cases, however, it is difficult to accept the notion that the average and the expected ratios belong to the same universe, with differences due only to normal statistical errors inherent in most economic observations, for a large value for the computed probability (associated with a low 't' value) might have resulted either from an unusually small difference or from an unusually large estimate of the standard error – or both. For example: the relatively satisfactory 't' values shown for Ceylon and the Philippines in table 1, and for Burma and Ceylon in table 2, seem to have resulted mainly from high values of the computed standard errors in col. 4 (and of the computed standard deviation in col. 3). Especially for Indonesia, little statistical meaning can be inferred from its 't' value in view of the wild implications of the other three measures.

Two exceptional cases, out of 13 in all, are Thailand's export ratio (table 1) and the Philippines' import ratio[5] (table 2) which indicate satisfactory and accept-

[4] For a description of this and other similar procedures see, for example, Moneta (1959).

[5] Actually, the use of the 10% difference for the Philippines is not correct since this country reports its imports valued at f.o.b. (which is reflected in the low average import ratio 0.99). But a similar resuit is obtained when 'no difference' in the two recordings is used.

Table 1.
A test on average export ratio (M_{ij}/X_{ji}), assuming expected value of 1.10.

Country j	No. of trading partners (i) compared (1)	Average ratio (M_{ij}/X_{ji}) (2)	Computed standard deviation (3)	Computed standard error (4)	Value of 't' (5)
Burma	20	1.43	0.71	0.16	2.08
Ceylon	21	1.44	1.30	0.28	1.21
Thailand	25	1.14	0.40	0.08	0.53
Malaya	27	2.11	2.17	0.42	4.31
Singapore	25	0.46	0.43	0.09	−7.53
Philippines	24	1.34	0.61	0.13	1.89
Indonesia	24	10.47	27.68	5.64	1.70

Note: Computations are based on data given in Appendix table A1. Ratios involving absolute values less than 20 000 in either X or M are excluded.

Table 2.
A test on average import ratio (M_{ji}/X_{ij}), assuming expected value of 1.10.

Country j	No. of trading partners (i) compared (1)	Average ratio (M_{ji}/X_{ij}) (2)	Computed standard deviation (3)	Computed standard error (4)	Value of 't' (5)
Burma	23	1.38	1.21	0.25	1.08
Ceylon	22	1.30	1.09	0.23	0.87
Thailand	26	1.46	0.78	0.15	2.37
Malaya	28	1.51	0.80	0.15	2.73
Singapore	25	1.49	0.52	0.10	3.67
Philippines	24	0.99	0.49	0.10	−1.10

Note: See table 1.

able results in terms of both the average ratio and the estimated standard error. (But for Thailand's import ratio and the Philippines' export ratio, the consistency does not exist.) With these two exceptions, therefore, we can reasonably regard the M_{ij}/X_{ji}s and M_{ji}/X_{ij}s of these countries as random samples with respect to the expected value of 1.10.

The assumption of the 10% margin used above, is arbitrary. Transport and other service costs vary according to such factors as value, volume and type of goods traded, as well as distance. Accurate information on these costs is not available. But these costs, even if available and accurate, could not explain the violence and directions of the deviations shown in many ratios (Appendix table A1) and the results of tables 1 and 2.

Our tests of trade data of Southeast Asian countries indicate frequent and large errors. But conclusions are less gloomy if we divide the M/X ratios into two groups: (a) their trade with other countries in the region, and (b) their trade with developed countries (DCs) including Japan. A statistical measure of the dispersion in terms of variance and 'F' ratio for individual Southeast Asian countries is given in table 3.

The import ratios for table 3 show variances for intra-regional trade (col. 1) uniformly higher than those with the DCs (col. 2). Also, the import ratio values of 'F' indicate that the probability of obtaining values of 'F' as large as those observed fails at the 5% criterion of significance. We conclude that the variances of import ratios for the two groups of countries differ significantly.

Table 3.
A test on variability of export and import ratios by grouping Southeast Asian trading partners into Asian and developed countries.

	Import ratio (M_{ji}/X_{ij})			Export ratio (M_{ij}/X_{ji})		
	Variance		'F' ratio	Variance		'F' ratio
	Asian (1)	Developed (2)	(3)	Asian (4)	Developed (5)	(6)
Burma	2.80 (11)	0.30 (12)	9.33	0.91 (10)	0.15 (10)	6.07
Ceylon	2.58 (10)	0.03 (12)	86.00	0.25 (9)	2.86 (12)	11.44
Thailand	1.03 (14)	0.05 (12)	20.60	0.15 (13)	0.16 (12)	1.07
Malaya	0.93 (16)	0.27 (12)	3.44	7.72 (15)	0.38 (12)	20.32
Singapore	0.42 (14)	0.08 (11)	5.25	0.25 (15)	0.05 (10)	5.00
Philippines	0.48 (12)	0.01 (12)	43.00	0.28 (12)	0.48 (12)	1.71
Indonesia				1353.01	2.88	469.80

Notes: Computations are based on data given in Appendix table A1. Ratios involving absolute values less than $20 000 in either X or M are excluded. The numbers in parentheses denote the number of trading partners (i) considered. Each 'F' ratio is computed by placing the larger variance in the numerator.

For the export ratios, the result is slightly different. Values of variance and 'F' for the intra-regional trade of Indonesia, Burma, Malaya, and Singapore are larger than those values for their trade with DCs. But for Ceylon, Thailand, and the

Philippines, the variance with developed countries is larger than that with Asian countries. The '*F*' ratio for the two latter countries is small enough, however, so that we can judge no significant difference exists between the variances of the two sets of data. Ceylon's '*F*' value indicates that the variance of its DC trade is significantly larger than that of its intra-regional trade. But this high variance with the DCs is to a great extent illusory since it is largely the result of one untypically high M_{ij}/X_{ji} ratio, 6.81 with Sweden. When Sweden is excluded, Ceylon's variance with the DCs is 0.05 and is significantly smaller than that with Asian countries.

We conclude that data on Southeast Asian countries' intra-regional trade suffers from more discrepancies than data for their trade with DCs[6]. This finding encourages the use of DC trade data to measure Southeast Asia's trade with them, especially when data from Southeast Asian countries are not directly available.

There has, in recent years, been rising interest in regional cooperation among ECAFE countries. The analysis presented so far implies that studies of the benefits and costs of any integration scheme for the region must rest on the shaky foundation of conspicuously inaccurate trade data. The shares of intra-regional trade, surprisingly high for these countries, save for the Philippines, vary substantially depending on which trade data are used. For example, the percentage figure for Indonesia's exports to developing Asian countries is 41% according to the country's data and 54% according to that of its trading partners. Similarly, intra-regional import shares of Malaya are 43% according to the country's data and 64% according to its partners'. There are also many vexing cases where a trade surplus (or deficit) in one recording reverses itself and becomes a trade deficit (or surplus) in the other recording.

On the other hand, in view of the substantial discrepancies in the sets of recordings we have observed, the differences are rather moderate between total trade figures reported by *j* country and the sum of the corresponding figures recorded by its trading partners. For total trade figures, export ratios vary from 1.53 for Indonesia to 0.34 for Singapore while import ratios range from 1.37 for Singapore to 0.92 for Malaya (see cols. 1 and 5 of table 4). Because we have come to expect a certain amount of error, this showing might be considered fairly good. But no great comfort should be placed in the tendency, nor firm reliance on the figures, even the totals. The cancelling of opposed error works out crudely, and one wonders why total imports of three out of six countries are less than reports of their trading partners.

[6] That DCs' trade data show an extremely small discrepancy is evident in Appendix table A2. Presented is a frequency distribution of bilateral ratios of exports and imports of the U.S., Canada, U.K., each of the Common Market countries, and Japan with 14 trading partners (all DCs). For almost all countries, 75% or more of both bilateral export and import ratios fall within 0.90 to 1.29. Most of the remaining 25% does not diverge much from the above range.

These total figures, unlike the unweighted average ratios given in tables 1 and 2, are heavily weighted by the discrepancies in paired recordings of large trade values. For, a large proportion of total exports and imports of each country is directed to and comes from relatively few trading partners: total export shares to the four largest trading partners range from 59% for Burma to 92% for the Philippines; similar import shares, from 56% for Malaya to 77% for the Philippines (see cols. 4 and 8 of table 4).

The lowest and highest ratios of paired recordings among the four largest trade values are also given in table 4. In a few cases, e.g. Thailand's exports, these ratios are small and uniform (1.05–1.17), contributing to and consistent with the 'satisfactory' total. But in many other cases, e.g. Malaya's import and Indonesia's export ratios, variations which are large and in opposing directions (0.25–1.61 and 0.27–1.79 respectively), cancel out each other to give 'satisfactory' totals.

The range and discrepancy in these four ratios tend to be somewhat small compared with extremely large distortions shown for some of the other bilateral

Table 4.
The ratios of total imports to exports and the high and low ratios among the four largest trade values.

Country j	Export ratio				Import ratio			
	ΣM_{ij}	4 largest X_{ji}s			ΣM_{ji}	4 largest M_{ji}s		
	ΣX_{ji} (number of i partners) (1)	Lowest $\frac{M_{ij}}{X_{ji}}$ (2)	Highest $\frac{M_{ij}}{X_{ji}}$ (3)	As a % of total export value (4)	ΣX_{ij} (number of i partners) (5)	Lowest $\frac{M_{ji}}{X_{ij}}$ (6)	Highest $\frac{M_{ji}}{X_{ij}}$ (7)	As a % of total import value (8)
Burma	1.11 (21)	0.50	1.19	59	0.98 (23)	0.90	1.27	67
Ceylon	1.05 (22)	0.88	1.07	71	1.02 (23)	0.91	1.11	64
Thailand	1.07 (26)	1.05	1.17	60	1.21 (27)	1.09	1.43	64
Malaya	1.41 (28)	0.90	1.49	69	0.92 (28)	0.25	1.61	56
Singapore	0.34 (25)	0.15	0.66	64	1.37 (26)	1.17	1.79	67
Philippines	1.08 (24)	0.39	1.24	92	0.93 (25)	0.86	1.12	77
Indonesia	1.53 (29)	0.27	1.79	71				

Source: Appendix table A1.

ratios, especially those associated with very small export or import values. The major reason for omitting those ratios involving absolute values less than $20 000 in either exports or imports in our earlier computations (tables 1 and 2) is the high errors shown for these ratios. Therefore, one might expect that the relative discrepancy in the paired recordings is negatively related to the absolute size of export and import values.

In order to examine this relationship, a rank-order correlation has been computed. Two rankings compared in this test are: (1) descending order of absolute trade values of a Southeast Asian country (X_{ji} and M_{ji}); and (2) ascending order of ratios of paired recordings. For those of M_{ij}/X_{ji} and M_{ji}/X_{ij} less than 1.0, the reciprocal of these ratios is used: an equal weighting is given to them as with those having ratios greater than 1.0. The result of the ranking test is given in table 5.

In most cases, e.g. Burma's exports and both the exports and imports of Malaya, the Philippines, Singapore, and Thailand, the relationship between the size of trade values and the relative discrepancy is statistically insignificant at a 5% level. (Even a negative value is shown for Singapore's export ratio.) But for Ceylon and especially for Indonesia, the correlation between the two orderings is high and significant even at the 1% level (and for Burma's exports, at the 5% level). These

Table 5.
Rank coefficients of correlation between descending order of trade values (X_{ji} and M_{ji}) and ascending order of export and import ratios[a].

Country j	Rank coefficient	
	Exports (number of ranks)	Imports (number of ranks)
Burma	0.342 (21)	0.419 (23)
Ceylon	0.596 (22)	0.524 (23)
Thailand	0.314 (26)	0.284 (27)
Malaya	0.264 (28)	0.079 (28)
Singapore	−0.257 (25)	0.298 (26)
Philippines	0.252 (24)	0.347 (25)
Indonesia	0.742 (29)	

Source: Appendix table A1.
[a] For those export and import ratios less than 1.0, the reciprocal of these ratios has been used.

latter cases, though few, are somewhat encouraging since comparatively small (positive or negative) differences are generally associated with relatively large trade values. For Indonesia, however, absolute sizes of the discrepancies even in these figures are simply too great to be relied on much.

3. Concluding remarks

There are a number of possible reasons for errors in trade data as follows. (1) Transport costs will, as we have seen, create a discrepancy between f.o.b. export and c.i.f. import values. (2) Different recording definitions are used by different countries. The entrepôt trade of Singapore with other countries of the region, as we have also seen, is not treated congruently in their respective records. And for specific trade commodities, sub-items may be differently defined and so be entered under different aggregated headings. Customs officers may have considerable discretion as to where among several plausible categories a given item should be listed.

But the discrepancies are often so large that these innocent explanations plainly fail. (3) There may be a simple error in counting and recording. (4) Countries with considerable tariffs and other trade barriers, and with poorly policed boundaries on land, or extensive shorelines on the ocean, invite attempts to smuggle. Smuggling enterprises in the Philippines are said to be notably successful; and Indonesia was, like England, made by heaven for 'free trade'. (5) Customs officers may be encouraged by suitable tokens of friendship to understate quantity and quality of imports, where these are taxed; similarly for exports, where these are taxed. (6) The major channel for illegal transfer of wealth between countries is underinvoicing of exports and overinvoicing of imports.

Much can be done by energetic customs administrations to correct the causes of discrepancies numbered (1), (2), and (3) above. But (4), (5), and (6) are more resistant. They will be less serious sources of error if tariffs and other trade restrictions are lowered, if exchange controls wane; and as economic development in general progresses and so probity and efficiency improve. (6) is a major source of error. It is said that in some countries a 10–20% misrepresentation of the quantity and/or quality of traded goods is normal. In one case that has come to our attention, a large export from a Southeast Asian country was underinvoiced by 90%.

Errors in trade data frequently are substantial and plainly can be overwhelmingly large. For countries with high tariffs or equivalent bars to the international movement of goods, and with legal or other bars to the export or import of capital, substantial errors in trade data are likely to continue. For some countries – those with inviting boundaries, high hurdles to the movement of goods or of capital, and lackadaisical administration – the best guess of an informed and conscientious outside student can be more trustworthy than the official figures.

For certain research and policy purposes, existing errors may not be of prime importance, but for many other purposes they are. There should be much greater awareness of the errors concealed in trade data, and much more effort in the customs administrations of various countries toward effecting such improvements in accuracy as are feasible.

Acknowledgements

The authors wish to express their appreciation to Everett Hawkins, Allen Kelley, Robert Lipsey, Nyle Spoelstra, and M. Abe for their useful comments.

The earlier version of this paper was financially supported by the Agency for International Development of the University of Wisconsin, and was presented at a meeting of SEADAG Regional Seminar, 1967.

Appendix

Table A1.
Ratios of recorded trade value of Southeast Asian countries (*j*) to that of their corresponding trading partners (*i*) based on average trade values of 1962 and 1963.

Partner *i*	Imports of *i* from *j*/exports of *j* to *i*						
	Country *j*:						
	Burma	Ceylon	Indonesia	Malaya	Philippines	Singapore	Thailand
Brunei	—	—	0.50*	2.44	0.41	0.32*	—
Burma	—	0.95	6.04*	0.91	—	0.34*	0.93
Cambodia	—	+3.00*	58.10*	2.57*	2.05*	1.90	+0.02*
Ceylon	1.11	—	+661.00*	1.27	1.42*	0.31	0.81
Taiwan	1.10*	—	+6.65*	1.50	1.10	0.56	1.00
Hong Kong	1.10	0.90	5.94*	11.02	1.13	—	1.07
India	0.97	1.17	5.52*	1.08	1.09	1.11	1.33
Indonesia	—	—	—	—	—	—	—
Korea	2.59**	—	2.47*	6.89	1.37	0.29	1.15
Laos	—	—	+568.66	+1.43*	—	0.31*	1.33
Malaya	2.14	1.33	1.61	—	1.51	0.25	1.17
North Borneo	—	—	9.28*	3.25	—	0.16*	0.54
Sarawak	—	2.41*	128.79*	2.07	—	0.32	—
Singapore	1.40	1.32	1.80*	1.40	2.20	—	1.05
Pakistan	0.50	1.24	+39.29*	1.71	0.51*	0.69	1.40
Philippines	0.81**	1.15*	2.33*	2.01	—	0.60*	0.05
Thailand	3.59	2.02	4.07*	0.33	0.88	1.25	—
Republic of Vietnam	—	—	2.64*	1.12	1.30*	0.02	1.44
Japan	1.29	1.08	2.22*	1.49	1.24	0.47	1.07
Australia	1.19	1.02	1.93*	1.87	1.01	0.26	1.01
New Zealand	+5.00*	0.83	5.86*	2.01	0.89*	0.43	1.02*
Canada	—	0.89	1.51*	1.46	1.61	—	2.05
U.S.	1.56	1.08	1.39*	1.45	1.09	0.15	1.07
Belgium–Luxembourg	0.89	1.11	0.35*	0.35	3.04	0.33	1.26
France	1.97	1.44	3.64*	1.74	2.13	0.04	2.01
West Germany	1.13	1.01	1.09*	1.59	1.07	0.08	1.26
Italy	1.19	0.99	2.91*	1.51	1.39	0.68	1.29
Netherlands	0.93	0.49	+4800.25*	0.37	0.39	0.60	0.74
Sweden	2.01	6.81	4.02*	2.44	2.00	—	1.48
U.K.	1.20	1.06	0.27*	1.00	1.24	0.66	0.95
Total	1.11	1.05	1.53	1.41	1.08	0.34	1.07

(contd.)

Table A1 (contd.)

Partner *i*	Imports of *j* from *i*/exports of *i* to *j* — Country *j*: Burma	Ceylon	Malaya	Philippines	Singapore	Thailand
Brunei	—	—	—	—	1.18	—
Burma	—	1.11	2.14	0.81**	1.40	3.59
Cambodia	0.95	—	1.49	—	1.34	+0.67
Ceylon	—	—	1.33	1.15*	1.32	2.03
Taiwan	1.81*	6.00	1.29	0.70	1.33	1.19
Hong Kong	1.19	1.73	0.60	1.73	—	1.19
India	0.92	0.91	0.96	0.94	1.03	1.44
Indonesia	6.04*	+661.00	1.61*	2.33*	1.80	4.07
Korea	3.32	—	2.01	0.22	1.68	1.51
Laos	—	—	1.88*	—	+24.17	1.17
Malaya	0.91	1.27	—	2.01	1.40	0.33
North Borneo	—	—	4.41*	0.58	—	1.51**
Sarawak	—	—	0.86	—	0.87	—
Singapore	0.34	0.31	0.25	0.60	—	1.25
Pakistan	1.09	1.08	1.21	1.98	2.76	1.96
Philippines	0.41	1.42*	1.51	—	2.20	0.89
Thailand	0.93	0.81	1.17	0.05	1.05	—
Republic of Vietnam	—	0.93**	2.68	+3.40*	3.03	1.10
Japan	0.90	1.08	1.70	0.86	1.17	1.09
Australia	1.14	1.05	1.35	0.88	1.28	1.08
New Zealand	2.73*	1.25	0.86	0.88	1.29	1.88*
Canada	0.95	1.01	0.68	0.89	—	1.25
U.S.	1.27	0.81	1.48	0.92	1.36	1.19
Belgium–Luxembourg	1.44	0.79	1.58	1.14	0.88	1.14
France	0.83	1.14	1.16	1.00	1.26	0.98
West Germany	0.92	1.19	1.12	1.12	1.93	1.43
Italy	0.60	1.06	1.08	0.98	1.62	1.19
Netherlands	1.01	1.25	1.37	1.03	1.12	1.24
Sweden	0.88	1.43	2.75	0.91	1.54	1.16
U.K.	1.04	1.01	1.44	0.97	1.31	1.23
Total	0.98	1.02	0.92	0.93	1.37	1.21

Notes: 1962 trade values of ECAFE countries are taken from United Nations (1965), and most of the remaining data are taken from United Nations (1962, 1963). For those cases where comparable data are not given in the above sources, data are mostly from United Nations (1964b) and partly from I.M.F. and I.B.R.D. (1961–1965).

* and ** refer to ratios based on 1962 and 1963 trade values respectively.

\+ indicates the ratio involving the average trade value of either *j* or *i* less than $20 000.

— indicates no recording of trade figures either of *j* or *i* or both.

Table A2.
Frequency distribution of bilateral export and import ratios of the U.S., Canada, U.K., the Common Market countries and Japan with 14 developed trading partner countries; based on average trade values of 1962 and 1963.

Country j	U.S.		Canada		U.K.		Belgium–Luxembourg		France		Netherlands		West Germany		Italy		Japan		Total	
Export ratio M_{ij}/X_{ji}* / Import ratio M_{ji}/X_{ij}*	X	M	X	M	X	M	X	M	X	M	X	M	X	M	X	M	X	M	X	M
Less than 0.699			2				1					2					1		4	2
0.700–0.799	1	1	1				1	1								1	1	1	4	4
0.800–0.899	1			1		1	1	1				2					2		4	4
0.900–0.999	2	3		5	6	1	8	4	5	6	5	2	9	5	5	7	2		42	33
1.000–1.099	1	10	3	6	5	6	3	5	8	3	3	6	4	4	5	4	3	2	35	46
1.100–1.199	2		1		1	5		2		3	2	2	1	3	4	1	2	3	13	19
1.200–1.299	5		3	1	1	1			1		3			1				6	13	9
1.300–1.399			3		1			1		2	1					1		1	5	5
1.400–1.499																				
1.500–1.599	1		1														2		4	
1.600–1.699	1													1			1		2	1
Larger than 1.700				1														1		2
Total no.	14	14	14	14	14	14	14	14	14	14	14	14	14	14	14	14	14	14	126	126
Total $\Sigma M/\Sigma X$	1.15	1.01	1.07	1.01	1.03	1.11	0.94	1.01	1.02	1.02	1.03	0.96	0.98	1.09	0.86	1.00	0.98	1.20		

Notes * j's export and import ratios are denoted as X and M respectively. Compiled from trade data given in I.M.F. and I.B.R.D. (1961–1965). 14 trading partner countries (i) of a given j country are those remaining countries listed above, along with Austria, Denmark, Finland, Norway, Sweden and Switzerland.

References

Allen, R. G. D. and J. E. Ely, eds., 1953, International Trade Statistics (John Wiley, New York).
Department of Statistics, States of Malaya, 1963, States of Malaya Annual Statistics of External Trade 1, 11.
International Monetary Fund and International Bank for Reconstruction and Development, 1961–1965, Direction of Trade, A Supplement to International Financial Statistics, Annual.
Lichtenberg, R., 1959, The role of middleman transactions in world trade, N.B.E.R. Occasional Paper 64 (New York).
Moneta, C., 1959, The estimation of transportation costs in international trade, Journal of Political Economy 67, 42–43.
Morgenstern, O., 1963, On the Accuracy of Economic Observations, 2nd ed. (Princeton University Press), 22.
United Nations, 1962, Commodity Trade Statistics, various issues.
United Nations, 1963, Commodity Trade Statistics, various issues.
United Nations, 1964a, Review of Long Term Economic Projections for Selected Countries in the ECAFE Region, 199.
United Nations, 1964b, Yearbook of International Trade Statistics.
United Nations, 1965, ECAFE, Foreign Trade Statistics of Asia and the Far East 1, 2.
United Nations, 1966, ECAFE, Foreign Trade Statistics of Asia and the Far East 1, 2.

Chapter 9

ON THE UNDERINVOICING OF IMPORTS*

Jagdish N. BHAGWATI

1. Introduction

In many developing countries, it is customary to rely on severe import and exchange control regimes. Typically these regimes give rise to 'black' markets for various prohibited or restricted uses of foreign exchange. It is well known, for instance, that in countries limiting allocations of exchange for foreign travel, black exchange leaks into this area; and so on.

The supply of illegal exchange comes from several sources. Underinvoicing of exports and overinvoicing of imports are the most obvious sources. For countries, such as Turkey, where the earnings of workers abroad constitute a major source of invisible receipts through remittances, this represents at least as important a source of foreign exchange in the black market[1].

The demand for illegal exchange, on the other hand, comes largely from tourists (as noted above) and from the flight of capital abroad[2]. It also comes from the underinvoicing of imports, which requires the purchase of black-market exchange to make the full payment to the foreign exporter.

* This paper was written during my assignment as an Organization for Economic Development and Co-operation (OECD) Consultant in Turkey during April–July 1964. Its originality consists neither in discovering that underinvoicing of imports can occur nor in finding out that c.i.f. import statistics can be less than the corresponding f.o.b. export statistics, a fact well known to statisticians of international trade. It consists in (i) inferring the former from the latter; (ii) linking it to the phenomenon of tariffs and import control; and (iii) using the exercise to make informed inferences about the areas into which 'black' exchange is leaking and hence to assess better the 'losses' imposed by such a leakage. In my statistical work on the Turkish trade data, I have profited greatly from conversation with R. Gross, who had already noticed discrepancies between Turkish c.i.f. and partner-countries' f.o.b. values for a single year. My thanks are also due to Professors Bent Hansen and Besim Ustunel for useful discussions in the preparation of this paper.

[1] In fact, it was while trying to assess where the remittances were leaking – the official remittances being well below the expected level – that I undertook the present exercise in Turkey.

[2] It is known, for example, that accounts in Swiss banks are operated by the nationals of many developing countries such as Turkey and India.

The present paper deals with this phenomenon of underinvoiced imports. Sect. 2 states the general analysis that explains such underinvoicing. Sect. 3 concerns the application of this analysis to recent Turkish experience.

2. Reasons for underinvoicing of imports

Underinvoicing of imports – a discrepancy between the stated value of imports and their actual value (payable to the exporter abroad), such that the latter exceeds the former – may arise characteristically in two cases: when the imported commodity carries a tariff duty; and when the imports of the commodity are strictly controlled, resulting in a premium on it in the domestic market.

Take the case of a tariff duty, to begin with. It will pay the importer to understate the value of his imports when the resulting saving in tariff duties outweighs the extra price that he must pay to purchase the foreign exchange in the black market. For the individual domestic importer, who may be assumed to have access to illegal foreign exchange at a given premium, and whose imports face an *ad valorem* duty, the understatement of import values will become profitable as soon as the tariff rate exceeds the premium.

There is, however, a risk attached both to the understatement of value and to engaging in illegal foreign exchange transactions. Hence the understatement will not occur unless the discrepancy between the tariff rate and the black-market premium exceeds the evaluated risk factor. The extent of understatement will also be constrained by the increasing risk attached to greater understatement and, failing that, by the degree of understatement it is reasonably possible to claim successfully under existing regulations.

Similar arguments apply to the case where quantitative import restrictions are in use. If the understatement of import unit values enables the importer to import a larger quantity under his licence (stating the permissible total import value) and if the premium on the imported commodity in the domestic market is higher than the premium to be paid for black-market exchange, underinvoicing becomes profitable.

3. An empirical investigation

An analysis of the Turkish situation is attempted here, with a view to investigating the presence of underinvoicing of imports and its possible causes and effects.

The analysis rests crucially on a comparison of the f.o.b. export values recorded by Turkey's principal trading partners with the c.i.f. import values recorded by

Turkey. One would expect the latter to exceed the former (by the amount of the insurance and freight). If the c.i.f. values turn out to be less than the f.o.b. statistics, and if we cannot produce any other reason to explain this, we may reasonably infer that underinvoicing of imports appears to have occurred. This conclusion would be strengthened if these commodities could also be shown to be carrying high tariff duties which exceed the black-market premium for foreign exchange[3], and if they were such as to make underinvoicing feasible and easy – manufactures, especially capital goods (usually made to order), qualify readily.

In this sequence of inferences, the requirement that other reasons explaining the perverse discrepancy between c.i.f. and f.o.b. statistics must be ruled out (before we can reasonably infer underinvoicing) is naturally the most difficult to fulfil. There are, in fact, several reasons which may explain such discrepancies:

(1) There are frequently errors of commodity classification: an item belonging to code no. 319 may be wrongly put under code no. 316, making for an understatement in 319 if the error is committed only by the importing country. This type of error, however, is usually easy to trace by checking the data carefully for it.

(2) There may be exports from (say) Italy which have not reached (say) Turkey or have not yet passed through customs and been recorded. The goods may then be recorded as exported to Turkey but not as imported by it, causing the discrepancy in the 'wrong' direction, i.e. making c.i.f. imports smaller than f.o.b. exports. This argument, however, will not be persuasive if the level of imports does not change over time: in this case, the imports of this year, which are not recorded currently but carry over into the next year's c.i.f. statistics, will be more or less offset by the imports of last year carried over into this year's statistics. If, however, imports are rising, there will be a tendency towards understatement though it is unlikely to be large enough to produce a perverse discrepancy[4].

(3) There may be a misallocation of imports by country: imports from (say) Italy are wrongly attributed to Germany, and so on. This happens frequently. It is to be traced usually to confusion over the origin and ownership of imported goods. For example, Malayan exports of rubber to Turkey may be wrongly attributed to the United Kingdom because an English exporter is handling the transaction; and so on. Though this sort of error can usually be detected, omissions cannot be ruled out.

[3] Alternatively, these commodities may be shown to be subject to stringent import control, carrying higher domestic premiums than the premium in the black market for foreign exchange.

[4] Thus, even if we assume that the carry-over applies to six months in every year, and equally generously that trade grows by 10% per annum, the understatement in import value will only be 4.5% of the actual import value and is unlikely to exceed the insurance and freight charges in international commerce (especially for machinery and other manufactures where we find the perverse discrepancies in Turkish statistics).

(4) We must not rule out the possibility of overinvoicing of exports at the other end.

Clearly all these complicating factors must be carefully considered. Bearing them in mind, I have found in the Turkish case that, for 1960 and 1961, there is strong evidence of understatement of import values of manufactures, especially in the field of transport equipment and machinery. Let me now state the analysis

Table 1.
1960 trade between France and Turkey (thousands of dollars).

SITC code no.	Commodities	France's exports	Turkey's imports	Dis-crepancy
313	Petroleum products	9 059	617	− 8 442
6	Main manufactured goods	3 212	3 196	− 16
66	Non-metallic mineral manufactures	343	266	− 77
68	Non-ferrous metals	4 412	3 464	− 948
69	Metal manufactures	3 915	544	− 3 371
7	Machinery and transport equipment	5 270	3 820	− 1 450
8	Miscellaneous manufactured goods	1 246	595	− 651
	Others	4 197	3 834	− 363
	Total	31 654	16 336	−15 318

Table 2.
1960 trade between Italy and Turkey (thousands of dollars).

SITC code no.	Commodities	Italy's exports	Turkey's imports	Dis-crepancy
313	Petroleum products	13 093	713	−12 380
6	Main manufactured goods	3 576	3 559	− 17
65	Files, textiles, etc.	2 737	1 590	− 1 147
66	Non-metallic minerals manufactures	265	173	− 92
68	Non-ferrous metals	4 700	1 317	− 3 383
69	Metal manufactures	3 151	2 258	− 893
7	Machinery and transport equipment	18 913	15 213	− 3 700
8	Miscellaneous manufactured goods	1 591	1 035	− 556
	Others	4 391	4 176	− 215
	Total	52 417	30 034	−22 383

Table 3.
1960 trade between Germany and Turkey (thousands of dollars).

SITC code no.	Commodities	Germany's exports	Turkey's imports	Dis-crepancy
6	Main manufactured goods	4 094	4 023	− 71
66	Non-metallic minerals manufactures	3 111	1 259	− 1 852
68	Non-ferrous metals	20 623	21 357	+ 734
69	Metal manufactures	7 620	5 260	− 2 360
7	Machinery and transport equipment	62 884	51 097	−11 787
8	Miscellaneous manufactured goods	6 916	4 043	− 2 873
	Others	9 984	10 987	+ 1 003
	Total	115 232	98 026	−17 206

Table 4.
1960 trade between U.S.A. and Turkey (thousands of dollars).

SITC code no.	Commodities	U.S.A.'s exports	Turkey's imports	Dis-crepancy
313	Petroleum products	7 130	24 660	+17 530
412	Vegetable oils	5 673	14 828	+ 9 155
5	Chemical products	4 424	3 894	− 530
6	Main manufactured goods	5 258	4 529	− 729
66	Non-metallic minerals manufactures	350	563	+ 213
68	Non-ferrous metals	4 599	4 108	− 491
69	Metal manufactures	1 084	922	− 162
7	Machinery and transport equipment	62 032	53 942	− 8 090
8	Miscellaneous manufactured goods	2 422	1 711	− 711
	Others	31 808	11 310	−20 498
	Total	124 780	120 467	− 4 313

Table 5.
1960 trade between Netherlands and Turkey (thousands of dollars).

SITC code no.	Commodities	Netherlands' exports	Turkey's imports	Dis-crepancy
6	Main manufactured goods	4 298	4 062	− 236
7	Machinery and transport equipment	5 400	3 561	− 1 839
8	Miscellaneous manufactured goods	498	382	− 116
	Others	3 402	4 094	+ 692
	Total	13 598	12 099	− 1 499

Table 6.
1961 trade between Germany and Turkey (thousands of dollars).

SITC code no.	Commodities	Germany's exports	Turkey's imports	Discrepancy
6	Main manufactured goods	3 726	3 710	− 16
66+67	Non-metallic mineral manufactures + Iron and steel	14 700	16 620	+ 1 920
68	Non-ferrous metals	949	1 211	+ 262
69	Metal manufactures	4 795	2 848	− 1 947
7	Machinery and transport equipment	52 629	46 158	− 6 471
8	Miscellaneous manufactured goods	4 410	3 377	− 1 033
	Others	12 079	11 152	− 927
	Total	93 288	85 076	− 8 212

Table 7.
1961 trade between Italy and Turkey (thousands of dollars).

SITC code no.	Commodities	Italy's exports	Turkey's imports	Discrepancy
352	Petroleum products	15 526	592	−14 934
6	Main manufactured goods	4 368	4 503	+ 135
65	Files, textiles, etc.	1 749	1 461	− 288
66	Non-metallic mineral manufactures	373	363	− 10
67	Iron and steel	2 579	2 169	− 410
69	Metal manufactures	1 450	1 188	− 262
7	Machinery and transport equipment	21 801	24 465	+ 2 664
8	Miscellaneous manufactured goods	1 719	1 660	− 59
	Others	6 468	6 473	+ 5
	Total	56 033	42 874	−13 159

Table 8.
1961 trade between U.S.A. and Turkey (thousands of dollars).

SITC code no.	Commodities	U.S.A.'s exports	Turkey's imports	Discrepancy
352	Petroleum products	7 167	21 722	+14 555
5	Chemical products	7 637	6 526	− 1 111
6	Main manufactured goods	12 850	12 161	− 689
7	Machinery and transport equipment	39 380	30 513	− 8 867
8	Miscellaneous manufactured goods	2 721	1 548	− 1 173
	Others	71 893	67 609	− 4 374
	Total	141 738	140 079	− 1 659

Table 9.
1961 trade between France and Turkey (thousands of dollars).

SITC code no.	Commodities	France's exports	Turkey's imports	Discrepancy
332	Petroleum products	8 601	127	− 8 474
6	Main manufactured goods	6 355	6 050	− 305
7	Machinery and transport equipment	9 063	6 874	− 2 189
	Others	5 409	4 648	− 761
	Total	29 428	17 699	−11 729

Table 10.
Turkey's imports of petroleum products, 1960 (thousands of dollars).

Exporting country	Exporting country's statistics	Turkey's statistics	Discrepancy
France	9 059	617	− 8 442
Italy	13 093	713	−12 380
United Kingdom	2 166	8 819	+ 6 653
United States	7 130	24 660	+17 530
Total	31 448	34 809	+ 3 361

Table 11.
Turkey's imports of petroleum products, 1961 (thousands of dollars) (SITC 332).

Exporting country	Exporting country's statistics	Turkey's statistics	Discrepancy
France	8 601	127	− 8 474
Italy	15 526	592	−14 934
United Kingdom	1 339	10 030	+ 8 691
United States	7 167	21 722	+14 555
Total	32 633	32 471	− 162

fully. The data for Turkey–Italy, Turkey–Germany, Turkey–United States, Turkey–France and Turkey–Netherlands (tables 1–9), relating to Turkey's principal trading partners, testify to substantial excesses of f.o.b. over c.i.f. values in petroleum products and in the categories of main manufactured goods (code no. 6), machinery and transport equipment (code no. 7) and miscellaneous manufactures (code no. 8).

Not all of these testify to underinvoicing of imports. The discrepancies in petroleum products, for instance, are offsetting between France, Italy, United States and United Kingdom (tables 10, 11). They arise from the misallocation of imports among sources, resulting from confusion over the ownership of refineries and petroleum[5]. But I have not been able to think of similar explanations for the other discrepancies[6].

It is not valid to argue that the time lag between exports and imports will explain the discrepancies observed[7]. Significant overinvoicing by exporters to Turkey is unlikely, given the existence of convertibility during this period for the relevant currencies and countries[8].

We are therefore left with some significant discrepancies for which the only explanation appears to be underinvoicing. How does this explanation stand up in relation to Turkey's organization of its international trade? Quite well, as it turns out.

Turkey, during the early 1960s, was operating a substantially 'liberalized' trade system. It relied on tariffs – other price-instruments such as devaluation, licence fees, stamp duty also being used occasionally – to regulate imports. I expected, therefore, that the underinvoicing would in this case turn out to be related to tariffs, rather than to import control. This turned out to be the case.

In the statement on Turkey's tariffs in 1961 (which also adequately serves our purpose for 1960), see sect. 4, the reader will find that the categories of goods which show perverse discrepancies (in tables 1–9) also generally had tariff rates ranging up to 30% and rarely below 10%[9].

As the black-market premium for foreign exchange has rarely exceeded 15% according to official observations, and has been usually below this level, it seems reasonable to conclude that the discrepancies represent underinvoicing of imports,

5 I am indebted to R. Gross, who spotted the offsetting nature of the petroleum discrepancies.

6 In ships and boats I found that the discrepancy was to be explained by foreign registration: but this, in turn, might be linked to high tariffs on import of ships.

7 This is for much the same reason as set out in footnote 4.

8 It is true that the relief from the cascading turn-over taxes in some Western European countries was related, during this period, to the *value* of exports. Hence there could have been some overinvoicing of exports to secure greater relief. But I doubt whether much can be made of this point.

9 Some puzzling tariffs seem to be those on non-ferrous metals – at 5%. I have not been able to think of a suitable explanation in these cases.

by and large. This conclusion is further reinforced by the fact that understatement of value in the field of manufactures – especially machinery, which is frequently made to order and rarely carries standard prices that the customs can readily check – is readily possible. And it is precisely in these areas that the perverse discrepancies occur in the Turkish case.

Let me emphasize again that the preceding analysis provides, not a conclusive proof, but only a strong indication of the presence of underinvoicing of imports in the Turkish case. Indeed, for many the case may appear totally convincing. What are we to conclude from this analysis? Some of the more interesting implications seem to me to be the following.

First of all, if black market foreign exchange is being used to buy manufactures, and in particular machinery and equipment, this is certainly less disastrous from the Turkish viewpoint than if it were leaking entirely into Turkish tourists' expenditure abroad and/or illegal export of capital. After all, even if the exchange had come into official channels, it would probably have been allocated for much the same uses as it gets into through illegal channels[10].

Secondly, certain fiscal measures may be of fortuitous assistance in reducing such underinvoicing. Take, for example, the accelerated depreciation allowance, introduced in Turkey in 1963. This type of measure is, in general, an 'inefficient' way of increasing investment in a country with an excess supply of labour (as Turkey is generally considered to be). Because it links the subsidy on investment to the value of (fixed) capital, it creates a bias in favour of capital-intensive techniques. In view of the understating of import values on equipment and machinery that appears to obtain in Turkey, however, it is possible to claim that the accelerated depreciation allowance has, in the Turkish case, the offsetting virtue of making undervaluation of capital goods imports less attractive: an undervaluation would mean a corresponding loss of the benefit from the accelerated depreciation allowance.

4. Turkish tariffs during 1961

There was a stamp duty, i.e. a *de facto* tariff, of 5% on all visible imports. Moreover, the tariff rates on the items covered in our analysis ranged up to 30–40%,

[10] Of course, this is not to argue that there is, therefore, *no* cost attached to illegal inflow of exchange. Aside from the usual costs, I may mention that nothing would seem to make the nations giving aid to Turkey happier, and more willing to support the Turkish developmental effort through large-scale aid, than the evidence of increasing exchange earnings which indicate the possibility of Turkish viability, without external aid, in the long run. One of the costs of exchange receipts going through illegal channels, therefore, could well be a reduction (even a sizeable reduction) in foreign aid.

in some cases going even higher. The only exceptions among the items which appear to have been understated in value were nickel, aluminium and zinc, which carried a duty of only 5%, and copper for which the duty was 10%.

Among transport equipment and different kinds of machinery, the following may be taken as illustrative: 20% on locomotives, trains, buses and wagons, 25% on tractors, 40% on automobiles, buses and pick-ups, 50% on ships and other craft, 20–25% on generators, motors and transformers, 20–30% on other machinery (including agricultural).

Some 'protective' duties were quite high and obviously related to categories of imports for which underinvoicing of imports seemed to be important. Examples are: 60% on knives, 70% on spoons and forks, 100% on lamps, 50% on bells, 50% on mirrors, 100% on metal necklaces, etc., 100% on decorative sculpture (figurines, etc.).

There is a minor complication in interpreting these duties. It was possible, in several cases, to get exemption from these duties and pay *lower* duties under certain circumstances. I have found it difficult to judge how important this exemption was, but my impression is that its effect was not significant from the viewpoint of the present analysis.

Chapter 10

CAPITAL FLIGHT FROM LDCs: A STATISTICAL ANALYSIS

Jagdish N. BHAGWATI, Anne KRUEGER and Chaiyawat WIBULSWASDI

1. Introduction

One important impact of exchange control in less developed countries (LDCs) is that capital flight would occur in illegal fashion. Whether, of course, such flight is still below the level that would occur in the absence of exchange control is an issue that is difficult to settle empirically, although we would be inclined to assume that the extra costs of illegal methods of capital outflow tend to reduce its level.

Can we, however, try to get an empirical indication of whether such capital flight is occurring at all? In this note, we explore the possibility of making partner-country trade-data comparisons to see whether the phenomena of overinvoicing imports and underinvoicing exports are used to effect such capital flight from the LDCs.

We confine our analysis to comparisons of the trade data of LDCs with the Organization for Economic Development and Co-operation (OECD) DCs, examining altogether 28 LDCs for 1966. This, of course, means that capital flight which occurs *among* LDCs cannot be shown up, even in principle, by our methods; and there is 'word-of-mouth' evidence of such flight occurring from some of the African countries to India by the Indian settlers, and from Indonesia, Malaysia and Philippines to Hong Kong and Taiwan by the overseas Chinese communities. Further, our method is subject to a lot of 'noise': as Morgenstern (1965) has already discussed in his classic study of the accuracy of economic statistics, there are a number of purely statistical reasons why partner-country data may not match.

Nonetheless, it is interesting to see whether on comparison, OECD imports from each LDC are sufficiently above that LDC's exports to the OECD countries to indicate underinvoicing of that LDC's exports and consequent presumption of capital flight; and whether each LDC's imports from OECD countries exceed the OECD exports to that LDC by a sufficient amount to indicate overinvoicing of imports and hence capital flight again from that LDC.

2. Analysis of findings

Table 1 summarizes for each of the 28 LDCs the percentage difference between imports and exports as a proportion of exports, the export figures being those recorded by the LDCs and the import figures being those recorded by the OECD countries. It is really quite remarkable that for all but 2 countries, we find that there is an excess of import figures over the corresponding export figures. However, note that the exports are f.o.b. and imports are generally c.i.f., so that the excess is actually smaller than it looks; but even if we estimate average insurance and freight at a maximum of 10% on f.o.b. value, it would still leave 20 LDCs as export-underinvoicers.

Noting that U.S.A. and Canada record their imports by *f.o.b.* values, we also calculated separately the trade-flow from each LDC to the two countries combined. Column 2 of table 1 shows the discrepancy between the combined imports of U.S.A. and Canada and the corresponding exports by LDCs as a percentage of the import figures. The excess of import figures over the corresponding export figures in this case would be presumptive evidence for export-underinvoicing practices in LDCs. Of the 20 countries noted earlier, such positive excess shows up for all but one (Pakistan). Moreover, the magnitudes of the discrepancies are quite significant: larger than 10% in eleven cases, and between 5 and 10% in five others. These nineteen countries may, therefore, be classified as 'clear' export-underinvoicers.

We would further argue that, unlike with the imports of LDCs which we shortly analyze, a significant part of the export sector is usually free from very *large* subsidies and taxes and the export duties on traditional exports are usually well-balanced by subsidies on non-traditional exports. Hence, no pronounced effect of trade tax and subsidy policies need be expected to affect the trade declarations in the direction of either net overinvoicing or net underinvoicing of exports[1].

We would thus presume that the above results strongly signify capital flight from LDCs, especially in light of the supplementary evidence concerning the black market premium of U.S. dollars in each LDC. The average black market rate for the year in question is presented in the last column of table 1. In view of its 'black' nature, the estimates of premiums on foreign exchange presented here may not be terribly reliable. They nevertheless substantiate our result quite well. Among the nineteen export-underinvoicers, eleven show black market premiums

[1] For an analysis of the influence of trade taxes and subsidies on the faking of trade transactions, and hence on the inferences that can be made from partner-country trade-data comparisons such as those being employed in the text above, see Bhagwati (1964; 1967), reproduced here as chapters 6 and 9. The several difficulties with the use of the partner-country-comparison technique are also discussed there in detail.

exceeding 10% (some as high as 100%), and four others smaller but still positive premiums. Only Honduras and Mexico have no functioning black markets, and in the cases of Colombia and Ivory Coast, information on black markets is not available.

A breakdown of the countries by the degree of underinvoicing of exports to U.S.A. and Canada and the height of black market premiums, based on columns 2 and 3, can be shown as follows:

Trade data discrepancy (%)	Black market premium (%) >20	10–19	1–9	0	No data
>10	5	1	3	1	1
5–10	3	—	1	—	1
1– 4	—	2	—	1	—

Using the height of black market premium as an indication of the profit from the illegal sales of foreign exchanges in the black market, we may then deduce that in more than half of the nineteen countries under consideration the incentives for export-underinvoicing are quite clearly evident.

The data in table 2, on the other hand, relate to LDCs' imports; we try to see if the same conclusion can be drawn from these statistics, with overinvoicing of imports being the instrument via which capital flight occurs from LDCs.

We did not expect to see, on the LDC-import side, a clear demonstration of capital flight for the following reasons: (1) The customs authorities are more vigilant about faking of transactions on the import side than on the export side because traditionally duties have been levied on a much wider range of imports than of exports in LDCs; hence the faking of import invoices is likely to be confined to essentially manufactured (Standard International Trade Classification (SITC) 5–8) imports where product differentiation etc. make it generally possible to 'get past the customs' with faked invoices. (2) Since imports are almost never subsidised at the customs point, there is always a net tariff on imports into any country, which acts *ceteris paribus* to reduce overinvoicing of imports (for overinvoicing implies paying more tariff duty); thus, depending on the relationship of the tariff structure to the import structure (since the same duty on different types of products can create different effects just because different products are differently susceptible to the possibility of faking trade declarations, as we have just argued), one may find the incentive to overinvoice imports, to facilitate capital flight, overcome in various degrees so as to result, in some cases, even in a net incentive to *underinvoice* imports[2].

[2] This, in effect, was observed in Bhagwati's (1964) study of Turkish trade data, where imports carrying high tariff duties were observed to be generally underinvoiced. In some countries, another motive for underinvoicing imports is that import licences are issued for a dollar value: thus, by understating price, the importer can buy more.

Table 1.
Exports of LDCs to OECD countries compared with corresponding imports by OECD countries from LDCs, and black market premium of U.S. dollars, for 28 LDCs: 1966.

Country (by region)	Total OECD $100 \cdot (M-X)/X$ (1)	U.S.A. and Canada $100 \cdot (M-X)/M$ (2)	Black market premium of U.S. $ (%) (3)
South America			
Argentina	24.2	17.5	23
Brazil[a]	14.0	4.1	10
Chile	4.5	4.4	49
Colombia[a]	14.2	9.3	n.a.
Mexico	37.0	14.0	0
Central America			
Costa Rica	6.8	6.6	17
El Salvador	0.1	−5.3	13
Guatemala	24.2	16.3	15
Honduras	27.3	3.8	0
Nicaragua	14.7	3.2	19
Africa			
Ethiopia[a]	14.6	15.1	24
Ivory Coast	26.9	19.2	n.a.
Libya	11.1	5.2	20
Nigeria	9.9	1.1	n.a.
Tunisia	47.2	34.7	67
Far East			
Hong Kong	13.7	9.6	1
Korea	−4.6	−16.7	0
Philippines	16.1	16.5	2
Taiwan	7.0	−2.1	3
Thailand[a]	6.4	3.6	0.6
South Asia and Middle East			
Ceylon[b]	20.1	12.9	94
Egypt	30.7	13.9	111
India	23.7	5.3	74
Iran	35.2	21.4	4
Pakistan	14.3	−3.5	75
Europe			
Greece	27.9	16.1	4
Turkey[a]	15.4	9.6	40
Yugoslavia	−1.0	−1.0	17

Notes: 1. OECD countries in tables 1 and 2 include only EFTA, EEC, U.S.A., Canada and Japan. 2. *M*, *X* represent imports and exports, respectively.

[a] 1967 data.

[b] 1968 data.

Sources: United Nations, *Statistical Papers*, Series D (Commodity Trade Statistics). OECD, *Statistics of Foreign Trade*, Series C (Commodity Trade). Pick, Franz, *Pick's Currency Yearbook*, Pick Publ. Co., N.Y.

Table 2.
Imports of LDCs from OECD countries compared with corresponding exports by OECD countries to LDCs for 28 LDCs: 1966.

Country (by region)	100 · (Imports − Exports)/Exports		Percentage share of SITC 5–8 in total LDC's imports
	Total trade	SITC 5–8	
South America			
Argentina	0.6	− 0.4	91.8
Brazil[a]	1.3	− 4.7	75.5
Chile	16.6	17.1	82.8
Colombia[a]	12.1	−12.1	68.8
Mexico[a]	− 7.7	− 4.4	85.7
Central America			
Costa Rica	19.0	17.9	86.6
El Salvador	8.1	10.5	87.9
Guatemala	− 0.6	2.4	87.6
Honduras	14.5	17.8	89.2
Nicaragua	7.8	8.5	88.4
Africa			
Ethiopia[a]	− 1.2	− 0.1	84.2
Ivory Coast	13.0	7.0	80.9
Libya	− 9.9	−10.9	83.4
Nigeria	14.9	15.2	85.4
Tunisia	0.1	1.4	75.2
Far East			
Hong Kong	−11.6	−11.4	84.1
Korea	− 0.4	−10.0	67.4
Philippines	− 7.6	− 8.3	80.1
Taiwan	− 3.3	− 3.4	75.4
Thailand[a]	14.0	11.0	88.5
South Asia and Middle East			
Ceylon[b]	− 5.7	−11.0	71.2
Egypt	8.3	6.4	60.6
India	− 1.0	−15.7	55.0
Iran	− 1.3	0.8	90.7
Pakistan	− 1.3	− 7.6	77.4
Europe			
Greece	− 0.2	− 0.2	81.7
Turkey[a]	−13.4	−10.2	91.1
Yugoslavia	− 1.3	6.2	72.6

Notes and Sources: Same as table 1.

3. Conclusion

Our expectation that the import side would show 'mixed' results was borne out in fact, as table 2 shows. Altogether 7 LDCs show a percentage excess of imports over exports, on exports, of over 10% for total trade, with 6 more LDCs having a positive (but less than 10%) excess and 15 LDCs having a negative excess figure. This would suggest, once we take into account the fact that imports are c.i.f. and exports are f.o.b. and that this discrepancy may be taken at an average figure of 10% on f.o.b. value, that 7 LDCs with excess on top of 10% in table 2 are 'clear' *overinvoicers* whereas all the rest are not, while those having negative figures are probably 'clear' *underinvoicers*. The same exercise, repeated for only SITC categories 5–8, shows that these conclusions roughly carry over, except that only 5 LDCs became 'clear' overinvoicers: Chile, Costa Rica, Honduras, Nigeria and Thailand[3]. If we could show that the average tariff level on SITC group 5–8 in these 5 LDCs is lower than in the remaining LDCs in our sample, we would have a reasonable presumption that these 5 LDCs are experiencing capital flight through overinvoicing, whereas in the other LDCs the higher tariff level is tending to create a counterincentive to underinvoice imports. However, neat as this would be, a failure to find a lower average tariff level in the 5 LDCs would still not rule out the presumption of capital flight for two reasons: (i) as argued above, it is not the usual average tariff level which is really relevant for our analysis but the tariffs weighted in such a way as to reflect the 'invoice-fakeability' of the importable commodities, and there is really no feasible way in which this could be done with available information; and (ii) what matters anyway, in determining whether imports will be overinvoiced or underinvoiced, is not just the tariff level but also the premium on black market foreign exchange[4]; and this premium is not uniform across the LDCs in our sample, as is evident in table 1, column 3. Hence, we have little choice except to infer from table 2 merely that the phenomenon of over-invoicing of imports, as a vehicle of capital flight, seems to be much more restricted

[3] It is interesting to note that Honduras is the only case where the 'faking' presumably occurs on both import and export sides. In all four other countries, export-underinvoicing may be practiced to only a limited scale as evidence shows up only in the export-trade with U.S.A. and Canada but not with total OECD countries. The Honduras case may seem peculiar since its liberal exchange control regime allows capital to be transferred rather freely. There is, however, a requirement (for statistical purposes) that buyers of exchange must file the applications stating how the exchange will be used (IMF, 19th Annual Report on Exchange Restrictions, p. 185); this may provide an incentive to 'fake' the invoices so that illegal uses of exchange can be concealed.

[4] For, if imports are overinvoiced (underinvoiced), the importer must sell (buy) in the black market an amount of foreign exchange equal to the difference between the correct and the faked price on the invoice. Hence, two critical variables in his decision will clearly be the duty and the black market premium on foreign exchange. See Bhagwati (1967).

than the phenomenon of underinvoicing of exports. This asymmetry of conduit-behaviour for capital flight, in the exports and imports of LDCs is, on the other hand, a conclusion of great interest to policymakers in these countries[5].

Acknowledgement

The research underlying this note has been supported by the National Bureau of Economic Research with financing provided by the United States Agency for International Development.

References

Bhagwati, J., 1964, On the underinvoicing of imports, Bulletin of the Oxford University Institute of Statistics, November; ch. 9 in this volume.

Bhagwati, J., 1967, Fiscal policies, the faking of foreign trade declarations, and the balance of payments, Bulletin of the Oxford University Institute of Statistics, February; ch. 6 in this volume.

Morgenstern, O., 1965. The Accuracy of Economic Observation (Princeton University Press); relevant material reprinted as ch. 7 in this volume.

[5] Note that some of the illegal outflow of foreign exchange, which we seem to have detected in our analysis, may well be for reasons other than capital flight in the usual sense: thus, it may partly be financing foreign travel by nationals. Thus, the reader should not allocate all the outflow of exchange to capital flight.

PART IV

DETECTING SMUGGLING

Chapter 11

INDONESIA'S UNRECORDED TRADE*†

C. G. F. SIMKIN

1. Introduction

It is seldom that attempts at analysing, forecasting or planning the Indonesian economy make more than marginal reference to that considerable part of its foreign trade which escapes official record. This neglect would not greatly matter if Indonesia's unrecorded trade, like that of some other Southeast Asian countries, were small relative to official exports and imports. But it is widely recognised that physical smuggling, deliberate undervaluation of declared exports, and under-invoicing of imports have been widespread, involving Indonesian peasants, Chinese or Sumatran merchants, corruptible customs men, and even local military commanders or provincial administrators who find Djakarta's grants quite inadequate for their public responsibilities.

There are obvious reasons for analysts and planners neglecting this unrecorded trade. It cannot be other than a politically sensitive problem in a country which a new government is striving to rehabilitate after a prolonged deterioration in economic and administrative conditions, and which badly needs foreign aid, in spite of smuggling, for rehabilitation. More important, the problem, by its very nature, is statistically obscure, so that attempts at quantitative estimation are

* Editor's note: The last section on *Incentives to Illegal Trade* in the original article has been omitted here.

† A first version of this paper was prepared in April 1969, after a two months' assignment in Indonesia. It suffered from the usual local difficulties of obtaining data, and also from the inadequacy of my own understanding of this country. Some gaps in the data were later filled, and I have had the benefit of criticism from Dr. W. Hollinger, Professor H. W. Arndt and Mrs. H. V. Richter. The present version has been adjusted to meet some of their criticisms, and uses, with acknowledgements, material prepared by Mrs. Richter for this purpose. Not all of the criticism, however, struck me as fully convincing or well based. I have tried to reduce possibilities of misunderstanding by putting disputed matters more clearly but fear that there are still points which will provoke objection or disagreement. Although, then, I gratefully acknowledge the help of my critics, no responsibility can be attributed to them for the defects of this article.

necessarily hazardous. Complete neglect, however, is much worse; it implies a zero estimate which, in the circumstances, would be absurd.

A few statements, of course, have been made, and they give some indication of the importance of the problem. *The Far Eastern Economic Review Year Book* of 1968, p. 201, refers to an announcement that 'smuggling costs the country at least $200 million a year'. A report from the International Bank for Reconstruction and Development (IBRD, 1968), says that 'smuggling has been publicly estimated at $100 million or more annually and has by all accounts increased dramatically since the ending of confrontation with Malaysia and Singapore'. These figures (which appear to emanate from some official source) are to be compared with recorded exports of $658 million in 1967 or, better, with recorded non-mineral exports of $365 million, because shipments of oil and tin are hardly affected by smuggling. Oil is exported by two American companies and a state company, all operating under the supervision of a Ministry of Mines, and tin, until quite recently, was wholly mined by state companies.

But there is plenty of opportunity for smuggling most agricultural products. Indonesia has 50 substantial and many more smaller ports, scattered over an archipelago the western end of which borders Malaya and the eastern end adjoins the Philippines. Malaya has a coastline which its own navy cannot effectively patrol, and the Philippines is unable to suppress the brisk smuggling trade between its myriad islands and Hong Kong. Nor is it in these countries' own interests to check trade, legal or illegal, with Indonesia, whose navy has had neither the capacity, nor always the enthusiasm, to police the archipelago's extensive waters. Thousands of small craft or coastal vessels ply between Indonesia, West Malaysia or Singapore, and East Malaysia or the Philippines. Moreover, although estates which are largely owned or supervised by the government, produce all the palm oil and half the tea, most of Indonesia's rubber and coffee, and practically all the copra, pepper and tobacco, come from smallholders, who often deal with merchants having strong business connections with firms in Penang, Singapore or Hong Kong.

Besides opportunity, there is motive. Legal exports bear tax, and have had to be surrendered at exchange rates well below the free market rate. Legal imports, it is true, may also be obtained at exchange rates below the free rate, but only for limited categories of goods and they, too, bear taxes. It will be shown later how strong has been the net economic incentive for a two-way smuggling trade. In addition, there have been other incentives to capital flight because of serious political disturbances, bad treatment of Chinese or foreign businesses, and a galloping inflation which almost wrecked the foreign exchanges.

Considerations of this sort persuaded me that it was important, both for understanding the Indonesian economy and for planning its development, to attempt estimates of unrecorded trade, and to make some exploration of the influences which govern it. But I have had neither the expertise nor the time for more than a rough survey, and offer it here only as a pioneering exploration of an important yet badly neglected problem.

2. Trade with partner countries

The obvious first step in obtaining such estimates is to use Indonesia's own official figures for exports and imports in conjunction with the corresponding figures of its trading partners. These are set out in table 1 for the period 1958–1967, but suffer after 1963 from two flaws. One is the omission of trade with Indonesia by Malaysia

Table 1.
Indonesia's exports and imports 1958–1967 (millions of dollars).

	X_i	M_p	$D_x{}^a$	$D_x{}^b$	M_i	X_p	D_m
1958	791	1085	186	240	544	617	135
1959	931	1143	98	155	483	542	113
1960	841	1130	176	233	574	701	197
1961	788	982	96	145	794	918	216
1962	682	939	163	210	647	741	168
Average	807	1056	144	197	608	704	166
1963	696	548	−203	−175	522	501	29
1964	724	731	− 66	− 30	691	513	−127
1965	707	759	− 24	14	718	547	−116
1966	679	839	76	118	689	512	−126
1967	658	812	73	113	649	612	24
Average	693	738	− 29	8	654	537	− 63

Notes: X_i = recorded exports of Indonesia.
M_p = corresponding imports of trading partners.
$D_x{}^a$ = (90% of M_p) − X_i.
$D_x{}^b$ = (95% of M_p) − X_i.
M_i = recorded imports of Indonesia.
X_p = corresponding exports of trading partners.
D_m = (110% of X_p) − M_i.

Sources: X_i, M_i: Biro Pusat Statistik.
M_p, X_p: IMF and IBRD (1958–1962); IMF and IBRD (1963–1967).

and Singapore in the IMF-IBRD Direction of Trade[1] (DOT) statistics; this is serious because much of Indonesia's unrecorded trade is connected with these two countries. The DOT statistics also omit trade with mainland China and other communist countries of Asia, but their omission hardly matters for the present problem as their Indonesian trade was substantial only in the years 1963–1965.

An estimate of Indonesia's unrecorded exports is obtained by deducting its recorded exports from the corresponding imports of partner countries after correction for freight, insurance and other transport costs. The usual allowance here (in the DOT and other statistics) is 10%, which leads to an estimated average of $144 million a year between 1958 and 1962. But there are two reasons for thinking that this is too low. One reason is that the 10% allowance is probably excessive for a country which exports mostly primary products, and a good deal of them to adjacent countries. A check was made here with data for Thailand, which is similarly placed to Indonesia in regard to trade; between 1958 and 1962 the ratio of Thailand's exports to world imports from this country averaged only 95%. If, then, we accept a 5% adjustment instead of 10%, Indonesia's unrecorded exports would average for this period not $144 million but $197 million. Even this may be too low because it assumes that Indonesia's trading partners fully and accurately record all their imports from it[2]. The assumption, of course, is highly doubtful in the case of Asian neighbours with which Indonesia conducted, in this period, at least two-fifths of its official export trade. It is difficult to suggest any correction in this respect, but $200 million certainly appears to be a low estimate of Indonesia's annual unrecorded exports in the five years preceding confrontation.

Similarly, an estimate of Indonesia's unrecorded imports is obtained from table 1 by applying a 10% adjustment to its recorded imports and subtracting from the result the corresponding exports of other countries. (This adjustment seems reasonable because a comparison with Thai data for imports gave a ratio of 11%.) It then appears that Indonesia's unrecorded imports could have averaged $166 million a year between 1958 and 1962, and so amounted to perhaps four-fifths of its unrecorded exports.

This indicates the markedly two-way nature of Indonesia's unrecorded trade in which operators often tempt illegal suppliers more by imported goods than by money – even foreign money. But it also allows a substantial balance of over $30 million a year for illegal capital flight, a minimum which would be raised if we knew what allowance to make in neighbouring countries for their unrecorded imports from Indonesia.

[1] Malaysia and Singapore ceased recording their Indonesian trade after August 1963, when Sukarno began his policy of confrontation. This statistical obscurity has continued even though the new Suharto regime officially ended confrontation in late 1967.

[2] I owe this point to Mrs. Richter and Professor Arndt.

A dramatic feature of table 1 is that both unrecorded exports and imports, estimated by the above methods, appear to have shrunk to negligible dimensions after 1962. This appearance, of course, is associated with the later omission from the DOT statistics of Indonesia's trade with Malaysia and Singapore, so that we need to look at what evidence is available about Indonesia's trade with Southeast Asian neighbours.

Table 2.
Indonesia's apparent trade with selected Asian countries, 1958–1962 (average annual values in millions of dollars).

	X_i	M_p	D_x^a	D_x^b	M_i	X_p	D_m
Singapore	178	309	100	116	13	71	66
West Malaysia	47	85	29	34	2	7	7
East Malaysia	—	3	3	3	5	6	2
Hong Kong	8	16	6	7	22	28	9
Sub-total	233	413	138	160	42	112	84
Philippines	19	30	8	10	—	—	—
South Vietnam	5	15	9	9	3	3	—
Thailand	9	19	8	9	18	21	5
Sub-total	33	64	25	28	21	24	5

Notes: X_i = recorded exports of Indonesia.
M_p = corresponding imports of trading partners.
D_x^a = (90% of M_p) − X_i.
D_x^b = (95% of M_p) − X_i.
M_i = recorded imports of Indonesia.
X_p = corresponding exports of trading partners.
D_m = (110% of X_p) − M_i.

Sources: X_i, M_i: Biro Pusat Statistik.
M_p, X_p: IMF and IBRD (1958–1962); IMF and IBRD (1963/1967); and United Nations (1966).

It would seem from table 2 that the greater part of Indonesia's unrecorded exports went to Singapore, some \$116 million as compared with the total D_x^b figure of \$197 million in table 1, and most of the remainder (\$37 million) to Malaysia. Smaller values may also have gone, in the period, to Hong Kong, the Philippines, South Vietnam and Thailand. For unrecorded imports the proportions appear less: \$66 million for Singapore and \$9 million for Malaysia.

But these figures are badly deceptive. Naya and Morgan (1967) have exposed considerable discrepancies in the trade returns of Southeast Asian countries, greater for their trade with one another than for that with developed countries. The reasons for discrepancy include differences between f.o.b. and c.i.f. values, differences in recording destinations of exports, and simple errors of compilation besides physical smuggling and undergrading of exports or overinvoicing of imports. They remark that 'smuggling enterprises in the Philippines are notably successful and Indonesia was, like England, made by heaven for free trade'. A major source of error, too, is undervaluing exports or overvaluing imports in order to achieve illegal transfers of capital. Results for Indonesia were far worse than for any other country, and by no means good for Singapore or Malaysia, but the authors point out that variations for these three countries went in opposite directions and cancelled out to give 'satisfactory' totals.

A peculiar difficulty arises about the differences in recording destinations of exports, as Richter (1966, p. 32) emphasized some years ago, when the term Malaya was used to include Singapore:

> Indonesian statistics present their exports according to the known destination... The system would classify, for example, a shipment of Sumatran rubber which was expected to go to France after storage or regrading in Singapore as an export to France. Malayan returns would show this rubber as a simple import from Sumatra.

In a subsequent communication Mrs. Richter writes further:

> Indonesia classifies exports by country of final destination, while Singapore-Malaysia classify entrepôt goods as simple imports and, after transshipment or processing, as simple Singapore-Malaysian exports. Thus Indonesian rubber imported by the United Kingdom via Singapore appears as exports to the United Kingdom on *both* the Indonesian and the Singapore-Malaysian export statistics. The apparent understatement of Indonesian exports to Singapore-Malaysia (as compared with the latter's imports from Indonesia) in table 2, therefore, is largely offset by overstatement of Indonesian exports to the United Kingdom (and perhaps to other ultimate consumers of Indonesian exports shipped via Singapore and other entrepôt ports).

This consideration shows that table 2 gives a badly inflated estimate of Indonesia's unrecorded exports to Singapore-Malaysia. According to calculations which Mrs. Richter has made for the period 1959–1963, Indonesia's recorded exports of rubber to this area averaged 152 000 tons a year as against corresponding import figures of 345 000 tons, and those to the United Kingdom 143 000 tons as against corresponding import figures of only 8000 tons; but there was little difference between the two figures for rubber shipped by Singapore-Malaysia to the United Kingdom. Two-thirds of Indonesia's apparently unrecorded exports of rubber to Singapore-Malaysia were thus accounted for by transit trade through this area to the United Kingdom.

Mrs. Richter's result, it should be noted, covers only physical shipments of rubber and so ignores the associated problem of undervaluation covered by the tables here. Nor does it cast direct doubt upon the result of table 1 because the double counting to which she draws attention necessarily cancels out in global estimates of Indonesia's unrecorded exports. But it does mean that table 2 is of little use, as it stands, for indicating the direction of this unrecorded trade. About all that it does is to strengthen the general impression that much of this trade, particularly physical smuggling (as distinct from undervaluation) is associated with Singapore, and to a lesser extent with Malaysia, and that some of it, even before confrontation, involved other neighbouring countries.

This perhaps appears more clearly from the figures for unrecorded imports which would be connected, to some extent, with physical smuggling on a quasi-barter basis. The estimates of table 2 for unrecorded imports from Singapore-Malaysia are only half the inflated estimates for unrecorded exports, and the corresponding proportion for the other Asian neighbours is nearer one-third.

3. Exports of major commodities

The global estimates of table 1 provide no breakdown of unrecorded exports by smuggling and undervaluation, nor by commodity, and go no further than 1962. In order both to obtain such a breakdown, and to carry estimates over the period of confrontation, a far riskier and more laborious method has to be used. Broadly speaking, it involves estimating smuggling as the difference between an assumed 'normal' export quantity and the recorded shipment, and estimating undervaluation by the difference between an appropriate foreign price and the recorded unit values applied to the recorded export quantity. The main risk is assuming 'normal' exports in such a disturbed period, and there are also acute difficulties in choosing appropriate world prices where products lack homogeneity and markets perfection. Nevertheless some such attempt has to be made for any quantitative perspective of this problem.

Estimates of possible smuggling and undervaluation are presented for the major export commodities in table 3. They are not to be taken literally as they stand because of various qualifications which will be mentioned in the text and taken into account when an attempt is made to reach conclusions from the evidence.

The most important commodity is rubber, two-thirds of which comes from

Table 3.
Possible unrecorded commodity exports, 1958–1962 and 1963–1966 (annual averages).

Commodity	Year	Quantities (thousands of tons)		Prices ($ per ton)			Value (millions of dollars)			
		Recorded (1)	Un-recorded (2)[a]	Unit value (3)	Foreign price (4)[b]	Difference (5)[c]	Smuggled (6)[d]	Under-valued (7)[e]	Total un-recorded (8)[f]	Total recorded (9)[a]
Rubber	1958–1962	674	76	531	577	46	49	31	80	333
	1963–1966	649	101	354	460	106	47	70	117	231
Copra	1958–1962	157	93	160	166	6	16	1	17	25
	1963–1966	125	126	125	174	49	22	7	28	17
Coffee	1958–1962	46	17	378	452	74	7	4	11	16
	1963–1966	83	3	274	562	288	1	22	23	27
Tobacco	1958–1962	18	3	1391	1442	51	5	1	6	25
	1963–1966	15	23	1451	1801	350	42	6	48	21
Tea	1958–1962	34	13	658	687	28	9	1	10	26
	1963–1966	30	39	445	663	218	26	6	32	16
Pepper	1958–1962	16	4	609	617	8	2	—	3	10
	1963–1966	21	—	617	643	26	—	—	—	13

[a] 'Normal' less recorded exports (volume)
'Normal': Rubber 750 000 tons
Copra 250 000 tons
Coffee (production) 30 000 tons
Tobacco (production) 50 000 tons
Tea (production) 32 000 tons
Pepper (production) 16 000 tons
Production figures for coffee, tobacco, tea and pepper have been obtained by extrapolating recorded production statistics for 1958–1960 on the basis of the volume indexes for estate and farm production (Bank Negara, 1968).

[b] Rubber: Thai unit value
Copra: Philippine unit value
Coffee: 90% of Uganda unit value
Tobacco: 110% of Greek unit value
Tea: 58% of Ceylon unit value as given in IMF (1966)
Pepper: Singapore wholesale price of black Lampong as given in United Nations (1968).

[c] Foreign price less unit value: (4)–(3).
[d] Unrecorded times foreign price: (2)×(4).
[e] Recorded volume times difference: (1)×(5).
[f] Smuggled plus undervalued: (6)+(7).

Sources: Cols. 1 and 9: Biro Pusat Statistik (BPS) (1961); BPS (1963); BPS (1964–1967).
Col. 3: Bank Negara (1960–1966).
Col. 4: IMF (1966), for rubber, copra, coffee, tobacco and tea; and United Nations (1968), for pepper.

Sumatra, and at least two-thirds of which is produced by smallholders. Nearly all the rubber produced is exported and, up to 1963, about one-third of recorded shipments went to Singapore and Penang. These two ports were particularly concerned with smallholders' rubber, which required cleaning, processing or grading, and much of it came from Sumatra and Kalimantan in small craft or coastal vessels (Richter, 1966, p. 31).

Recorded shipments of *rubber* reached a peak of 774 000 tons in 1951, and another peak of 777 000 tons in 1962, just prior to confrontation. In 1958 they were 660 000 tons, but unrecorded shipments in that year were estimated at 83 000 tons by the International Rubber Study Group, see Richter (1966, p. 34), so that total shipments may then have been 743 000 tons. Higgins, B. and Higgins, J. (1962), refer to 'large-scale smuggling amounting to perhaps a fifth of the total export'. A similar ratio is mentioned by the *Economic Survey of Asia and the Far East, 1963*, which says that 'it has been estimated, unofficial exports of rubber are more than one-quarter of official exports' (United Nations, 1964); this ratio, applied to the 1960–1961 average recorded shipment of 606 000 tons gives an estimate of 758 000 tons for total shipments. Richter (1966, p. 44), moreover, notes that '. . . Malaya had during 1964 roughly 120 000 tons more rubber available for sale than could be accounted for by recorded imports, production or carry-over stocks'; in that year Indonesia's recorded shipment was 627 000 tons. These various estimates thus converge to a figure of 750 000 tons for Indonesia's total annual export of rubber between 1958 and 1964, so that table 3 takes it as the 'normal' level, in spite of the likelihood that it may be somewhat too low in view of the peak figure for 1962.

This view has been questioned on the ground that the Indonesian rubber output was declining, and particularly that of estates which are thought to indulge in smuggling less than smallholders do, so that the assumption of a constant normal export must be wrong. Whatever may have been the situation before 1960 I find it hard to believe that there was any marked decline of output thereafter as official indexes of rubber production (admittedly imperfect) show, between 1960 and 1966, a rise of 15% for smallholders and a decline of only 1% for estates.

The variety of grades for rubber present a difficulty in deciding upon the appropriate foreign price for realisations of Indonesia's rubber shipments. It seems best here to take the unit value of Thai rubber exports as these also come from smallholders, and the two producing areas are not dissimilar in regard to this trade. Acceptance of the Thai unit value does not exaggerate Indonesia's realised price as, between 1960 and 1967, the Thai price was about 7% less than the New York price of RSS III after deduction of $50 a ton for freight (the value used for official estimates of the rubber 'overprice' under Indonesia's bonus export scheme). It should, however, be stressed that the measurement attempted here for rubber and the other commodities, too, is a gross price differential from which the costs of smuggling must be met. The measurements, that is, relate to Indonesia's loss of official export receipts rather than to the net returns to Indonesians who participate in unrecorded trade.

Between 1958 and 1962, table 3 indicates smuggled rubber as averaging 76 000 tons a year, or more than a tenth of recorded shipments. The value, at Thai prices, was $49 million and the corresponding average for undervaluation of declared exports $31 million. The combined average of $80 million was about one-quarter of the value of recorded rubber exports, but only two-fifths of the estimate for total unrecorded exports given by table 1. If this estimate is acceptable, the present result seems to be on the low, not the high, side in view of rubber's importance in Indonesian exports.

Both types of illegal trade appear, from table 3, to have increased during the period of confrontation. Smuggling appears to have risen by one-quarter to an annual average of 101 000 tons, or somewhat less than one-sixth of recorded shipments but, since rubber prices fell, had about the same average value at $47 million. Undervaluation appears to have doubled to $70 million, and faster growth would be expected here in view of the peculiar difficulties in keeping up the old transit trade with Singapore-Malaysia. Total unrecorded exports of rubber are thus given as $117 million, one-half of the recorded value. This estimate, however, is almost certainly too high because there were increasing transport difficulties over the period and some decline in the quality of rubber shipped; at the same time, there was an increasing gap between the world price and that received by illegal exporters. I do not know what allowance to make for these complications, but it seems a reasonably cautious conclusion that confrontation did not reduce overall, Indonesia's unrecorded trade in rubber.

Copra is the next most important export and practically all of it is supplied by smallholders. Sumatra produces more than a third of the crop and the remainder comes in roughly equal proportions from Java and Sulawesi. Exports of Sumatra copra went to Singapore and Penang, and supplies from Sulawesi and Kalimantan to the Philippines, East Malaysia or Hong Kong. Most of the crop is used within Indonesia as average production between 1955 and 1959 was recorded at 1 075 000 tons and average exports at only 215 000 tons. But this figure for exports is too low because the corresponding average for 1951–1954 was 375 000 tons and the official 1961 export was 247 000 tons. It seems quite conservative, therefore, to take the 'normal' export as 250 000 tons, and reasonable to regard it as steady because official figures for copra output show little variation after 1958. Using this norm, table 3 finds that smuggling averaged 93 000 tons a year from 1958 to 1962, and recorded shipments 157 000 tons. For 1962 the figures were 140 000 tons for smuggling and 110 000 tons for recorded shipments, so that our estimate is in line with an observation (United Nations, 1964), that the ratio of unofficial to official copra exports was near to unity.

The best measure of realised price is the unit value of copra exports from the neighbouring Philippines. (This unit value has been close to the London price of copra less \$30 a ton for transport used in official Indonesian calculations for the overprice for copra.) Applied to table 3, it leads to an estimate of \$16 million a year for smuggling between 1958 and 1962, and of \$1 million a year for undervaluation of declared copra exports, i.e. \$17 million for the unrecorded export as against \$25 million for the recorded export.

Table 3 shows a drastic change in these illegal exports over the period of confrontation; whereas the recorded export fell to \$17 million a year, smuggling appears to have reached \$22 million a year and undervaluation rose to \$7 million. This suggests that more than three-fifths of copra exports escaped official recording if not official knowledge. But the estimate for the confrontation period is probably also exaggerated through neglect of transport difficulties and possible decline of quality. Even so, we would have to reduce this estimate for unrecorded copra exports from \$28 million to \$17 million in order to assert that there was no increase of illegal trade in copra between 1962 and 1966.

Most of Indonesia's *coffee* exports come from smallholders in Sumatra, although plantations in Java provide just under one-quarter of the recorded export. The official figures show an average production of 70 000 tons a year between 1955 and 1959, 41 000 tons of which was exported and 29 000 tons consumed locally. Assuming that domestic consumption remained at this level, table 3 puts 'normal' exports at recorded production (average 1958–1962) of 89 000 tons, less 30 000 tons for domestic consumption. This is a very rough assumption but has to serve for want of a better one[3]. It leads, as table 3 shows, to an estimate of smuggling as averaging 17 000 tons a year between 1958 and 1962, or a bit more than one-third of the recorded shipment.

There is also difficulty about choosing an appropriate world price for Indonesia's coffee. Here we take 90% of the unit value of Uganda's coffee export, because this was the ratio between the two unit values between 1955 and 1959 and, from 1960 to 1967, the same relation held approximately between the Singapore wholesale price of API coffee and the Uganda unit value. We have then, an estimate of \$7 million a year for smuggling of Indonesian coffee between 1958 and 1962, and one of \$4 million a year for undervaluation of the declared export. These estimates compare with \$16 million a year for the average value of the recorded export.

[3] The calculations in the text assume that the official statistics for production of smallholder crops and of domestic consumption are both independently estimated. At the time of writing it has not been possible to ascertain how far this has been the case between 1955 and 1959.

Smuggling and undervaluation appear to have risen sharply in 1963, when they came to around $37 million or double the recorded export. Thereafter smuggling appears, from table 3, to have declined to very small proportions, perhaps because Indonesia was being allowed, and using, more favourable quotas under the International Coffee Agreement made in 1962 and finally ratified in 1964. The recorded export rose from an average of 46 000 tons in 1958–1962 to one of 83 000 tons in 1963–1966. But the position is obscure regarding undervaluation, given by table 3 as $22 million a year in this later period, only $5 million short of the recorded export value. Here, too, there could well have been some decline in quality, and Indonesia may have had to cut the export price so severely, in order to push bigger official exports into new as well as old markets, that table 3 gives an exaggerated price differential for estimating undervaluation. We should, however, have to halve it in order to make unrecorded coffee exports in 1963–1966 no greater than they were in 1958–1962.

Tobacco is about as valuable an export as coffee to Indonesia, and comes very largely from smallholders most of whom are in Java, which supplies four-fifths of the recorded export. Examination of the official statistics for 1955–1959 suggests an average domestic consumption of 50 000 tons a year. This figure, accordingly, is deducted from the production statistics in order to estimate unrecorded shipments of Indonesian tobacco in table 3. The estimate is on the modest side, giving smuggling as little more than 3000 tons a year between 1958 and 1962, or less than one-fifth of the recorded shipment.

There is again difficulty in selecting an appropriate world price. The unit value of the Greek export seems to be nearest, but over 1958–1960 averaged only 90% of the Indonesian unit value. Table 3 therefore, takes as the world price from 1958 to 1966, 110% of the Greek unit value. We then obtain $5 million as the average estimate for smuggling between 1958 and 1962, and a mere $1 million for undervaluation, as against nearly $25 million for the recorded export. These estimates for unrecorded trade may seem rather low. But those for 1963–1966 seem far too high – over $42 million a year for smuggling and $6 million for undervaluation as against $21 million for recorded exports.

Tea is produced in roughly equal proportions by estates and smallholders, and most of it in Java. Here, on the basis of 1955–1959 data, it has been decided to allow an average of 32 000 tons a year for domestic consumption, and to estimate smuggling as the difference between official figures for tea production less 32 000 tons and recorded shipments. This estimate, probably too conservative, points to smuggling of 13 000 tons a year for 1958–1962, as compared with an average recorded export of 34 000 tons.

The foreign price adopted is 58% of Ceylon's unit value, as this was the average ratio of the Indonesian unit value to that of Ceylon between 1955 and 1959. It leads to an estimate of $9 million a year for the value of smuggling between 1958 and 1962, and $1 million for undervaluation of declared tea exports, making the unrecorded export two-fifths of the recorded. Here, too, there was a big apparent increase of the unrecorded export between 1963 and 1966 – to $26 million a year for smuggling and to $6 million for undervaluation, raising the ratio of the unrecorded to the recorded export to over 150 %. But this is an exaggeration, as Indonesia faced considerable difficulties in marketing tea, legally or illegally, after confrontation lost it the British market which had previously taken one-third of the recorded export.

Pepper, wholly a smallholders' crop, subject to wide swings of output according to climatic changes, is largely produced in South Sumatra. Average production over the period 1955–1959 was 33 400 tons, recorded exports 17 800 tons, and domestic consumption 16 000 tons a year. Unrecorded exports are then the official estimates of production less 16 000 tons for domestic consumption and less recorded exports, although the production estimates must be subject to a very large margin of error. Our resulting estimate for unrecorded exports of pepper is 4000 tons a year for the period 1958–1962, or one-third of the average recorded export, but is exceptionally uncertain.

The foreign price is a good deal better, as we have figures for the wholesale price of Black Lampong at Singapore. Applied to the quantity estimates, it gives smuggling an average value of over $2 million between 1958 and 1963, and undervaluation as being negligible.

Palm Oil is the remaining agricultural export of any importance, and is wholly produced by estates in North Sumatra. A comparison of the Indonesian unit value here with the Singapore wholesale price gives no indication of any significant undervaluation. Nor does a comparison of export and production figures point to regular or substantial smuggling of palm oil. There is, perhaps, an indication that something like 16 000 tons may have been smuggled in 1958 when the Sumatran rebellion broke out, and lesser quantities in 1962 and 1963. But the indications are too uncertain for use.

4. Conclusions

Bringing these results together, we obtain from table 3 an estimate of $127 million a year for Indonesia's unrecorded exports of these six primary commodities between 1958 and 1963 against a figure of $435 million for their recorded export. This gives a somewhat higher ratio for illegal trade than did table 1, but is $70 million below the conservative upper estimate for total unrecorded exports (although only $17 million below the lower estimate) given earlier. Other agricultural exports have, of course, to be considered: of which palm kernels, sugar, hard fibres, kapok, tapioca products, cinchona bark and spices have been the most important. It is difficult to attempt for them any similar estimate of unrecorded trade because their individual contributions are so small and relevant data are incomplete. The combined annual average of their recorded export was $12 million for 1958–1962 and $18 million for 1963–1966. If we could suppose, in the light of table 1, that another quarter of them were smuggled or undervalued, the estimate for unrecorded agricultural exports would rise to $130 million for 1958–1962, only $14 million less than the lower estimate in table 1, but $67 million less than its upper estimate.

Various interpretations of these results are possible. I do not, myself, see much reason for doubting that the upper estimate of $197 million in table 1 is low because of the assumption that all partner countries fully recorded their Indonesian imports. For the same reasons, the assumptions used for table 3 may be unduly cautious, leading to underestimates, at least for the period 1958–1962. An acceptable conclusion could be that in this period, Indonesia's unrecorded exports were probably not less than $140 million and may have exceeded $200 million. Smuggling may have accounted for two-thirds of this illegal trade, and undervaluation of declared exports for the remainder. On the commodity side, rubber could have accounted for over one-half of total unrecorded exports and copra for over one-eighth, with lesser proportions attributable to other exports.

We have seen how difficult it is to carry such estimates over the disturbed period of confrontation; table 1 is incomplete for this purpose and table 3 becomes more dubious. Its estimates for rubber and copra, the two most important commodities here, indicate no great change in smuggling but a sharp increase of undervaluation which might have raised their joint unrecorded export from $97 million a year to $145 million, while their joint recorded export fell from $358 million to $248 million. Transport difficulties, some decline in quality, and other factors mentioned above make it hard to accept such a figure for unrecorded exports of rubber, copra, and other commodities after 1962. I am content to draw the cautious conclusion that unrecorded exports probably increased during confrontation, mainly because of greater resort to practices of undervaluation.

References

Bank Negara, 1960–1966, Indonesian Financial Statistics (Indonesia), various issues.
Bank Negara, 1968, Indonesian Financial Statistics (Indonesia), Nov., 82–83.
Biro Pusat Statistik, 1961, Statistical Pocketbook of Indonesia (Djakarta).
Biro Pusat Statistik, 1963, Statistical Pocketbook of Indonesia (Djakarta).
Biro Pusat Statistik, 1964–1967, Statistical Pocketbook of Indonesia (Djakarta).

Higgins, B. and J. Higgins, 1962, Indonesia: The Crisis of the Millstones, 112.
International Bank for Reconstruction and Development and International Development Association, 1968, Economic Development of Indonesia I, Feb., 18.
International Monetary Fund and International Bank for Reconstruction and Development, 1958–1962, Direction of Trade.
International Monetary Fund and International Bank for Reconstruction and Development, 1963–1967, Direction of Trade.
International Monetary Fund, 1966, International Financial Statistics (Washington, D.C.).
Naya, S. and T. Morgan, 1967, The accuracy of international trade data: the case of Southeast Asian countries, in: Journal of the American Statistical Association, 1969; ch. 8 in this volume.
Richter, H. V., 1966, Indonesia's share in the entrepôt trade of Malaya and Singapore prior to confrontation, The Malayan Economic Review XI, no. 2, Oct.
United Nations, 1964, Economic Survey of Asia and the Far East (Bangkok), 170.
United Nations, 1966, Yearbook of International Trade Statistics.
United Nations, 1968, Economic Survey of Asia and the Far East (Bangkok).
United Nations, 1968, Far Eastern Economic Review Yearbook (Hong Kong), 201.

Chapter 12

PROBLEMS OF ASSESSING UNRECORDED TRADE*

H. V. RICHTER

1. Introduction

This paper is designed to supplement Professor Simkin's article on 'Indonesia's Unrecorded Trade' to clarify and bring up to date some aspects of my earlier estimates of Indonesia's trade with Singapore and Malaysia to which Professor Simkin makes reference (Richter, 1966).

There seems little doubt that Professor Simkin is right in stating that a good deal of unrecorded foreign trade has been carried on for many years in Indonesia[1]. Attempts to measure the quantities likely to be involved are, however, fraught with difficulties; those to measure values still more so. His pioneering effort to measure unrecorded trade with some precision is thus most valuable, as presenting a basis for discussion.

Professor Simkin seeks to establish likely levels of Indonesian unrecorded trade by alternative methods. The first consists in confronting the trade accounts of Indonesia with those of its partners, suitably adjusted, and so establishing discrepancies shown in the total value of trade. The second is to compare the volume of recorded exports of individual commodities with estimates of 'normal' export volumes defined as the difference between estimates of production and domestic consumption, and then to value any discrepancies shown at world prices. This second method Professor Simkin uses to demonstrate, for example, the possibility that over 100 000 tons of unrecorded rubber was shipped out of Indonesia annually between 1963 and 1966.

* Editor's note: A section on Indonesia's trade with Sino-Soviet countries has been omitted from the original article.

[1] By unrecorded trade, Professor Simkin means both smuggling and private trade which is recorded at false values. In this article the term will be used more broadly at times to cover, in addition, official trade which is not recorded in the returns.

2. Estimating exports from production

To deal first briefly with his latter method of equating smuggling roughly with the difference between normal production on the one hand and recorded exports plus domestic consumption on the other. Such a method must necessarily rely to a large extent on official estimates of production, consumption and exports for some historic period, in order to establish what is 'normal'. It is difficult, however, to feel confident that Indonesian official data are yet strong enough to bear the weight of evidence placed upon them. This is especially so when dealing with the smallholder sector from which the bulk of supplies for smuggling come. It has not been possible to discover how consumption estimates, which often remain unchanged for many years, are arrived at. Smallholder production, apart from the eight main food crops, is rarely estimated in the field, and data are usually based partly on deliveries to factories and estates for processing (tea, tobacco) and partly on exports plus an allowance for domestic use.

Rubber production may be taken as an example. According to the International Rubber Study Group (IRSG), 'Figures for estate production represent reported production; no production figures are available for smallholdings. Total production is taken as equivalent to total net exports plus an allowance for internal consumption' (IRSG, RSB, table 10). It should be noted that in calculating production in this way, the IRSG in some years (1949–1960, 1966–1967) uses as a base 'net exports' as adjusted by the group to include its own unofficial allowance for non-reported exports and in other years (1961–1965) uses reported exports, unadjusted. Nugroho cites two alternative Indonesian official estimates of smallholder rubber production calculated by similar methods, one of which was dropped in 1960 'for serious incompleteness of coverage' (Biro Pusat Statistik, 1968, p. 246).

Similar difficulties are encountered in interpreting export returns, especially as the Bureau of Statistics and the IRSG have used varying methods from year to year in deriving their estimates. Extracts from both sets of figures are given in table 1. It will be seen that during some years the IRSG somewhat arbitrarily adjusts Indonesian official export returns to take into account unreported exports (a useful service that it has performed since smuggling became significant during the Stevenson restriction scheme of the 1920s). Again, as explained in note *j* to table 1, the *Statistical Pocketbook 1964–1967* appears inadvertently to have added 117 000 tons to recorded exports of 1962, bringing the total up to the 777 000 tons cited by Professor Simkin as a peak. Similarly Professor Simkin was perhaps misled by IRSG 1958 returns, for the 660 000 tons he cites for recorded exports already includes the 83 000 tons IRSG estimate for unrecorded shipments, so that it is counted twice in his total of 743 000. Nor must this 1958 83 000 ton figure be taken as the IRSG normal estimate for unrecorded rubber shipments. This was

Table 1.
Indonesian rubber exports, 1949–1968.

	International Rubber Study Group (thousands of long tons, dry weight)				Conversion net exports (m.kg)	Indonesian official returns		
	Reported exports[a]	Adjustments[b]	Net exports[c]			Biro Pusat Statistik[d]	Nugroho[e] dry gross (m.kg)	
1949	390.3	+31.7	422.1	=	428.9	n.a.		
1950	659.4	+32.3	691.7	=	702.8	677.8		
1951	743.2	+50.6	793.8	=	806.5	754.9		
1952	743.2	+ 5.9	749.1	=	761.1	754.8		
1953	653.9	+17.1	674.0	=	684.8	674.6		
1954	698.7	+30[f]	728.7	=	740.4	723.1		
1955	691.8	+30[f]	721.1	=	732.7	707.3		
1956	638.7	+30[f]	668.7	=	679.4	659.9		
1957	636.9	+30[f]	666.5	=	677.2	646.4		
1958	566.6	+83[g]	649.6[k]	=	660.0	577.0		
1959	678.9	+30[f]	681.3[h]	=	692.2	692.2		
1960	547.5	+30[f]	577.3	=	586.5	556.0	577.6	556.0
1961	666.5	—	666.5	=	677.2	656.7	681.1	656.7
1962	649.8[i]	—	649.8	=	660.2	660.2[j]	691.9	660.2
1963	552.1	—	552.1	=	561.0	581.1	582.6	560.9
1964	617.5	—	617.5	=	627.4	627.4	659.1	641.5
1965	683.7	—	683.7	=	694.7	707.9	707.3	707.3
1966	653[l]	+27	680	=	691	679.8		
1967	623[l]	+103	726[l]	=	738	642[m]		
1968	713[l]	n.a.	717[l]	=	728	728[m]		

[a] Data in this column from IRSG (RSB, various issues, table 10), 'Current Rubber Position in Indonesia', taken from official Indonesian returns of exports by country of destination.

[b] 1949–1953: Adjusted by the IRSG by the difference between Malayan imports from Indonesia and Indonesian reported exports to Malaya. 1954–1960: IRSG adjustments. 1966–1967: Adjustment made by author (difference between tables 3 and 10 of IRSG (RSB).

[c] IRSG (RSB, table 3) (world) 'Net Exports'.

[d] 1950–1960, net weight, from Biro Pusat Statistik (1963). 1963–1966, gross weight, from Biro Pusat Statistik (1968, p. 227). Curiously enough, net figures given in the 1963 *Pocketbook* are identical with gross figures in the 1964–1967 *Pocketbook* for the years that overlap, i.e. 1960 and 1961.

[e] Biro Pusat Statistik (1969, pp. 402, 421).

[f] 2500 tons per month included for smallholder rubber.

[g] The 1958 increase was presumably due to the Sumatran rebellion.

[h] Figures do not add in the original.

[i] Revised figures for total reported exports, May 1964, issue. Details of exports by destination remain unrevised at 637 627.

[j] This figure is from Biro Pusat Statistik (1963, p. 145). In the 1964–1967 issue, this figure was erroneously altered to 777.2 m.kg, the subtotal for Germany apparently having been transposed from 13.2 m.kg to 130.2 m.kg, and this 117 000 tons discrepancy was carried through into the total. Value figures were identical in both issues.

[k] Revised estimate, thought to be incomplete.

[l] Provisional estimate.

[m] Biro Pusat Statistik as quoted by IBRD.

the year of the Sumatran rebellion. For years immediately prior to and after 1958 the IRSG allowance for unrecorded shipments was 30 000 tons a year.

3. Complications in comparing partners' trade accounts

The other method used by Professor Simkin, that of confronting trade accounts, in practice runs into a number of snags. To turn first to the problem of differing systems of trade classification adopted by the various trade partners. Any effort to estimate data is confused by the broad interpretation adopted by Indonesia (varying at different periods), when classifying exports by country of final consumption and imports by country of production. Thus products which are offloaded at Singapore may at times be recorded by Indonesia as an export to (or import from) a third country, which in turn recognises the goods as an import from (or export to) Singapore.

To obtain a true picture of Indonesia's trade with individual partner countries, overstated Indonesian recorded trade with the industrial countries of final consumption and production must therefore be offset against under-recorded trade with countries of immediate consignment. Thus, as Professor Simkin points out, Indonesian unrecorded trade cannot be measured by confronting its trade accounts individually or regionally with those of its trade partners, especially where dealing with commodities which flow through entrepôt centres.

4. Differing systems of recording rubber

These technicalities are illustrated by drawing on the statistics of the rubber trade between Britain, Malaya[2] and Indonesia in the period prior to confrontation. Figures of volume traded (table 2) show that there was an annual average Malayan surplus of 193 400 tons of rubber imported from Indonesia over recorded Indonesian exports to Malaya for the years 1959–1963. But table 3 shows that during the same period the combined recorded exports by Indonesia and Malaya of rubber to the U.K., exceeded U.K. imports from these two countries, as given in the United Kingdom Trade Accounts, by an annual average of 130 800 tons. In other words, it would seem that during this period some two-thirds of the Indonesian–Malayan discrepancy in the rubber trade was accounted for by an

[2] Up to 1966 the present West Malaysian and Singapore issued joint trade statistics for 'Malaya' are taken as one unit. Inter-trade between them was excluded from these returns and trade with present East Malaysia treated as foreign trade. The bulk of trade between 'Malaya' and Indonesia was conducted by Singapore for rubber and most other products, except for tin.

Table 2.
Recorded Malayan imports from Indonesia and recorded Indonesian exports to Malaya of raw rubber (thousands of long tons).

	Malayan[a] imports	Indonesian exports	Malayan import surplus[b]
1957	301.9	182.5	119.4
1958	348.3	176.2	172.1
1959	372.4	165.1	207.5
1960	322.5	170.2	152.3
1961	350.0	182.8	167.2
1962	398.1	166.4	231.7
1963	282.9	74.5	208.4
Average			
1959–1963	345.2	151.8	193.4
1964	4.2	—	4.2
1965	—	—	—
1966	5.4	—	5.4
1967	14.8	73.1	−58.3
1968	8.6	360.6[c]	−352.0

[a] 'Malaya' refers to the present West Malaysia and Singapore taken as one unit.
[b] No account is taken of time lags for shipping, which should not greatly affect the average of several years.
[c] This is an annual rate, based on actual exports, January–November, of 330 600 tons.

Source: Malaya 1957–1963, Statistics Department 1958 —; 1964–8, Department of Statistics 1963 —. Indonesia IRSG (RSB).

Indonesian overstatement of trade with the U.K. alone. Examination of the trade returns of other industrial countries shows a similar excess of recorded Indonesian exports over the industrial countries' imports from Indonesia, suggesting that overstatement occurred there, too.

Since October 1963, the method used for tracing this statistical discrepancy for the period 1959–1963 has no longer been available because Singapore ceased to record any imports from Indonesia[3] (rubber imports shown in table 2 for 1964–1968 were recorded by Malaysia). Curiously enough, this Singapore practice of concealment has been continued even after the ending of confrontation. It can, however, be demonstrated that Singapore/Malaysia imported rubber, presumably from Indonesia, on a large scale. In 1966, I published calculations up to 1965, comparing total supplies available in Singapore/Malaysia from domestic production, recorded imports and decline in stocks, with uses of rubber in exports,

[3] This means that the 'Malaya' Trade Statistics, referred to in footnote 2 above, are to this extent incomplete.

Table 3.
Recorded exports of Indonesia and Malaya[a] to U.K. and U.K. imports of raw rubber (thousands of long tons).

	Recorded exports to U.K. from			U.K. imports from			Discrepancy[b] (surplus exports = double counting?)
	Malaya	Indo-nesia	Total	Malaya	Indo-nesia	Total	
1959	159.3	218.8	378.1	161.0	9.3	170.3	207.8
1960	164.4	67.4	231.8	155.9	8.5	164.4	64.4
1961	170.6	52.0	222.6	183.6	11.9	195.5	27.1
1962	135.8	180.6	316.4	140.6	7.5	148.1	168.3
1963	125.1	190.7	315.8	127.4	4.9	132.3	183.5
Average 1959–1963			292.9			162.1	130.8
1964	122.2	33.7	155.9	122.1	11.1	133.2	22.7
1965	110.2	15.2	125.4	116.1	14.9	131.0	−5.6
1966	99.2	43.7	142.9	102.0	22.5	124.5	18.4
1967	93.9	76.7	170.6	118.1	20.2	138.3	32.3
Average 1964–1967			148.7			131.7	17.0

[a] Malaya refers to the present West Malaysia and Singapore.
[b] No account is taken of time lag for shipping, which should not greatly affect the average of several years.

Sources: Exports to U.K. by Malaya and Indonesia: IRSG (RSB), U.K. imports: HMSO (1959–1967).

domestic consumption and increase in stocks (Richter, 1966, p. 43). These showed an unexplained surplus of supplies of 122 000 tons in 1964. In table 4 this calculation has been brought up to date, showing unexplained Singapore/Malaysia supplies, almost certainly mainly imported from Indonesia, of 127 000 tons in 1966, 307 000 tons in 1967 and 425 000 tons in 1968.

Indonesia resumed recording exports to Singapore/Malaysia in 1967 and between January and November 1968 recorded exports there of 330 600 tons of rubber, a larger recorded amount than at any time since the early 1950s, and 50% of Indonesia's total recorded rubber shipments. By deducting recorded Indonesian exports from unexplained Singapore/Malaysian supplies, one can derive a rough guide to Indonesian exports to Singapore/Malaysia which were not recorded as going to these markets 1964–1968. This calculation is shown in the last row of table 4.

Table 5 brings together the evidence on statistical discrepancies in relation to Indonesian exports of rubber between 1959 and 1968. (It should be stressed that

Table 4.
Supplies and use of West Malaysian and Singapore rubber, 1964–1969 (thousands of long tons).

	1964	1965	1966	1967	1968	1969 (Jan.–June)
Supplies						
Production	818	861	927	935	1046	525
Stocks[a]	113	134	115	146	185	160
Recorded imports						
a. from Indonesia	4	—	5	15	9	5
b. from other countries	71	105	102	79	76	49
Total	1006	1100	1149	1175	1316	739
Use						
Exports	982	1024	1115	1280	1562	860
Stocks[a]	134	115	146	185	160	125
Domestic use	12	15	15	17	19	8[b]
Total	1128	1154	1276	1482	1741	993
Discrepancy						
(unexplained supplies)	122	54	127	307	425	254
Recorded imports from Indonesia	4	—	5	15	9	5
Total possible imports from Indonesia, of which:	126	54	132	322	434	259
a. recorded by Indonesia as exports to Malaya/Singapore	—	—	—	73	361	n.a.
b. unrecorded Indonesian exports to Malaya/Singapore	126	54	132	249	73	n.a.

[a] Stocks in the *supply* sector refer to stocks at the beginning of the year and those in the *use* sector to stocks at the end of the year.
[b] West Malaysia only.

Source: Supplies and use, IRSG (RSB, various issues).

the calculation is not only in its nature shaky but also takes no account of shipping time lags, losses in processing and other such complications.) For what it is worth, however, it suggests that much the larger part of the discrepancy in the Indonesian/Malayan rubber trade in the years before 1963 is due to overstatement elsewhere, mainly in trade with the U.K., but perhaps also with other countries. The same may be true also for the years after 1964, although here the share of U.K. trade is certainly much smaller and the whole calculation more uncertain.

5. Measuring recorded values of all products

When value rather than volume figures are considered, whether for rubber or for

Table 5.
Indonesian rubber trade discrepancies, 1959–1968 (thousands of long tons).

	Understatement of exports to Malaya	Overstatement of exports to U.K.	Residual (over-statement with other countries?)
1959	207.5	207.8	−0.3
1960	152.3	67.4	84.9
1961	167.2	27.1	140.1
1962	231.7	168.3	63.4
1963	208.4	183.5	24.9
Average 1959–1963	193.4	130.8	62.6
1964	126	22.7	103.3
1965	54	−5.6	59.6
1966	132	18.4	113.6
1967	249	32.3	216.7
1968	73	n.a.	n.a.

Sources: Col. 1: 1959–1963, table 2; 1964–1968, table 4.
Col. 2: table 3.

any other commodity, two further complications must be taken into account; the fact that Indonesian exports are often valued at check prices rather than at realised prices; and that value is added on transhipped or transformed goods in the entrepôt centres[4].

A similar accounting discrepancy can creep into individual trade accounts through Indonesia's practice, since 1947, of treating its shipments to its own free ports of Riau and Sabang as exports (because foreign currencies circulate there). Between 1958 and 1962, the period covered by Professor Simkin's table 2, Indonesian exports to Riau amounted to an average of only $14.4 million a year, less than 2% of total exports. Their exclusion from his table thus creates only a minor discrepancy compared to the figures he cites of an annual average of $266 million for recorded Indonesian exports to Asian countries in the region. However, any study of the regional pattern of trade during the following few years would have to include Indonesian exports to Riau, since they rose significantly. They reached a peak of $58 million in 1965, possibly because Riau was used to put an acceptable

[4] Value added in Singapore entrepôt on all goods coming from or going to Indonesia prior to confrontation has been estimated at over $70 million a year, of which at least half was added in processing, mainly of rubber, coffee and spices, see Richter (1966, pp. 39–43), in which calculations are based mainly on data from IBRD (1963).

label on to continuing shipments to Singapore during times of stress[5]. Indonesian products transhipped to world markets via Riau or consigned via Riau to Singapore might appear on the industrial country's import returns as coming either from Indonesia or from Singapore[6].

This problem of diverse systems of recording the destination and origin of goods traded applies equally to Indonesian imports. Textiles originating in Japan, for example, and imported via Singapore, would be classified as imports from Japan by Indonesia, but as exports to Indonesia by Singapore. The discrepancy between the trade accounts of the regional partners, shown in Professor Simkin's table 2, cannot therefore, as he admits, be used to establish the degree of unrecorded trade, either on the import or export side.

6. Global trade comparisons

Logically, differences arising out of alternative methods of recording trade flowing through entrepôt centres should disappear when trade is examined globally. Any remaining discrepancies could then be equated roughly with unrecorded trade (i.e. trade smuggled or falsely valued) as Professor Simkin does in his table 1, after making due allowances for freight costs and so on. Such a global confrontation of trade accounts he shows to reveal discrepancies ranging between $96 and $240 million a year between Indonesia's recorded trade and that of its world partners between 1958 and 1962, the Indonesian deficit being roughly equally large when comparing both its import and export returns with those of its partners.

When global estimates of trade are examined, however, a number of other difficulties in the official returns arise. On the Indonesian import side probably the most significant is that goods imported by the armed forces, imports of military goods and certain ships are excluded from the import returns[7] (United Nations, 1967), whereas they usually, but by no means always, appear in the export returns of the country of origin. Indonesia is thought to have bought, under military credits, some $600 million worth of military equipment during the years of the Sukarno regime; $520 million from the U.S.S.R., according to an unofficial Indonesian estimate for Soviet military credit used in 1960–1962 (FEER, 1967),

[5] According to Biro Pusat Statistik (1963—), shipments to Riau and Sabang were 2.4% of total export value in 1963, 3.8% in 1964 and 8.5% in 1965. For 1966 data are given only for Sabang, 0.6%.

[6] Shipments of tin, tin ore and bauxite produced in Riau are included in Indonesian exports, but Riau exports of other products, such as food-stuffs to Singapore, are excluded from Indonesian returns.

[7] The United Nations series, in rupiah, are the same as those used in the IMF *Direction of Trade*.

and $69 million from the U.S.A., given as the total of military assistance between 1946 and 1965 (U.S.A.I.D., 1967), and fairly small sums from other East and West European suppliers[8]. Only part of any such sum would, however, have to be taken into account in calculating global discrepancies of trade accounts. This is mainly because, as far as can be discovered, only a small share of Soviet military shipments were included in their trade returns, so that there are offsetting omissions on both sides of a global balance sheet.

Foreign suppliers of goods to the Indonesian forces record such exports in diverse ways, although all would classify non-military goods so purchased (trucks, cloth and so on) as normal exports. Treatment of strictly military supplies, however, differs. The U.S. includes the value of all goods, against grant or credit, military 'hardware' or otherwise, in the total of exports to each country, although certain commodities might not be separately identified. This is also the practice of Britain and most other Western countries.

Again, recorded Indonesian exports may not always be identifiable as imports elsewhere. Indonesian 'special category' exports, such as bunker fuels, occasionally assume importance, as in 1962, when they amounted to $78.5 million, or 11% of recorded DOT exports.

7. Summary

The various factors discussed above, inadequacies of official production and consumption data, differences in partners' recording systems, omissions from official trade returns and so on, make the task of the private research worker trying to assess with any precision the total value of Indonesia's foreign trade over the past decade difficult if not impossible. Nevertheless the alternative methods which Professor Simkin has used to estimate unrecorded trade might well be utilised by the Indonesian authorities themselves to form some judgement on the likely size of the foreign exchange leakage through smuggling and falsification of values. They presumably already have access to some of the missing data, imports for military authorities, for example, and the real destination of recorded shipments. Moreover the methods proposed by Professor Simkin to measure unrecorded

[8] Some sources put the total of military credits by communist bloc countries to Indonesia during the years 1960–1962 at nearly $1000 million. This is certainly an overstatement of actual supplies obtained by Indonesia. According to the IMF, $233 million of military credits by the U.S.S.R. were cancelled in 1967 as having remained unused. No information is available on supplies under military credits said to have been obtained by Indonesia from other European countries during 1960–1962, but such evidence as there is suggests that they were not very substantial.

trade should in future become more practicable generally, since the obscurities of the past decade are lessening. As things are at present, however, the general impression arising out of the present study is that the methods used by Professor Simkin may result in a substantial overestimate of the volume and value of Indonesia's unrecorded (private) trade because they cannot take sufficiently into account overlappings and omissions in official data of Indonesia and of its trade partners.

References

Biro Pusat Statistik, 1963, Statistical Pocketbook of Indonesia 1957–1963 (Djakarta).
Biro Pusat Statistik, 1963 —, Ekspor (Djakarta), annual.
Biro Pusat Statistik, 1968, Statistical Pocketbook of Indonesia 1964–1967 (Djakarta).
Biro Pusat Statistik, undated c. 1969, Indonesia, Facts and Figures (Djakarta).
Department of Statistics, 1963 —, Monthly Statistical Bulletin of West Malaysia (Kuala Lumpur), monthly.
Far Eastern Economic Review (FEER), 1967, 3 Sept. (Hong Kong), weekly.
H.M.S.O., Annual Statement of Trade of the United Kingdom (London), annual.
International Bank for Reconstruction and Development, 1963, Report on the Economic Aspects of Malaysia (Kuala Lumpur).
International Rubber Study Group, Rubber Statistical Bulletin (RSB), (London), monthly.
Richter, H. V., 1966, Indonesia's share in the entrepôt trade of Malaya and Singapore prior to confrontation, Malayan Economic Review, Oct.
Statistics Department, 1958 —, Malaya, External Trade Statistics (State of Singapore and Federation of Malaya), (Singapore), annual.
United Nations, 1967, Yearbook of International Trade Statistics, 389.
United States Agency of International Development, undated, c. 1967, U.S. Economic Assistance to Indonesia 1946–1965 (mimeo).

Chapter 13

TARIFFS AND SMUGGLING IN INDONESIA

Richard N. COOPER

1. Introduction

Smuggling was allegedly rife in Indonesia in the late sixties. With its 30 000 miles of coastline, its proximity to the great entrepôt centers of Singapore and Hong Kong, and its extensive ties of family and finance between Indonesian Chinese and Chinese elsewhere in Southeast Asia, smuggling would seem to be exceptionally easy there. But smuggling is an illegal activity, not lightly undertaken if it is not lucrative as well as easy. Smuggling was made attractive in Indonesia by the extraordinarily high tariffs (up to 300 percent) levied on many imports, combined with lax and corruptible enforcement. This combination, which can be found to a lesser degree in many developing countries, meant that an inspection of Indonesia's economic *policies*, and especially its tariff and tax policies, offered little guide to what was actually happening in Indonesia's economy. High statutory tariffs do affect economic behavior, but not necessarily in the intended direction. Indonesia's high tariffs neither protected Indonesia's industry nor produced tariff revenues commensurate with their height. Instead, they induced smuggling.

2. Types of smuggling

The notion of 'smuggling' conjures up images of smugglers' lairs and small boats operating stealthily in the night. The dictionary defines smuggling as 'clandestinely importing dutiable goods without paying the customs'. Boats landing quietly in the night constitute only one form of smuggling, however. For purposes of analyzing evasion of import duties in Indonesia, it is useful to distinguish four types of smuggling, or methods of evasion of import duties.

First, imports may not be recorded by customs officials. This can arise either because they are landed outside the official ports of entry, or because they are moved covertly with or without the complicity of customs officials through the official ports of entry. The latter possibility is especially important for types of goods that are large and require the specialized equipment (e.g. cranes) that is available only in major ports. But surveillance may be sufficiently lax that facilities may be used without leading to a record of the imports, and without payment of duty. (We call this category Type I smuggling.)

Second, goods may come through the customs post, but be falsely declared as to value. When tariffs are high, there is an incentive to *under*-invoice imports so as to reduce their dutiable value. Extensive exchange controls on payments to foreigners, e.g. on remittances of profits or repatriation of capital by foreign-owned firms, creates an incentive in the opposite direction, to *over*-invoice imports in order to export funds illegally. But Indonesia, unusual among developing countries, had virtually no controls on the transfer of funds across the foreign exchanges, so this incentive was absent except for foreign investors who wanted to exaggerate their equity investment in the country. The tariff-induced incentives to under-invoice, on the other hand, were powerful.

Third, goods may come through the customs post but be falsely declared with regard to their nature (e.g. automobiles declared as tractors) or to their quality (e.g. silk goods declared as cotton goods – and possibly wrapped in cotton goods), so as to lower the applicable duty. This type can be called 'misclassification'.

Fourth, goods may come through the customs post properly declared, but the duties actually assessed are below those that are legally applicable. We call this 'under-assessment'.

Needless to say, the probability of success in using these various forms of evasion depends on the degree of complicity or the gullibility of the customs service, with these attributes becoming more important as one moves through the list from the first to the fourth. But when duties are high, customs officials are badly paid, and traditions of honesty do not pervade government officialdom, this complicity may not be difficult to obtain.

In terms of their local market effects, there is perhaps not much difference among these different types of smuggling. But their welfare effects may be greatly different. In a recent essay on the welfare implications of smuggling, Bhagwati and Hansen have argued that smuggling in the presence of legal imports may reduce economic welfare and under conditions of increasing smuggling costs is bound to reduce economic welfare (Bhagwati and Hansen, 1973). This result depends critically on the explicit assumption that there are *social* costs associated with smuggling, as indeed might be generally expected to be the case when smuggling is of the 'motorboat in the night' variety. (Even here, however, there may be *greater* social cost in routing some goods through official ports of entry in a country like Indonesia than simply landing them near the point of local sale; so the assumption even that type I smuggling is socially more costly than legal trade may be questioned.) But it is clearly not true of the last three types of smuggling. There the additional social costs may be negligible or literally zero. Of course, where the complicity of customs officials is involved, importers may have to bribe them into non-enforcement. But these bribes are transfer payments, not social costs that absorb resources.

Under these circumstances, smuggling of the last three types – and possibly smuggling of the first type as well – will lead neither to gain nor to loss of welfare in the Bhagwati–Hansen framework. And of course to the extent that smuggling of all types actually eliminates *full* duty-paid imports, there will be a welfare gain, for tariff-induced price distortions will have been reduced.

However, the neo-classical framework they use for their analysis of the welfare effects of smuggling sorely neglects a key factor of tariff policy in most developing countries, viz. the need to rely on tariffs as a relatively low-cost source of government revenue. Indonesia in the late sixties drew one-third of its total (non-aid) revenues from import and export duties. To the extent that governments need to raise revenues to finance public goods, a welfare loss is incurred by any development that either reduces those revenues or forces the government to increase its expenditures on collection. A welfare analysis of smuggling is surely incomplete without taking this important factor into account. (Bhagwati and Srinivasan (1973) do analyze some of the revenue implications of smuggling.)

3. Methods for detecting smuggling

What can one say about the relative importance of the different types of smuggling noted above? Unfortunately, not much. It is in the nature of illegal transactions that they do not get accurately recorded, so any evidence on their magnitude is necessarily circumstantial and inferential, based on incomplete and indirect sources of information.

The first type of smuggling is not recorded at all, for instance. But the goods must be paid for. This means that they must appear somewhere in a complete set of the importing country's balance-of-payments accounts, if only in the errors and omissions. Thus the balance-of-payments accounts might seem to put at least circumstantial limits on the amount of smuggling. In the late sixties, however, Indonesia's balance of payments showed a *positive* balancing item, rather than a negative one which unrecorded payment for smuggled imports would require. Several explanations are possible, such as that the value of smuggled exports (to evade a modest tax on exported rubber) exceeded that of smuggled imports. The most probable explanation, however, is that Indonesian-owned assets, which had left the country during the political turmoil of the early and mid-sixties, were returning both in the form of unrecorded capital inflows and in the form of unrecorded imports. Inferences from balance-of-payments figures can be no better than those figures, and for many developing countries most of the accounts, especially for capital and service transactions, represent at best crude approximations of what is really happening.

An alternative approach to estimate the magnitude of smuggling is to rely on the trade figures of partner countries. This technique, while perhaps better than none, places great burdens on the accuracy of those figures, and is exceptionally difficult in the case of Indonesia because of the lack of uniform treatment in trade statistics of entrepôt centers such as Singapore, through which a substantial portion of Indonesia's trade flows.

The second type of smuggling, under-invoicing, can also be expected to be reflected in the errors and omissions of the balance-of-payments accounts. In addition, however, a more direct check can be made through comparison of unit values of imports (c.i.f. import value divided by some measure of quantity or even weight) with known foreign prices. Many imports are sufficiently idiosyncratic (e.g. a made-to-order piece of machinery) that foreign prices different from those shown on the invoice are difficult or impossible to obtain. But other prices are quite standard, and still others are subject to ranges of common-sense plausibility. Comparisons of this type suggest that under-invoicing into Indonesia was quite common in the late sixties, although it is impossible to say just how great was its magnitude. To give only a few examples, drawn from the imports recorded by customs: gold imports, dutiable at 8 percent, carried an import unit value of under $23 an ounce; motorcycles, dutiable at 50–100 percent, had a unit value of $129; motorcycle tires, a unit value of $2.27; table salt, dutiable at 140 percent, a unit value of 1.5¢ a kilogram; and so on. Some of these may be the result of careless recording of the quantity data. But there were enough examples to suggest under-invoicing was widespread. This practice lowers the effective rate of duty.

The third type of smuggling cannot be detected at all through indirect processes: the correct value is declared and the correct duty is paid for the merchandise declared. Direct inspection is required to see whether the goods have been misclassified.

Sometimes the several types of smuggling are used together. For example, automobiles were being imported into Indonesia at suspiciously low unit values. They were however declared as *used* automobiles at those values. Later a smuggling ring involving several customs officials was discovered to be engaged in this misdeclaration, and a number of persons were jailed for the offense.

The fourth type of smuggling, under-assessment of legal duty, can be discovered by comparing revenues collected, declared values and statutory duties, commodity by commodity. This comparison requires that the import statistics be kept on the same basis as the tariff schedule, otherwise discrepancies in classification will mar

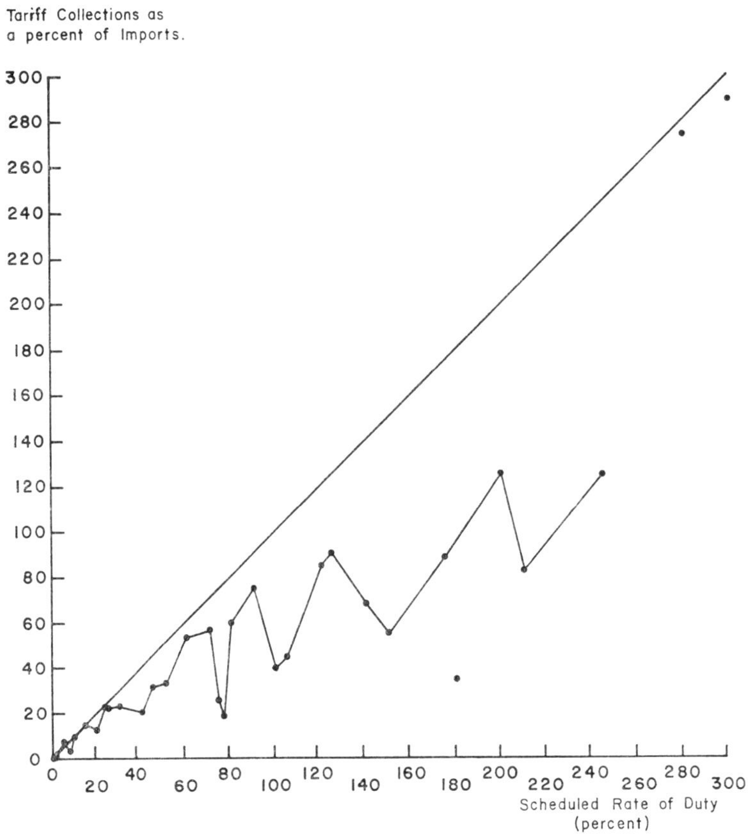

Fig. 1. Relationship between scheduled duties and actual tariff collections.

the comparison. The data displayed in fig. 1 are not entirely free from this last difficulty, but they probably offer a reasonable approximation to the discrepancy between statutory duties and duties actually collected. Association of these discrepancies with illicit activity is further complicated by the fact that certain classes of importers (some government agencies, foreign or domestic investors in 'pioneer' industries, etc.) are entitled to exemption from duties on imports essential for their activities. As a rule, however, imports of capital goods and raw and intermediate materials carry only low duties, so this complicating factor is not sufficient to explain the marked shortfall of collections in the range of commodities subject to high duties. It is noteworthy that the proportionate extent of shortfall tends to increase with the statutory duty, a point that will be discussed further below[1].

[1] The points that have not been connected to the rest are *de minimus* (under $500 000) in recorded import value; the two goods carrying duties of 280 and 300 percent – drinking glasses and matches – were believed to have been subject to extensive under-invoicing.

4. Market impact of smuggling

While we cannot be sure of the total amount of smuggling or of the relative importance of the different types, except that in Indonesia all were present to some degree, we can measure more directly the effects of all types of smuggling on the marketplace. To this end, local wholesale prices for about 70 commodities were collected and compared with estimates of the c.i.f. prices augmented by the tariff and other taxes on imported goods. The results are shown in fig. 2, which has a basic format similar to fig. 1. Statutory duties are measured along the horizontal axis, while the vertical axis shows the local wholesale price as a percentage of the c.i.f. price. The 45-degree line indicates what the c.i.f. price inclusive of duty and tax would be, before allowance for importer and wholesale mark-ups. Thus if all imports were fully duty-paid, all the points (each of which represents a single,

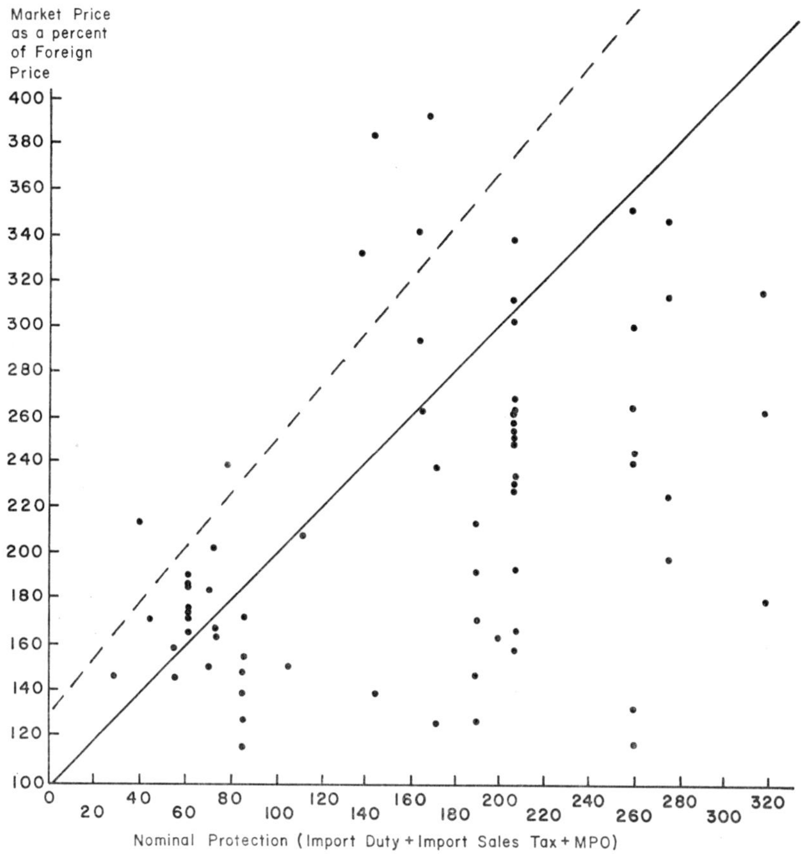

Fig. 2. Ratio of domestic to foreign price of imports in relation to duties plus taxes.

well-specified good, e.g. a room fan of a certain brand and model) would lie above, presumably well above, the 45-degree line. As can be seen, most of the points in fact lie below the line, and virtually all the points lie below the dashed line, which would be the price with a uniform 25 percent mark-up on tariff-inclusive prices.

Moreover, the extent to which they lie below the 45-degree line seems to depend on the level of the tariff, i.e., the higher the tariff plus other applicable taxes, the greater the proportionate shortfall – the same phenomenon that we observed in connection with under-assessment of duties. A linear regression of the observed wholesale price as a percentage of the hypothetical full duty-paid price on the level of the tariff plus taxes (a transformation of the points shown on fig. 2) suggests that the shortfall increases by 18 percent of higher statutory duties plus taxes. At taxes plus duty of 61 percent, the market price is just equal (on average) to the full duty-paid price (implying a domestic mark-up on average of 11 percent, which seems low); at taxes plus duty of 120 percent, the market price falls to only 88 percent of the full duty-paid price. To put the point another way, as the tariff plus taxes are raised from zero to 100 percent, only 82 percent (on average) is actually reflected in the market price; and as the tariff plus taxes are raised further to 200 percent, only 39 percent of this increment is actually reflected in the market price. Increases in tariffs above 258 percent will result (on average) in an actual reduction of market price[2]. Revenue collections will of course fare even worse, for the market price reflects not only tax collections but also other costs (including bribes) that may be associated with importing the goods in question. Variation around these averages is of course wide, as the scatter in fig. 2 indicates. But the underlying tendency of market prices to rise with duties, but less than proportionately, is unmistakable.

5. Interpretation of the data

What explains this pattern of behavior? One plausible model involves a threshold

[2] The linear regression result was $p/f = 1.11 - 0.18t$, where p is the observed market price, $f = c(1 + t)$ is the hypothetical full duty-paid price, t is the rate of duty plus indirect taxes, and c is the c.i.f. price. Multiplying through by f and substituting yields a market price quadratic in the tariff rate: $p = [1.11 + 0.93\,t - 0.18\,t^2]c.p/c$ reaches a maximum at $t = 258\%$. The total explanatory power of this regression is low ($R^2 = 0.19$), as can be inferred from the wide scatter in fig. 2, which shows the same underlying data in a different transformation. But the coefficient on t is significantly different from zero at the level of one-tenth of one percent (t-ratio = 4.1 for 72 observations), so the relationship between p/f and t is a strong one.

The basic empirical work reported here was done for Harvard's Development Advisory Service with the collaboration of Lawrence White of Princeton University, to whom I am grateful for assistance.

of illegality which importers are reluctant to cross, but once it is crossed illicit activity dominates the market. Thus if the costs of smuggling were the same (per unit value) for all goods, all imports dutiable below a threshold tariff would enter the country legally, with full duty being paid, while all goods dutiable above that threshold would pay no duties. In terms of fig. 2, all the points below the threshold tariff would lie on the 45-degree line (before allowance for domestic mark-ups), while all the points beyond the threshold tariff would lie along a horizontal line somewhat below the market price ratio of the goods dutiable just at the threshold (reflecting the conjecture that importers are willing to incur some cost to remain law-abiding).

Reality is not so clear cut. Undoubtedly there is a threshold of law-abidingness below which smuggling will be negligible. Penalties for breaking the law are not proportional to the benefits; indeed they arise even if benefits are nil. Breaking the law also exposes one to blackmail, damages reputation and hence business goodwill, and so on. So importers are likely to be willing to pay a full duty so long as it is 'small', even when it exceeds the direct costs of smuggling. How small is 'small' will vary from culture to culture, for the traditions of law-abidingness, and the social penalties associated with being caught breaking the law, vary substantially from country to country.

Once tariffs and taxes rise above this threshold level, smuggling is not in fact likely to replace legal trade altogether. This is in part because the costs of smuggling will vary from commodity to commodity (whereas the threshold tariff is not likely to vary so much, if at all), so the gains from smuggling at the threshold will vary substantially from commodity to commodity. Furthermore, some importers are likely to want to remain as close to the law as possible and still remain in business, whereas others will leave it more quickly. Risk aversion will differ from businessman to businessman, and there is no insurance market to hedge against getting caught in violation of the law. Thus some importers, instead of abandoning legal entry altogether, will begin to 'trim' through modest under-invoicing or through small bribes to achieve under-assessment or misclassification to qualify for a lower duty. But they continue to import through a customs post and they continue to pay some duty. As the tariffs rise relative to the cost of the first type of smuggling, the amount of 'trimming' will also increase, and probably more than proportionately, for two reasons. First, the incentives to trim rise with the duty. Second, it becomes increasingly difficult for any one importer to stay in business as the extent of tariff evasion grows. With competition from smuggling of any type, what appears to be an indirect tax, the tariff, becomes a direct tax on the income of he who pays it, for he cannot pass it on to his customers. As the pervasiveness of evasion increases, this fact becomes increasingly apparent, even to the customs officials, and their willingness to provide some relief to the relatively law-abiding importer, enough at least to keep him in business, will result in systematic under-assessment or other forms of permitted evasion. The result of this process is something like the observed pattern: import costs that rise with the statutory tariff, but less than proportionately.

Various possible cases can be expressed in algebraic terms. Let s_i be the constant cost of smuggling commodity *i*, as a proportion of its c.i.f. price, c_i. Let $r_i = p_i/c_i$ be the ratio of the local market price to the c.i.f. price. Then if we make no allowance for local mark-ups or for law-abidingness, $r_i = 1 + t_i$ if $s_i > t_i$ and $r_i = 1 + s_i$ if $s_i < t_i$, where t_i is the *ad valorem* tariff and other applicable taxes on commodity *i*.

A general schedule relating *r* to *t* then depends on the relationship between *s* and *t*. If *s* and *t* are uncorrelated over all commodities, then the general relationship between *r* and *t* will be $r = (1 + t)$ up to some threshold of law-abidingness, t^* (where t^* may exceed the median value of *s*), and $r = (1 + \mathbf{s})$ for still higher values of *t*, where **s** is the median value of *s*.

If, to take another extreme case, *s* and *t* are perfectly correlated, as might be the case if the tariff was aimed at protection rather than revenue and took 'smuggl-ability' into account, then $r = 1 + t$ up to the threshold of law-abidingness, and $r = 1 + kt$ for still higher values of *t*, where $k < 1$ is the constant of proportionality between s_i and t_i.

These alternative formulations would show the following general patterns, where t^* indicates the threshold of law-abidingness:

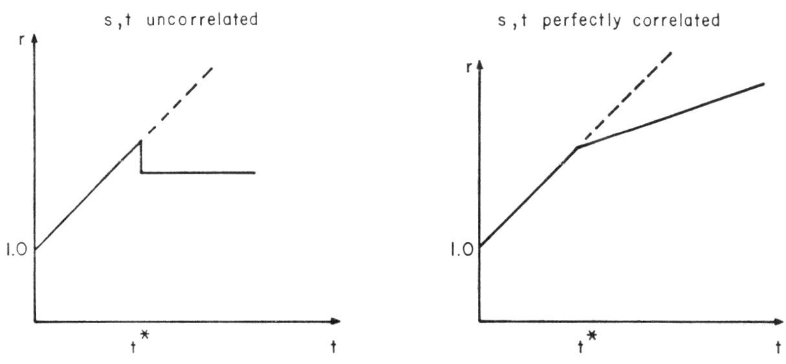

Fig. 3.

A combination of the two patterns would hold if importers drew a sharp distinction, say, between Type I smuggling and under-invoicing (as they might do, for instance, if the penalties for the former were much stiffer than for the latter). Then importers would continue to pay a fraction of the legal tariff, a fraction

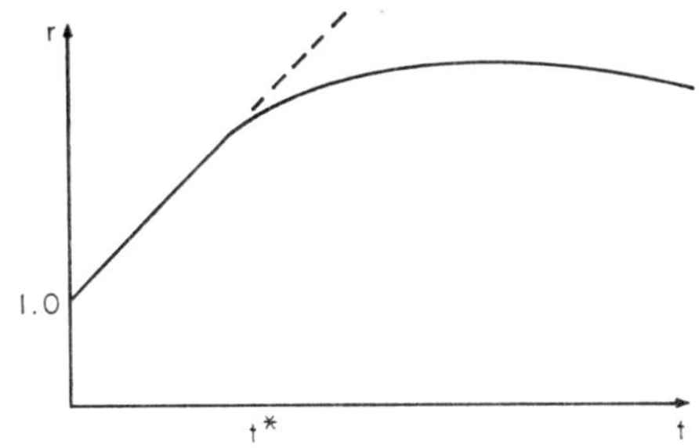

Fig. 4.

that might be expected to decline with higher and higher tariffs because of the alternative possibility of Type I smuggling.

Thus we have a mixed system, in which several types of smuggling take place simultaneously, in which many importers pay some but less than full duty, and in which the government collects as revenue not only less than regulations call for but also less than importers pay. Moreover, the protection provided by tariffs to local industries is less, sometimes substantially less, than the nominal tariff schedule would suggest. The welfare consequences of such a mixed system cannot be determined *a priori.* The efficiency gains from lower protection must be set against the real resource costs (if any) of smuggling plus the incremental cost of raising government revenue elsewhere or foregoing government expenditure.

In these cases national welfare would be improved if tariffs could be lowered to levels at which they seem 'reasonable' to the law-abiding business community and are not too costly to enforce against remaining smugglers. If this is done, government revenues will rise by inducing a higher proportion of imports to enter through legal channels. The protective effect of duties may also rise, to the extent that a threshold of law-abidingness exists and exceeds the cost of smuggling. Thus it may not serve the interests even of protectionist policy-makers to set tariffs as high as possible.

References

Bhagwati, J. and B. Hansen, 1973, A theoretical analysis of smuggling, Quarterly Journal of Economics LXXXVII, May, 172–187; ch. 1 in this volume.

Bhagwati, J. and T. N. Srinivasan, 1973, Smuggling and trade policy, Journal of Public Economics 2, no. 4; ch. 3 in this volume.

PART V

MISCELLANY

Chapter 14

UNIT VALUES OF U.S. MACHINERY EXPORTS

G. C. HUFBAUER and J. P. O'NEILL

1. Introduction

The reliability of export unit values for measuring either prevailing prices or price trends is often questioned. For example, Kravis and Lipsey (1971) open their pioneering work with the remark:

> Unit values are values per unit of quantity within detailed export or import classifications. However, since the classifications must in total cover every item of trade, they cannot be narrowly specified unless their numbers is increased far beyond any practical limit. As a result of the lack of close specification, there is never any certainty that a change in unit value represents a change in price; the unit value of a trade classification can change, even though all prices are constant, if there is a shift from one quality or type of item to another.

Our purpose here is not to defend the use of unit values as price level or price trend indicators, but rather to investigate the large variance in the unit values of the 'same' seven-digit Standard International Trade Classification (SITC) item shipped to different countries in a given year. Kravis and Lipsey mention one important reason for the variance: qualitative differences within an SITC category. Part of these qualitative differences might be systematically related to the attributes of the importing country, in particular, its level of development. Countries with high *per capita* income are likely to want rather different product characteristics than countries with low *per capita* income, a point emphasized by Linder (1961). Many qualitative differences within a seven-digit SITC group, however, might be unrelated to the attributes of different importing countries. This seems to be the essence of the Kravis–Lipsey criticism, although those authors cite oil pipe shipments as a case where quality is related to country destination.

Apart from qualitative differences, other causes have also been suggested for the intercountry variance in export unit values. Knight (1968) raised the possibility of price discrimination between purchasers, while Bhagwati (1964, 1967) and Winston (1970) have suggested that tariffs and overvalued currencies could lead to fake invoices, and thus to apparent variations in export unit values.

As a beginning contribution to the explanation of unit value variance, we performed a statistical analysis on the data relating to selected U.S. machinery exports in 1970, taken from United States Bureau of the Census (1971). Machinery exports were chosen for two reasons. First, the intercountry coefficients of variation for machinery unit values are quite large. Hence, there is a good deal of 'explaining' to be done. Table 1, based on 1965 data, gives the average coefficients of variation for the three-digit SITC groups which constitute the present object of study. The average coefficients (average of the component seven-digit SITC group coefficients) often exceed one, a value larger than that observed for most other three-digit groups.

The second reason for investigating machinery exports is that both the incentives and the opportunities for bogus invoicing are especially great in the machinery field. Incentives are great because large sums of money, often provided by the government in long-term, low-interest loans, are involved in single transactions. Opportunities are great because the non-standardized nature of machinery makes it difficult to detect fake invoices.

2. Alternative explanatory variables

From the three-digit SITC groups listed in table 1, 102 seven-digit SITC machinery products were selected. In total, these three-digit SITC groups contain some 466 seven-digit products; hence about one-fifth of the possible products were selected for study. The sample products were selected in a manner that ensured proportionality with the 1970 United States export values accounted for by the four-digit parent group[1].

For the analysis, 41 importing countries were chosen, and are listed in Appendix table A1. These countries were deliberately selected to represent a wide variety of sizes, *per capita* income levels, currency and tariff practices, and geographic location.

Of course, each of the 41 chosen countries does not import every seven-digit SITC product. In fact, the total number of country observations was 2099, or about 21 chosen countries per product. On average, each of the 102 products was exported to approximately 37 countries, so the country coverage is about half the possible country population.

[1] A list of the seven-digit SITC groups will be furnished by the authors on request.

Our working hypothesis is that part of the variance in unit values of exports of the 'same' product to different countries can be explained by four explicit product and country variables. These four variables are related to the explanations of Linder, Knight, Bhagwati, and Winston mentioned earlier.

The first variable is the relative quantity of the product sold to the particular country. If the country is a large buyer (relative to other importing countries) of a certain type of machinery, it should enjoy, as Knight suggested, a better bargaining position *vis-à-vis* American and other exporters. Also, the costs of establishing a sales and service network will be substantially lower, per unit of machinery, when large volumes are involved. The relative quantity variable was thus originally intended to reflect price discrimination based either on bargaining considerations or based on cost differences related to quantity sold (a good deal of price discrimination might be unrelated to quantity sold, so the relative quantity variable need not reflect the entire range of discriminatory practices). However, the relative quantity variable may reflect, not price discrimination, but rather the sale of special items within a seven-digit group. This possibility, suggested by Lipsey (1972), is explained in more detail later.

The second variable is the *per capita* income, gross domestic product, (GDP) of the importing country (Appendix table A1). This variable is intended to pick up those types of qualitative differences within a product group which were stressed by Linder. The assumption is that higher wages will impel the selection of more automated or more durable forms of machinery. Machinery which is more automated and durable is also more expensive, but since it permits the substitution of capital for labor, it can be attractive to high-income countries. Of course, there are other qualitative variations besides those linked to capital–labor substitution, and these other differences need not be reflected in the *per capita* income variable. Indeed, many important qualitative differences might not be associated in any systematic way with the attributes of importing countries, and this seems to be the thrust of the Kravis–Lipsey position.

The third variable, one emphasized by Bhagwati and Winston, is the extent of currency overvaluation. The 1970 edition of *Pick's Currency Yearbook* was used for the estimates of currency overvaluation which appear in Appendix table A1. If a machinery importer can secure foreign exchange at a 'low' official rate, and later resell it at a 'high' free or black-market rate, the incentive to overinvoice machinery imports will be strong. Acting in concert with the importer (more or less as a condition of sale), the foreign supplier will overinvoice the product and then pay a foreign exchange rebate to the importer. The importer might bank the foreign exchange in Switzerland, or perhaps convert it at the black-market rate to his own currency, repay part of his local currency loan at the official rate, and collect the exchange rate difference.

We make the assumption that the overinvoicing game starts with the documents submitted to the U.S. customs' authorities, so that any overinvoicing will be reflected in U.S. export statistics. Instead, a second set of papers might be prepared on the high seas, for the benefit of the customs and banking authorities in the foreign country; but this alternative seems more cumbersome, and hence less likely.

The fourth and final variable, one stressed by Bhagwati, is the *ad valorem* tariff plus internal tax rate charged on the machinery product. A higher *ad valorem* rate provides more incentive for underinvoicing. In order to reduce his tariff and internal tax payments, the importer may arrange with the foreign supplier to underinvoice the product. In this case, the importer would have to pay something beyond the invoice price to the foreign supplier.

3. Results

Bhagwati (1967) has pointed out that a high tariff rate and an overvalued currency pose opposite incentives to the importer. In principle, the overinvoicing incentive afforded by a currency overvalued some 20% is just offset by an *ad valorem* tariff of 20%. Thus, if the shipment is overinvoiced by \$100 000, the exchange rate gain of \$20 000 is counterbalanced by an additional tariff payment of \$20 000.

The tariff and internal tax rates given in Appendix table A2 are perhaps the least satisfactory figures used in the analysis. It was impossible to obtain tariffs and tax rates on a seven-digit SITC basis. Therefore, the rates were estimated for three-digit SITC groups, and all seven-digit products within the group were assumed to pay the same tariff-tax rate. (In the case of group 711, a distinction was made between steam generating machinery (711.1, 711.2, and 711.3) and internal combustion engines (711.4 and 711.5), since most countries charge higher duties on internal combustion engines.) The three-digit tariff–tax estimates were based on a survey of national tariff schedules, the *Douanes* published in Brussels, and the *Overseas Business Reports* issued by the U.S. Bureau of International Commerce. We used no formal system of weights in making the estimates. Because of this feature, together with various classification problems and the common practice of allowing special exemptions from the published tariff rates, the figures which appear in table A2 are, to a large extent, impressionistic guesses.

Experimentation with linear and logarithmic equation forms showed that a double logarithmic approach gave the best results:

$$\log U_{ij} = \alpha_0 + \alpha_1 \log Q_{ij} + \alpha_2 \log Y_j + \alpha_3 \log E_j + \alpha_4 \log(T_{ij} + 1), \tag{1}$$

where i = seven-digit SITC product subscript, j = importing country subscript, and U = ratio between the unit value of exports (f.o.b.) to a given country in calendar 1970 and the unweighted average unit value of exports (f.o.b.) to all countries in the sample. Q = ratio between the quantity of shipments to the country in calendar 1970 and the average quantity of exports to all countries in the sample, and Y = *per capita* gross domestic product for the country in about 1968. E = ratio of the average July 1969 through June 1970 black- or free-market exchange rate to the official exchange rate applicable to capital goods imports during the same period. (Note: the period July 1969–June 1970 was chosen on the assumption of a six-month lag between machinery orders and their delivery; the

Table 1.
Three-digit SITC machinery groups and their 1965 coefficients of variation in unit values.

Three-digit SITC group	Brief description	1965 coefficient of variation in unit values
711	Power generating machinery	0.99
712	Agricultural machinery	0.57
714	Office machines	0.60
715	Metalworking machinery	1.32
717	Textile and leather machinery	1.20
718	Machines for special industries	1.22
719	Machinery and appliances, n.e.s.	1.20
722	Electric power machinery and switchgear	1.75
723	Equipment for distributing electricity	0.88
724	Telecommunications apparatus	0.96
729	Other electrical machinery and apparatus	1.52

Source: G. C. Hufbauer (1970).

Table 2.
Parameter estimates from the regression equation[a].

	Constant term	Relative quantity	*Per capita* income	Currency over-valuation	Tariff–tax rate	R^2
Trial I	−0.49	−0.23[b]	0.08[b]	0.01	0.12	0.16[b]
Trial II	−0.49	−0.23[b]	0.08[b]	0.08	deleted	0.16[b]
Trial III	−0.46	−0.23[b]	0.08[b]	deleted	deleted	0.16[b]

[a] The results are based on the double logarithmic eq. (1), applied to 2099 observations. Logarithms to the base 10 were used. The parameters may be interpreted as elasticities.

[b] The parameter or multiple correlation coefficient is significantly different from zero at the 1% (or better) confidence level.

unit value figures pertain to calendar 1970.) T = *ad valorem* tariff and internal tax rate imposed by the importing country. (Note: The variable in eq. (1) is $(T_{ij} + 1)$ because some countries charge no tariffs, or very low tariffs, and hence the logarithm of T_{ij} alone would become a very large negative number.)

The dependent variable in eq. (1) is expressed as a ratio to facilitate the pooling of data on different seven-digit products which exhibit a wide range of average unit values. The results of the regression equation appear in table 2 as Trial I. A striking feature is the wrong sign of α_4, the parameter attached to the tariff–tax variable. Since the parameter is positive it suggests that unit values *increase* with a higher tariff rate. This result makes little sense. It could reflect the faulty nature of the tariff–tax estimates. Or perhaps it merely indicates that tariff and internal tax rates exert little impact on invoicing practices. As table 3 shows, higher tariffs are correlated with greater currency overvaluation, and it could be that tariffs and taxes themselves have little effect, but because of their positive correlation with currency overvaluation, the regression analysis gives a 'false' α_4 parameter[2].

Table 3.
Matrix of simple correlation coefficients between the variables.

	Relative unit value $\log U_{ij}$	Relative quantity $\log Q_{ij}$	*Per capita* income $\log Y_j$	Currency over-valuation $\log E_j$	Tariff–tax rate $\log (T_{ij} + 1)$
$\log U_{ij}$	1.000				
$\log Q_{ij}$	−0.393	1.000			
$\log Y_j$	−0.072	0.389	1.000		
$\log E_j$	0.071	−0.259	−0.560	1.000	
$\log (T_{ij} + 1)$	0.064	−0.113	−0.137	0.444	1.000

Whatever the reason for the wrong-signed α_4 parameter, the tariff–tax variable was dropped in the Trial II calculations. The currency overvaluation parameter, α_3, takes on a larger value, but the other parameters are hardly affected by the deletion of the $(T_{ij} + 1)$ variable.

Even with its larger value (of the correct sign) the currency overvaluation parameter has little statistical significance. These results do not support the widespread belief that overinvoicing is significantly stimulated by currency overvaluation. But

[2] The positive correlation between E_j and $(T_{ij} + 1)$ may reflect government awareness of the potential windfall import profits created by an overvalued currency, and the consequent imposition of compensatory tariffs.

the mesh of our statistical net may be far too coarse to detect the subtleties of fake invoicing. After all, the regression equation explains only 16% of the intercountry variance in unit values. While an R^2 value of 0.16 is highly significant for 2099 observations, 84% of the unit value variance remains unexplained. Part of the unexplained variance could be fake invoicing which has not been captured by the overvaluation and tariff–tax variables.

As a matter of interest, both the currency overvaluation term, E_j, and the tariff–tax variable, T_{ij}, were combined into a single term in one experimental regression run. The combined term was $(E_j - T_{ij} + 1)$; this particular form was dictated by the need to avoid negative variables in a logarithmic equation. The elasticity parameter of the combined term was -0.12, suggesting that either an increase in overvaluation or a decrease in the tariff rate would *reduce* the reported unit value. Thus, the parameter for the combined term, like the parameter for the tariff–tax term in isolation, makes no economic sense.

Although the statistical analysis reveals a wrong-signed tariff–tax effect and only a weak overvaluation effect, it might be interesting to contrast the estimated value of $(\overline{T}_j + 1)$ and E_j, an exercise suggested by Bhagwati[3]. $(\overline{T}_j + 1)$ is comparable to E_j in the sense that an average 30% *ad valorem* tariff will give a $(\overline{T}_j + 1)$ value of 1.30, while a 30% currency overvaluation will likewise give an E_j value of 1.30. An average tariff of 30% should approximately offset the overinvoicing incentive generated by a currency overvaluation of 30%. Thus, if the $\overline{T}_j$ and E_j estimates can be trusted, the net overinvoicing incentive generated by exchange rate, tariff, and tax policies is $\{E_j - (\overline{T}_j + 1)\}$. If this expression is negative, a net underinvoicing incentive exists.

Equally important as the fake invoicing incentive, however, is the stimulus to imported capital equipment purchases afforded by the exchange rate, tariff, and tax policies. This point was stressed by Winston (1970). When $\{E_j - (\overline{T}_j + 1)\}$ is positive, the public policies are working to subsidize machinery imports (assuming, of course, that the free-market exchange rate correctly measures the economic cost of foreign exchange). When the expression is negative, the net impact of public policies is to tax machinery imports.

Among the sample countries, there are only four which offer a net subsidy exceeding 20% $[\{E_j - (\overline{T}_j + 1)\} > 20\%]$: Pakistan, Egypt, Ghana, and Nigeria. On the other hand, there are 12 countries in the sample, including several in Latin America, which impose a net tax of 20% or more $[\{E_j - (\overline{T}_j + 1)\} < -20\%]$. Subsidized machinery imports may pose a serious problem in some countries, but judging from this sample of countries and the admittedly imperfect data on exchange rates, tariffs, and internal taxes, the problem was not widespread in 1970.

[3] $\overline{T}_j$ is the simple average for country j of the three-digit SITC tariff rates appearing in table A2.

In Trial III of table 2, the currency overvaluation variable is dropped, and the regression equation is reduced to two explanatory variables. Measured by their t values, each of these variables is highly significant in explaining export unit values. The parameters (which both have the right sign) and the constant term are practically unchanged from the Trial I and II estimates.

4. Summary

A noteworthy feature of the regression analysis is the strong and highly significant effect of the quantity variable. The elasticity of -0.23 may reflect price discrimination based on lower sales and service costs for the larger buyer or discrimination based on orthodox monopoly considerations. On the other hand, Lipsey has argued that the negative relationship between unit value and quantity exported is not discrimination, but something quite different. Most buyers want the ordinary variety; only a few want the superversion. Thus, a country purchasing a large number of cars from Germany would be more likely to import Volkswagens than Mercedes-Benz. And any country importing 100 airplanes is more likely to be buying business jets than 747s. If this line of reasoning is extended to seven-digit product categories, it follows that any country with large imports will be buying mostly standard products, while *some* of those countries with small imports will be purchasing mainly the special items. This phenomenon alone could give a negative regression coefficient between unit value and quantity.

It might be possible to distinguish between Knight's discrimination hypothesis and Lipsey's special item phenomenon by examining the month-to-month unit values of shipments to a single large importing country, for example, Germany or the U.K. To the extent such month-to-month unit values display the same negative relationship as cross-country unit values, it is very likely that Lipsey's special item explanation accounts for the results.

Obviously the quantity effect has policy importance only to the extent that it reflects discrimination. If discrimination is present, the small importing country pays more for its machinery. The unweighted average coefficient of variation in export quantities for the 102 products was 1.87. In the unlikely event that the quantity effect is entirely explained by discrimination, rather than by special items, a country which purchased one standard deviation less than the mean quantity for a particular product would pay on average about 40% more per unit.

The quality effect, as measured by *per capita* income in the importing country, is not so strong as the quantity effect. The richer country pays more per unit, presumably to get a more durable and automated piece of machinery, but the elasticity parameter is only 0.08. The coefficient of variation of GDP *per capita* for the sample countries is 1.07. A country enjoying *per capita* income one standard deviation greater than the mean would thus pay about 9% more per unit of machinery.

Finally, the fact that 84% of unit value variance is *not* explained by the regression equation tends to support the Kravis–Lipsey contention that very different products get put under the same statistical label, more or less on a random basis. We analyzed the residuals from eq. (1) for a subset of 27 products and 27 countries, using Kendall's rank correlation coefficient of concordance (1962)[4]. The coefficient had a value of only 0.09, which indicates that the ranking of residuals by country from one product to another is not very similar. Thus, a large part of the unexplained unit value variance is probably not connected with country attributes, but instead reflects the inherent diversity of goods within a seven-digit classification.

Acknowledgements

We are indebted to Mumtaz Pehlivanli, Hassan Balky and Angus Hone for their comments on the overinvoicing problem, and to J. N. Bhagwati for editorial improvements. The Bureau of Foreign Trade of the U.S. Department of Commerce was most helpful in supplying tariff and internal tax data.

References

Bhagwati, J., 1964, On the under-invoicing of imports, Bulletin of the Oxford University Institute of Economics and Statistics, November.

Bhagwati, J., 1967, Fiscal policies, the faking of foreign trade declarations, and the balance of payments, Bulletin of the Oxford University Institute of Economics and Statistics, February.

Hufbauer, G. C., 1970, The impact of national characteristics and technology on the commodity composition of trade in manufactured goods, in: Vernon, R., ed., The Technology Factor in International Trade (National Bureau of Economic Research, Columbia University Press, New York).

International Monetary Fund, 1970, International Financial Statistics, Washington, D.C., September.

Kendall, M. G., 1962, Rank Correlation Methods (Charles Griffin, London) third edition.

Knight, P. T., 1968, Private communication.

Kravis, I. B. and R. E. Lipsey, 1971, Price Competitiveness in World Trade (National Bureau of Economic Research, Columbia University Press, New York).

Linder, S. B., 1961, An Essay on Trade and Transformation (Almqvist and Wiksell, Stockholm).

Lipsey, R. E., 1972, Private communication.

[4] A subset of products and countries was selected for the analysis of residuals because many products are exported to only a few countries, and some countries import very few products. Even in the subset, each product was not exported to every country; in the case of no exports, that country was assigned the median rank value in the residual analysis.

Pick, F., 1970, 1970 Pick's Currency Yearbook (Pick Publishing, New York).
United Nations, 1970, Statistical Office, Yearbook of International Accounts Statistics: 1969 II, International Tables, New York.
United States Bureau of the Census, U.S. Exports – Schedule B Commodity and Country, Report FT 410 (U.S. Government Printing Office, Washington, D.C.).
Winston, G. C., 1970, Overinvoicing, underutilization, and distorted industrial growth, Pakistan Development Review, Winter 1970.

Appendix

Table A1.
Country variables.

Country	Y_j	E_j	$(\bar{T}_j+1)$	Country	Y_j	E_j	$(\bar{T}_j+1)$
Canada	2621	0.99	1.12	India	77	1.55	1.38
Mexico	553	1.00	1.14	Pakistan	130	2.14	1.36
Guatemala	297	1.09	1.17	Thailand	150	1.00	1.17
Nicaragua	357	1.18	1.19	South Vietnam	173	2.54	2.55
Haiti	86	1.14	1.11	Malaysia	280	1.00	1.07
Colombia	338	1.12	1.34	Indonesia	93	1.14	1.17
Venezuela	977	1.00	1.11	Philippine Rep.	282	1.17	1.19
Ecuador	214	1.23	1.52	Korean Rep.	173	1.14	1.02
Peru	268	1.09	1.37	Hong Kong	525[a]	1.00	1.00
Chile	518	1.54	1.81	Japan	1306	1.04	1.09
Brazil	291	1.13	1.77	Australia	2264	1.00	1.39
Argentina	657	1.00	1.95				
				Egypt	161	2.11	1.20
Norway	2145	1.00	1.24	Ivory Coast	231	1.04	1.29
United Kingdom	1573	1.03	1.11	Ghana	219	1.63	1.15
Netherlands	1764	1.00	1.24	Nigeria	75	1.62	1.22
West Germany	1928	0.99	1.21	Congo	69	1.25	1.24
Spain	719	1.01	1.45	Kenya	118	1.29	1.12
Italy	1257	1.01	1.20	Tanzania	67	1.29	1.13
Greece	713	1.04	1.25				
Turkey	338	1.51	1.86				
Iran	299	1.03	1.18				
Israel	1324	1.22	1.15				
Saudi Arabia	448	1.00	1.08				

Sources: Y_j values: United Nations (1970, table 18), latest available year (usually 1968). E_j values: F. Pick (1970) and International Monetary Fund (1970), average of free- or black-market rates, July 1969 through June 1970 divided by official capital goods exchange rate. $(\bar{T}_j + 1)$ values: Unweighted average of T_{ij} values in table A2, plus one.

[a] Extrapolated from 1963 using the Korean growth rate.

Table A2.
Ad valorem tariff and internal tax rates (*circa* 1970) by country and SITC category.

Country	711.1 to 711.3	711.4 to 711.5	712	714	715	717	718	719	722	723	724	729
Canada	0.00	0.12	0.00	0.28	0.00	0.00	0.05	0.17	0.10	0.23	0.23	0.23
Mexico	0.13	0.11	0.06	0.16	0.16	0.16	0.16	0.16	0.18	0.24	0.08	0.13
Guatemala	0.10	0.16	0.10	0.42	0.10	0.10	0.10	0.16	0.16	0.23	0.29	0.16
Nicaragua	0.12	0.18	0.12	0.45	0.12	0.12	0.12	0.18	0.18	0.25	0.31	0.18
Haiti	0.10	0.10	0.00	0.26	0.05	0.00	0.10	0.10	0.13	0.16	0.12	0.16
Colombia	0.29	0.29	0.09	0.84	0.19	0.24	0.29	0.34	0.44	0.49	0.29	0.34
Venezuela	0.03	0.08	0.03	0.13	0.03	0.03	0.08	0.08	0.20	0.20	0.19	0.19
Ecuador	0.45	0.50	0.40	0.85	0.40	0.45	0.45	0.50	0.45	0.60	0.60	0.65
Peru	0.37	0.32	0.32	0.47	0.37	0.37	0.37	0.37	0.37	0.37	0.37	0.37
Chile	0.47	0.67	0.67	1.57	0.57	0.77	0.77	0.87	1.07	0.57	0.97	0.77
Brazil	0.64	0.81	0.58	0.70	0.81	0.76	0.75	0.75	0.87	0.93	0.87	0.75
Argentina	1.00	1.00	1.00	0.77	0.67	0.94	1.00	1.00	1.00	1.00	1.00	1.10
Norway	0.24	0.22	0.18	0.22	0.31	0.22	0.26	0.26	0.24	0.24	0.30	0.24
U.K.	0.10	0.10	0.10	0.10	0.12	0.10	0.10	0.10	0.10	0.10	0.15	0.12
Netherlands	0.23	0.25	0.27	0.23	0.23	0.23	0.24	0.24	0.25	0.27	0.25	0.25
West Germany	0.20	0.22	0.24	0.20	0.20	0.20	0.21	0.21	0.22	0.24	0.22	0.22
Spain	0.51	0.67	0.45	0.24	0.40	0.40	0.45	0.45	0.50	0.45	0.45	0.40
Italy	0.19	0.21	0.22	0.19	0.19	0.19	0.20	0.20	0.21	0.23	0.21	0.21
Greece	0.21	0.26	0.23	0.26	0.17	0.19	0.21	0.21	0.26	0.37	0.26	0.26
Turkey	1.12	1.06	0.80	0.56	0.80	0.72	0.72	0.81	0.72	1.04	1.04	0.90
Iran	0.05	0.10	0.05	0.30	0.15	0.05	0.10	0.15	0.15	0.30	0.40	0.40
Israel	0.00	0.50	0.00	0.20	0.05	0.10	0.05	0.15	0.10	0.20	0.20	0.25
Saudi Arabia	0.05	0.05	0.02	0.16	0.05	0.05	0.05	0.08	0.05	0.10	0.15	0.10
India	0.43	0.43	0.30	0.54	0.30	0.30	0.30	0.30	0.30	0.60	0.40	0.40
Pakistan	0.40	0.40	0.05	0.30	0.40	0.40	0.40	0.40	0.40	0.40	0.40	0.40
Thailand	0.17	0.17	0.12	0.17	0.17	0.29	0.17	0.17	0.23	0.23	0.17	0.23
South Vietnam	0.83	2.39	0.48	1.12	1.88	0.58	0.86	0.86	1.97	2.90	1.96	2.81
Malaysia	0.00	0.00	0.00	0.22	0.00	0.00	0.00	0.00	0.22	0.17	0.17	0.12
Indonesia	0.10	0.20	0.10	0.30	0.10	0.20	0.10	0.10	0.15	0.15	0.30	0.20
Philippine Rep.	0.18	0.18	0.18	0.23	0.18	0.10	0.18	0.10	0.30	0.23	0.23	0.15
Korean Rep.	0.02	0.02	0.02	0.02	0.02	0.07	0.02	0.00	0.02	0.02	0.02	0.02
Hong Kong	0.00	0.00	0.00	0.00	0.00	0.00	0.00	0.00	0.00	0.00	0.00	0.00
Japan	0.10	0.10	0.10	0.08	0.12	0.08	0.08	0.08	0.10	0.10	0.08	0.10
Australia	0.46	0.60	0.52	0.14	0.25	0.36	0.47	0.47	0.25	0.42	0.30	0.41
Egypt	0.13	0.26	0.13	0.36	0.13	0.19	0.13	0.13	0.16	0.31	0.26	0.21
Ivory Coast	0.13	0.36	0.13	0.47	0.38	0.13	0.13	0.36	0.30	0.15	0.47	0.47
Ghana	0.05	0.10	0.00	0.50	0.05	0.05	0.05	0.15	0.10	0.20	0.25	0.30
Nigeria	0.16	0.16	0.00	0.43	0.11	0.16	0.16	0.22	0.27	0.27	0.43	0.32
Congo	0.21	0.21	0.16	0.36	0.21	0.21	0.21	0.21	0.26	0.31	0.31	0.26
Kenya	0.00	0.00	0.00	0.30	0.00	0.00	0.00	0.10	0.20	0.20	0.30	0.30
Tanzania	0.00	0.00	0.00	0.35	0.00	0.00	0.00	0.10	0.20	0.20	0.43	0.32

Sources: International Customs Tariffs Bureau, Bulletin International des Douanes, Brussels, various issues; United States Bureau of International Commerce, Overseas Business Reports, U.S. Government Printing Office, Washington, D.C., various issues; various tariff and tax schedules supplied by the Bureau of Foreign Trade of the U.S. Department of Commerce.

INDEX

Abe, M., 133
Afghanistan, 9, 11
Allen, L., 70, 124
Arndt, H., 157, 160

Balance of Payments, 74
Beccaria, Marchese di, 9, 10
Bhagwati, J., 5, 20, 21, 23, 27, 30, 39, 42, 46, 49, 51, 53, 64, 67, 71, 79, 148, 149, 150, 153, 154, 184, 185, 192, 196, 197, 203
Bodio, L., 88
Bowley, A., 88

Clark, C., 88
Cooper, R., 1, 5, 183
Corden, W. M., 20

Desai, Padma, 21

Ely, J., 122, 124

Ferraris, C., 88
Furlan, V., 109

Gardner, W., 91
Graham, F. D., 88
Gross, R., 138
Guisinger, S., 64

Hansen, B., 1, 23, 27, 39, 42, 46, 79, 138, 184, 192
Hawkins, E., 133
Higgins, B., 171
Hollinger, W., 157
Hufbauer, G., 5, 195, 203

India, 68, 78
Indonesia, 9, 157–171, 172–182, 183–192
Industrial capacity utilization, 49, 58
Industrial growth, 49, 61, 62
Iran, 11

Johnson, H. G., 2, 28, 66

Karreman, H., 122
Kearl, J., 10
Kemp, M., 22
Khan, A. R., 56
King, T., 5
Knight, P., 197
Kravis, I., 195, 203
Krueger, A., 5, 148

Lerner, A. P., 2, 22
Lewis, S., 51
Lichtenberg, R., 124
Linder, F., 90
Linder, S., 195, 203
Lipsey, R., 133, 195, 197, 203

Manne, A., 9
Maximal-revenue tariffs, 32, 34, 43
Meade, J., 66
Mexico, 5
Moneta, C., 122, 126
Morgan, T., 4, 161
Morgenstern, O., 4, 70, 89, 91, 93, 94, 110, 123, 148
Musgrave, R., 66

Nadel, E., 22
Naya, S., 4, 161
Non-economic objectives, 30
O'Neill, J., 5, 195
Optimal tariffs, 33, 34
Overinvoicing, 21, 49, 66–83, 184

Pal, M., 51
Pakistan, 4, 11, 49
Pettengill, J., 13

Revenue collection, 35, 36, 43, 187
Ricci, U., 88
Richter, H., 5, 157, 160, 162, 163, 172
Rolph, E., 22

Salant, W., 66
Shelling, T., 53

Simkin, C. G. F., 5, 157, 172
Spolestra, N., 133
Srinivasan, T. N., 2, 6, 20, 30, 46, 185, 192

Turkey, 4, 71, 78, 138–147

Underinvoicing, 21, 49, 51, 138–147
Ustunel, B., 138

Vandendorpe, A., 2, 3, 6

White, L., 189
Wibulswasdi, C., 5, 148
Wilks, S., 122
Winston, G., 4, 21, 65, 196, 197

Young, G., 110